UNBOUND

UNBOUND

*Unforgettable True Stories from
the World of Endurance Sports*

BILL DONAHUE

FOREWORD BY ALEX HUTCHINSON

ROWMAN & LITTLEFIELD
Lanham • Boulder • New York • London

Published by Rowman & Littlefield
An imprint of The Rowman & Littlefield Publishing Group, Inc.
4501 Forbes Boulevard, Suite 200, Lanham, Maryland 20706
www.rowman.com

86-90 Paul Street, London EC2A 4NE, United Kingdom

British Library Cataloguing in Publication Information Available

Library of Congress Cataloging-in-Publication Data

Names: Donahue, Bill, 1964– author.
Title: Unbound : unforgettable true stories from the world of endurance sports / Bill Donahue ; foreword by Alex Hutchinson.
Description: Lanham, Maryland : Rowman & Littlefield, 2024. | Includes bibliographical references and index. | Summary: "Unbound is a fascinating collection of stories from the world of endurance sports, written by award-winning journalist Bill Donahue. They include the daring travels of Swiss explorer Sarah Marquis, cross-country skiing in Alaska with the U.S. military, a visit with Tour de France contender Nairo Quintana in his Colombian village, and much more"—Provided by publisher.
Identifiers: LCCN 2023044067 (print) | LCCN 2023044068 (ebook) | ISBN 9781538189726 (cloth) | ISBN 9781538189733 (epub)
Subjects: LCSH: Endurance sports. | Endurance sports—Training. | Athletes—Biographpy.
Classification: LCC GV749.5 .D66 2024 (print) | LCC GV749.5 (ebook) | DDC 796.04—dc23/eng/20231026
LC record available at https://lccn.loc.gov/2023044067
LC ebook record available at https://lccn.loc.gov/2023044068

♾️™ The paper used in this publication meets the minimum requirements of American National Standard for Information Sciences—Permanence of Paper for Printed Library Materials, ANSI/NISO Z39.48-1992.

For Verna

Contents

Foreword

A few years ago, while writing a book about the limits of endurance, I realized that I needed a definition of the concept—one with a little more gravitas and versatility than "what happens when you can't sprint anymore." It turned out to be a trickier challenge than I anticipated. I sat in at an international conference in Australia where physiologists from around the world spent several rancorous days debating what the word *fatigue* meant. *Endurance* seemed like an even slipperier notion.

I needed to nail down the *what* in order to wrestle with the *how*. How was it possible for a human to run a marathon in two hours, or hold his breath for 11 minutes, or—this is foreshadowing—bounce 17,354 times on a pogo stick? What alchemy of muscle fibers and corpuscles and neurons separated the Eliud Kipchoges and Bill Donahues of the world from the rest of us? The phrase I eventually settled on, borrowing from the work of Italian psychobiologist Samuele Marcora, was "the struggle to continue against a mounting desire to stop."

Marcora's definition may seem a little vague, scientifically speaking. But it's not. The limits of endurance, in his view, are precisely and tautologically defined by the point at which you give up the struggle. As a lifelong distance runner who has been wrestling with my own limits since childhood, I found that this perspective required some mental adjustment. The *how* of endurance suddenly became a question of how the mind responded to the body's signals rather than the other way around.

The real action, in other words, is in the mind. The pages you're about to read explore this insight through the eyes of some of the most remarkable people on the planet: a 4-year-old boy who ran 43 miles without stopping, in the blistering heat, the Spam-fueled military skiers defending the Arctic, an ultrarunning star whose career took off after surgery removed a portion of her brain. In the last case, the cognitive changes wrought by Diane Van Deren's surgery may have changed how her mind processes the body's signals, offering some tantalizing hints about how endurance works, and how we negotiate with that mounting desire to stop.

But the deeper theme that unites the stories in this collection isn't the *how* of endurance. It's the *why*, which is a much harder question—and one that those of us bitten by the endurance bug tend to studiously avoid. "Those questions had been considered a long time ago, decisions were made, answers recorded, and the book closed," muses Quenton Cassidy, the protagonist of John L. Parker Jr.'s cult running classic, *Once a Runner*. "If it had to be re-opened every time the going got rough, he would spend more time rationalizing than training."

In fact, the truth is—and I don't mean to project my personal neuroses onto you, dear reader—that I suspect there's a lot of self-deception going on when it comes to our reasons for heading out the door in pursuit of suffering. We're doing it for physical fitness, or mental health, or camaraderie, or to defy the sands of time. Those are the explanations we offer to ourselves or to our long-suffering spouses, and there's certainly some truth to them. That stuff will get you to the finish line of a 5K. But it won't get you through an ultramarathon, much less along the entire 2,190-mile length of the Appalachian Trail with a 5-year-old.

Fortunately, Bill Donahue doesn't buy those pat answers, and he's willing to ask harder questions—of others, and even more so of himself. Not everyone appreciates it. Van Deren disputes Donahue's analysis of her endurance prowess. Henry Rono, once the greatest runner in the world, hangs up on him. "With every question and answer, I felt more depraved," Donahue writes after tracking down Nairo Quintana in rural Colombia and quizzing his mother. There's no simple epiphany waiting on the other side of these questions, but in asking them Donahue elicits moments of reflection and self-knowledge in his subjects, and in us too.

I've been reading and admiring Donahue's writing for nearly two decades now, so it's a long overdue treat to have all these pieces collected in one place, including some rare gems from deep in the archives.

By the time you finish, you'll have encountered some hitherto obscure subcultures and unforgettable characters. You'll have peered deep into Donahue's heart, and come away with the conclusion that he's a seriously unusual dude. And perhaps, next time you glance at your reflection in a passing mirror, you'll catch a glimmer of something you hadn't previously recognized or understood staring back at you.

Alex Hutchinson
Toronto
January 2023

A one-time runner for the Canadian national team, Alex Hutchinson is the author of *Endure: Mind, Body, and the Curiously Elastic Limits of Human Performance,* a *New York Times* bestseller.

INTRODUCTION

Hello, my name is Bill and I'm an addict. The problem began, as these things so often do, innocently, when I was 10 years old and decided, one torpid summer afternoon, to pursue the world pogo stick jumping record. That was my first taste of the sweet pain that endurance sports can yield—my first foray into that long, lonely tunnel we addicts crave to inhabit each time we go running, hop on our bicycles, lace up our long-distance ice skates, whatever.

Two hours in, my glutes ached, and my quads, and my hamstrings, and the inside of my knees were raw from rubbing the shaft of the pogo stick. I was thirsty and starving (this was long before gels and Power-Bars), and still my eyes were fixed on the record—17,323 jumps, set by Danny Kloster of Clinton, Michigan, on June 17, 1972. How long would it take to reach 17,323? I had no idea. I felt trapped in a misery that would never cease. But I also knew, even then, that I was on a beautiful journey. I'd traveled away from the world into a clean, focused quadrant of the mind. I'd woken that morning as just another bored kid weary of summer vacation, weary of the humidity and of tussling with my siblings, and now, suddenly, I'd transcended the puniness of my life. Carried along by my own muscles and grit, nothing more, I was doing something that I never thought I was capable of. The power in that, the glory surge—that, more than anything else, was the needle I needed.

And I kept finding my fix. The next year—fifth grade, in gym class—we took the Presidential Fitness Test and ran the 600: three squarish laps around the soccer field on the third level of our terraced suburban playground. None of us involved even knew what training was, and we were ignorant of racing spikes and even pacing, but we'd all watched enough

Wide World of Sports to know that real runners need to be light on their feet. And so, pre-run, the cool kids decided to race barefoot in the grass.

Going without shoes that morning signaled a commitment, a seriousness and a self-importance, and I still can't fathom how I mustered the cojones to peel off my sneakers and socks and join the shoeless elite. I was a withdrawn kid—socially awkward, with zero chops in the playground sports that mattered, kickball and dodgeball. But when I stepped to the starting line and felt the grass cool and wet under my toes, still coated with dew, the moment seemed somehow right, and keen. It would all come down to this: "On your marks, get set, go."

By the first turn, I was in the lead pack. By the next straightaway, the only person before me was the coolest boy in the class. Rick was bigger than the rest of us, and more poised. His legs had actual muscles, and he ran up on his toes, hungry. There was no way I could close, but the gap wasn't much, and I felt lucky to be bony and lean. My body could kill space. My heels slammed the hard, sandy soil, and I ran along faster than almost anyone else, lapping kids, gasping, floating once again into that cave of pain and delight. I finished second that day. My social stock skyrocketed.

And it was not long before my life became largely a pursuit of the high I felt after I ran the 600. I ran on the team in high school and in college as well. I trained obsessively. I felt guilty if I took a zero day, and in my 20s, when I suffered back problems that ended running for me, I felt desolate and lost. For a few years, actually.

I'm almost 60 now, and I've switched to sports that are easier on the joints. I'm a cyclist these days and a cross-country ski racer. But have I grown wiser? I'm afraid not. I still have this sick, ingrown tendency to overtrain, to hit 170 or 175 on the heart rate monitor as I attack a hill on an "easy" day.

The only thing I've learned is that, in the long arc of an athlete's life, there is metaphor. The arc begins with an early glimpse of bliss. There follows a long, dogged quest to recapture that first Edenic moment. Then there is the taste of disappointment and failure and then, hopefully, in the end, there is some recognition of how sweet and big life is, how lucky we are to be involved in something as superfluous and as joyful as endurance sports.

The arc of the athlete's life is the story of human frailty and human absurdity distilled, and it's a story that, in my 30-plus years as a journalist, I've kept tuning into. This book collects 23 pieces I've written about endurance sports, mostly for national magazines, since 1989. These stories are reported from seven countries on five continents, from the slums of Bhubaneswar, India, to the windswept tundra of the Alaskan Arctic.

I never set out to write such a book, but as I hunted about for stories that went deep, that carried a Greek resonance, endurance athletes kept cropping up for me, like so many bright, emaciated insects come to the party. These are my people. Somehow I couldn't *not* write about them.

But enough preamble, enough warm-up. Now I want to take you on a journey along the roads and trails of the world. For if you've read this far, you too are probably an addict. And you too need to get out there. Let's go.

Bill Donahue
Gilmanton, New Hampshire
July 2023

RUNNING

Wonder Boy

Runner's World, *August 2008*

IF YOU STAND LONG ENOUGH BY THE TEMPLE COMPLEX, YOU SEE them—the pilgrims—weaving on bare feet through the choked, filthy side streets, past bone-thin wandering cows and past amputee beggars and street children and mangy dogs sprawled on their backs on the cobblestone.

Patiently, the pilgrims pick their way through the mayhem of Puri, India, until they catch sight of the terraced white spires of Jagannath, a labyrinth of some 120 temples. Then they drop to their knees and pray—and, watching, you see how the gritty physical world and the shimmering spiritual realm are deeply intertwined in India, sometimes in strange ways.

On the morning of May 2, 2006, a little boy stepped into the streets of Puri, in running shoes. Budhia Singh was 4 years, 3 months old. A slum kid from a nearby city, Bhubaneswar, he wore bright red socks and a collared white tennis shirt that drooped to midthigh. His task that morning, as prescribed by his coach Biranchi Das, a one-time all-India judo champ, was to run home: 43 miles back to Bhubaneswar, the largest city in the state of Orissa, through the rising heat of Northeast India's most sweltering season.

If all this sounds stranger than a fairy tale, consider that Budhia is now, at age 6, a celebrity in India. He's starred in a popular music video in which he runs, does judo, and unleashes a hip-hop chant, "I am Budhia, son of Orissa." Indian newspapers regularly hail him as a "wonder boy" bound for the Olympics.

As he stood in Puri, Budhia was said to have run six half-marathons and train 120-plus miles a week. Sometimes he ran barefoot on asphalt. Almost always, he ran without hydrating. "If he drinks while running," reasoned Das, "he will go weak."

This run wasn't a race; it was a test with a spiritual resonance. Budhia was traveling a route that millions of pilgrims had ridden in buses: running north from Puri, with its 900-year-old holy shrine, and past the Sun Temple, a World Heritage site boasting exquisite stone carvings. Das had alerted the media and worked his connections with the Central Reserve police force. A squadron of officers and cadets in khaki shorts was ready to run with the boy. Budhia stood hip high among them. He looked little and fragile.

In time, Das would be pilloried by critics arguing that no 4-year-old should be forced to endure the ardors of long-distance running. Three days after Budhia's Puri run, Orissa's minister for women and child development would sweep in to arrest Das, who was also the boy's foster father, on charges of child cruelty. Later, newspapers would air lurid accusations. Budhia's mother alleged last summer that Das hung her son upside down from a ceiling fan, splashed him with hot water, and branded his skin with the words "Biranchi Sir." Budhia himself told reporters, "He locked me in a room for two days without food." Sukanti Singh took her son back from the coach.

All very damning, except that a medical report, conducted by a neutral forensics specialist, Sarbeswar Acharya, revealed that the scars on Budhia's body were three to six months old. They were not caused by scalding water, Acharya opined, and not corroborative of Sukanti's claims. And a newsbreak this spring only deepened the mystery.

On April 13, Biranchi Das, 41, was murdered—shot dead outside his judo hall. The prime suspect, a gangster named Raja Acharya, who faces some 30 unrelated counts of extortion, murder, and kidnapping, is now in jail, awaiting trial. He was infatuated with a lovely Indian actress, Leslie Tripathy. Police speculate that Das irked the gangster by cautioning him to stop harassing Tripathy. If they're right, perhaps Das died for honor. Then again, you could ask why he was hanging out with a violent thug like Acharya in the first place. And was he himself the sort of tough who might thrash a child?

No one (except Budhia himself) will ever know for sure, and there's an outside chance that the boy's scars could have accrued without anyone striking him: In Bhubaneswar's slums, open cook fires are always burning, and rusty nails and broken glass are heaped by the roadside. All that's clear is that nearly every adult in Budhia's life has caused the boy harm.

There is something about kids—their magic innocence, maybe—that can make adults go crazy. Anyone who has ever endured a child-custody battle knows how covetous grown-ups can get. And this is a story about adults going crazy—and about a child trying to remain whole amid the chaos. It's a story about a sort of custody battle, one lacking moral clarity. Biranchi Das wasn't a pure villain; in some ways he shined as devoted.

Back in Puri, he bent to the ground and tied Budhia's shoes. Budhia started to run, at roughly 10 minutes a mile, up a long, slight incline, past roadside shops where vendors sold milky chai for 10 cents a cup and past bald patches of land where long-tailed monkeys crouched by the road, watchful and still.

The police officers surrounded Budhia, their boots scuffing the pavement with a militarized rhythm, and TV cameras craned in at the boy, shooting footage that would later verify that this run was no hoax. Thousands stood at the roadside. Later, everyone in Orissa would speak of how the crowds felicitated Budhia, and that word, carrying hints of fervor and ecstasy, seems to fit. Several times, spectators rushed toward the boy, attempting to garland him with a necklace of orange and red marigolds—the flowers that abound in Indian temples.

Budhia kept going. He crossed a bridge over the River Kushabhadra and passed the fishing village of Chandrabagha. With temperatures climbing into the 90s, Budhia drank only a touch of lemony water. He tired. Then, three miles short of his goal—seven hours, two minutes into his run—Budhia collapsed from exhaustion. He began vomiting and convulsing. Over and over, he bit at the arms of Jyotsna Nayak, the doctor tending to him.

Nayak later told a British filmmaker, "Brain irritation was there. Had I not been there, he certainly would have died." And large questions seemed to hang in the air: Do coaches and parents have the right to conscript children to chase after glory? Who sets the rules? And why are we so transfixed by the bizarre achievements of a 4-year-old boy? Sitting here in the world's most affluent nation, fretting over what type of soy milk our kids are drinking, are we entitled to dictate how the talent of a desperate Indian slum kid ought to be nurtured?

Budhia was thirsty. Nayak gave him water. And before long, the boy bounced back. After all, he'd seen hardship before.

* * *

Budhia Singh was born in Bhubaneswar's Gautam Nagar slum, in a shanty that has since been razed to make way for the railroad. His mother worked, in Indian parlance, as a peon. She did domestic chores, earning $6 a month. Budhia's father, meanwhile, was an alcoholic addicted to ginger—dirt-flecked firewater that women sell from battered metal bowls by the roadside in India. He was unemployed, a beggar who contributed nothing to his family's welfare.

Budhia's parents knew Biranchi Das, who was the president of their slum in Bhubaneswar, the owner of a hotel, and a partner in his family's taxi business. For more than a decade, Das had run an esteemed judo hall, handpicking athletically promising boys and girls from the slums and subjecting them to an almost paramilitary training regimen with twice-daily workouts, strict dietary rules, and classes on combat theory. Seven of his students have become national champions, and more than 1,200 have launched careers with the Central Reserve police force.

I met Das four months before he was killed. He was stout and bearded, rippling with muscles despite a little potbelly, and he exuded the dark, burly beneficence of a Mafia don.

In 2003, he said, Sukanti asked if 1-year-old Budhia could bunk at the judo hall. "She had three daughters, all older than Budhia," Das said, "and already she'd sold the two oldest into servitude, as maids. She told me, 'I can't afford this boy. I can't feed him. Take him.'"

Das said no—Budhia was too young for judo. But about six months later, according to Das, the boy suffered an accident. Riding the crossbar of a neighbor's bicycle, he crashed, fracturing his ankle and shredding the skin on his leg. Untended, the wound festered and got infected. When Sukanti at last took her son to the hospital, doctors advised amputation. Terrified, she returned to Das. This time he said he'd care for the boy. Budhia lived with Das and his wife for six months, until his leg healed.

Then the boy went back to his mother, only to be hit by tragedy. Inside a month, Budhia's father died. Soon after, Das asserted, Sukanti sold her son to a bangle vendor, a man who sold peanuts and gum from his bicycle, with the expectation that, in time, Budhia would work as an assistant. "The vendor didn't take care of Budhia," Das said. "When Budhia visited me after one month, his skin was pale, his clothes were dirty, and he had sores on his body." Das said he bought the boy back for $20. Then one day when Budhia was just 3, the boy cussed. Das punished him, forcing him to run around a dirt oval "until I get back."

Five hours later, Budhia was still running. Soon Das decided that Budhia would become the first Indian runner to win an Olympic medal. He began training the boy, riding on his bicycle as Budhia ran—four miles a day at first, then six, then 10. In time, crowds of adoring fans joined the runs, trotting behind the boy or rolling beside him on bikes.

In October 2005, Das took Budhia, then 3, to his first race—a half-marathon in Delhi. Race officials forbade Budhia to start, but no matter. He was the darling of the 6K fun run, and the It Boy of a postrace gala. British decathlete Daley Thompson tried to score a kiss from Budhia, but Tim Hutchings, international administrator for the London Marathon, fulminated, "For a child of 3 to be training hard is verging on criminal."

By now, a British filmmaker was tracking Budhia's story, making a half-hour TV documentary, and Das was hatching intricate plans. He decreed that, after the Puri run, Budhia would run a marathon in Nayagarh. "After that," he said, "he'll go to Madras, and then there's a race in Cochin, and on to Guwahati. After this we will take him to some events abroad."

He never competed in these races. After his Puri run, Orissa's child welfare department issued a medical report finding him "undernourished, anemic, and under cardiological stress." The agency banned all children from entering distance races before the age of 14. In India, the ruling was largely seen as ridiculous. "How self-indulgent and naive can our liberalism be?" railed *Khaleej Times* columnist Barkha Dutt. "This is a chance for a poor slum child to break down the class divide and travel on the same superhighway to success as everyone else."

Snubbing officials, a public poll named Budhia the second most popular person in Orissa. A steel company hired the boy as a spokesmascot, and a Dubai businessman flew Budhia and his coach to the Emirates for a splashy getaway at an amusement park. Then came the video that nearly deified Budhia. "We hoped the song would clear many misconceptions about the child," said producer Rajesh Kumar Mohanty. "We have tried to compare him with the mythological Lord Krishna."

* * *

Over the following year, Budhia's prospects seemed to brighten. With his mother's permission, in September 2006, he'd moved to a state-run sports hostel, where he lived and trained with more than 100 other sports hopefuls, most of them teens. He had a new coach named Arun Das (no relation to Biranchi Das), who promised further glory. Then, on a scholarship, he enrolled at the DAV Public School, arguably Bhubaneswar's most prestigious academy. He was treated like a celebrity on his first day. After his classmates, all dressed in uniform plaid pinafore shorts, clambered to kiss him on the cheek, he addressed the entire student body, from a stage, chirping, "I am Budhia Singh. You will all be my friends. I will help you to learn running."

I arrived in Bhubaneswar on a warm day last winter. The city is loud 24/7, teeming with a vitality that is both joyful and desperate. From my hotel room, I heard hundreds of garbage-eating crows cawing in a tree, the low throttle of auto rickshaws, and a nightclub downstairs where middle-aged men paid teenage girls to sing for them.

I later moved to a quieter hotel. I also began counting dead dogs I saw smooshed on the roads. In one week, I saw eight. Once, when I was riding with an interpreter, he ran over a puppy and never let the conversation falter. "So your brother," he said, "he is staying in New York?"

Crossing the street was life threatening. There were few public bathrooms, so men peed by the roadside; the stink of urine was everywhere.

Orissa has the worst child mortality rate in India, and several times, young mothers trailed me, tugging at my shirt and begging me to buy food for their infants.

Biranchi Das's judo hall was an oasis, secreted behind high concrete walls on the spacious grounds of the state museum. One day in the coolness just after dawn, recorded chant music echoed over the grounds. Das stood outside the hall, fresh from a six-mile run, dancing in place like a boxer, then vaulting into a handstand. He plucked a little branch off the ground and began using it, as many Indians do, as an improvised toothbrush.

"How's Budhia?" he asked. "What did Budhia say?" I hadn't yet met the boy, but Das continued. "Budhia is a good child," he said. "I miss him. He and I had a dream. It was not fulfilled. That is agony for me. In Japan and Korea, they start training athletes at age 3. If you don't take risks, you don't get results. I am the person who took risks with Budhia, and I got results."

As he spoke, a friend of his stood nearby, radiating his own athletic vigor. Ashwini Das, 55, is a devout yogi and an Art of Living instructor with the regal bearing and prominent clavicle that comes from a lifetime of Ashtanga and belly breaths. A few years ago, he told me, "I became interested in how Biranchi is growing up this Budhia. This child has an inner facility, and Biranchi just explored it."

Biranchi drifted off, and Ashwini and I wandered through the deserted museum grounds. "When Budhia came to him," Ashwini said, "the child had a physical problem, and Biranchi worked for Budhia as no parent can. Look, there are hundreds of millions of kids like Budhia in India—starving, without even a meal—and among all these children, Budhia alone became an inspiration."

He halted and abruptly asked: "What is the nature of the mind?" I had no earthly idea, so I let him answer his own question. "Whatever you resist," he said, "that persists. If you say, 'I want to sleep,' you can't sleep. Meditation means deconcentration—and Budhia achieved this, as few people can. He had an inner quality."

"You mean he was wise?" I asked.

Ashwini looked at me like I was a total idiot. "No," he said. "Budhia is a small child. He knows nothing of the world. I believe that he had a gift inculcated from a past life—a gift beyond imagination. He can run, and Biranchi brought that talent to life. He is the one who put the petrol in the Budhia vehicle."

* * *

Sukanti felt otherwise. I met with her one afternoon in a lawyer's office. Budhia's mother looks about 40. Slender and fine-featured, she wore a Bindi (a red dot traditionally worn by married women on their foreheads). Her bony brow jutted out of her yellow sari. She was quiet, keeping her eyes downcast as men yelled around her.

"She's illiterate," said the lawyer, Suresh Routray, dismissively waving a hand toward Singh. "She knows nothing."

Singh's boyfriend also spoke over her. "Biranchi Das is a goon," said Pranakrushna Khatua, a convicted bank robber, according to Bhubaneswar police records. "He threatened to kill Sukanti and her three daughters. He told her that if she said anything about the money, she would die."

We were there to discuss the donations and endorsement money that Budhia had received during the 18 or so months he trained under Das. This past December, Singh told police that Das had embezzled more than 60 million rupees, about $1.4 million, from the Budhia Singh Trust. Routray, a corpulent man, about 40, with drowsy eyes and a broad mustache, prepared the legal papers. He did so because he's the president of Salia Sahi (the slum Sukanti Singh now lives in) and also a prominent member of Orissa's Communist Party.

Twice, I'd meet Routray in my hotel lobby, to probe him for details on how he arrived at 60 million rupees. His air was breezy and jocular. "Ah, Meester Bill," he said, hailing me with bearish effusion, "Meester Bill! You want the papers? I will get you the papers." He never got me any documents. Biranchi Das said that Routray was showboating to garner publicity for the Communist Party.

Now, in his office, I asked him, "What companies gave Budhia money?"

"Ah, there were so many companies, so many companies," he responded. He named three, each of which, he reckoned, gave $500 or so. Then he repeated himself: "So many companies."

I wanted to hear what Singh thought, and she bitterly lambasted Das. "When they stopped Budhia from competing," she said, speaking to my interpreter, "he couldn't make any more money for Biranchi. So Biranchi started torturing Budhia. There is no other reason."

Singh argued that Das had bullied her into lying to the media. "That story about me selling Budhia," she said, "it wasn't true. I never sold my son. Biranchi just made me say stupid things. I said them because I was depressed."

Singh talked of her husband's death. "He left me without one pie," she said. "My neighbors had to pay for the cremation. When they demolished my house to make way for the railroad, I asked Biranchi for money. I said, 'You have taken all the money that my son earned. You should give me money to rent a house.' He said, 'There is no money left. We spent it on Budhia's training.' He is a liar."

Suddenly Khatua's cell phone rang. Budhia was calling from school. He'd just won a 100-meter race for kindergartners. I could hear his joyous voice coming out of the phone—and it seemed that he'd called to talk to his mother. They were still in touch, after all. Press photos have captured her cradling her slender boy in her own slender arms. She visits Budhia once a week, scraping together 10 rupees for the rickshaw ride.

But this was a big meeting for Sukanti Singh. An unfathomable pile of money was at stake, as she saw it, so she did not get on the phone to say hi. She just sat there stooped over the desk, staring dully ahead as she stewed in disdain for Biranchi Das.

* * *

Two years after his 40-mile Puri run, Budhia is still famous in Bhubaneswar. On the streets, he is a one-name hero. "Ah, Budhia!" people will say. "Marathon boy!" "Ah, Budhia, he is a miracle!" Once, when I went to meet him at a DAV Public School picnic, he wasn't present. His minders at the sports hostel forbade him to go out in public without a security guard, and on that day, the guard had a holiday.

I finally met Budhia in his classroom. He sat at a desk in his plaid pinafore and brown V-neck sweater. Budhia was watchful, with the whittled, ropy look of a runner, and he fidgeted—overwhelmed, perhaps, by my looming, pale presence. "This man has come all the way from America to see you," the teacher proclaimed in the singsong universal to kindergarten instructors.

Budhia said nothing; he just looked up at me, skeptically. I'd brought a present for him—a book about children of the world. I'd tried to make the gift speak to his worldview: Pasted to the wrapping paper were pictures of Budhia himself, running. He picked open the paper as the teacher translated my questions. "Do you like running?" she asked, vigorously nodding her head. "Yes, you like running. It is very fun, isn't it?"

I looked at Budhia and rolled my eyes. Tentatively, he smiled—and for a while, he seemed amused by me. We went back to the sports hostel, where he sleeps in a large concrete room, and he played a little cricket with me, waving a mop handle as I bowled him a yellow ping-pong ball. At one point, he sprinted into the kitchen and came sprinting back, giddy as he pressed his fist toward my hip. "Want apple?" he said in faltering English, his voice tiny and high as he skittered away.

Soon, though, I was no longer a novelty. Budhia sat down in the corner. I thought that maybe now he'd read the book that I'd given him, but no, very carefully he plucked a piece of paper from out of his pinafore and stared at it, delighted. It was the picture of Budhia himself, running and waving to fans.

* * *

"You talked to Budhia? What did he say?" I'd expected that Biranchi Das, facing the torture accusations, would shun all my calls and refuse to be interviewed. But in fact he was the most media-friendly person I met in Bhubaneswar. He was polished and genial, and it seemed that impoverished slum dwellers considered his office a small fount of hope. One afternoon I found him meeting with a man who needed money for his sister's wedding dowry. Without the money, his sister couldn't marry; her future would be cast into doubt. "Five minutes," Das told me.

The meeting lasted for half an hour, and when the man emerged, he was smiling. Das had promised he would help, personally, in a couple of weeks. "Right now," Das explained to me, "I only have 700 rupees [about $16] in my bank account. I am a poor man. I didn't get rich from Budhia. All the money we got came to 1.32 lakh rupees [about $3,100], and we spent it on Budhia's training."

Yet on another occasion Das hinted that he had profited from Budhia. "I adopted him," he said. "If he makes some money, I deserve some of it, don't I?" Later, Das fed me what seemed an outright lie. "This judo hall," he said, "is the production center for Budhias. Right now I am training four new Budhia runners. They are all between 3 and 5 years old. They are training every day. They are practicing. I have videotapes, but I cannot show you. It is all very secret right now, but when the day comes—when it is time for them to perform—I will tell everybody."

I asked at least five children at the judo hall if they'd seen any preschoolers besides Budhia Singh training as runners. They all looked at me with blank stares. No, they had not seen the new Budhias.

Even when he was joking, Das oozed swagger and bravado. One morning, he smugly summoned me to lie on the judo mat. Then he sicced one of his young behemoths on me as I struggled to break free of the boy's hold. When the farce was over and I lay there, whipped, Das chuckled and tossed me a little tip—a two-rupee coin.

Das's police record was not pretty. After the Child Welfare Committee for Orissa's Khurda District took Budhia out of Das's house, the judo coach allegedly organized a mob of 200 protesters to rally outside the home of Rabi Shankar Misra, the agency's chairman. Misra contends that some protesters burned his effigy, climbed a wall into his property, and surrounded his house for several hours. Misra also accused Das of using Budhia. "He got a free trip to Dubai out of him," Misra told me. "Would he be able to go to Dubai otherwise?" (It was a valid critique, but a few days later Misra himself tried to milk the Budhia story for a free trip. In answering Runner's World's request that he e-mail some legal documents. Misra demurred. "I can give you a presentation on the complex issues," he wrote, "in your office in USA, if invited for this presentation.")

Later, in August 2007, after a street accident that saw Das's 7-year-old son get harmlessly clipped by a motorcyclist named Sabeer Ekram, Das allegedly burst into the man's home with 30-odd henchmen. Ekram's mother, M. D. Manju, told police that Das beat her son up. "He pelted us with filthy expletives and threatened to set our house on fire," she told the police.

Still, Das had close ties to the police. One afternoon, he brought me across town to visit his top contact at the Central Reserve police force—deputy inspector G. P. Mastana.

Mastana's building was guarded by several machine-gun-toting officers who wore full khaki uniforms topped by brilliant indigo tricornered hats. Scores of young recruits were training as we arrived, running along in lockstep on a sandy dirt road. We went inside. Mastana's office was grand, with a large desk bearing four black telephones and, above that, a plaque honoring men who'd preceded him as deputies. Mastana, who's a Sikh, was sitting there in a turban, very erect—a bristling, fit 60-year-old.

The mood was a bit stiff, so I tried to break the ice. "Jeez." I said to Mastana, "I wouldn't want to wrestle you." He did not laugh, but after a few minutes he spoke warmly of Budhia. "I admire the boy," he said, "and one time I advised him. I told him he could be a supreme athlete, and I said, 'After that, then you can do something good. You can bring glory to the nation—you can become an officer with us and set an example for others.'"

Das was leaning forward in his chair now, listening with rapt appreciation. The troops scuffed by on the roadway outside, and it seemed almost forgotten that we were talking about a little boy who was still learning to read. "What did Budhia say?" I asked.

Mastana stared me down, somber and earnest. "Budhia said he was willing."

* * *

Two days later, I saw Budhia on the track at Kalinga Stadium, but he didn't seem particularly focused on athletic supremacy or national service. He was dribbling a soccer ball as some teenage girls in full soccer regalia made pretend futile attempts to steal the ball. He was laughing.

"Budhia is doing his training," his new coach, Arun Das, told me before detailing the boy's current regimen: seven or eight miles a week, a little stretching, a little hopping and bounding, a little horseplay with the soccer ball and the discus.

Arun Das is a genial and wrinkled man, about 60 and a tad flabby, dressed in a blue nylon track suit. As his older runners muscled their way through a speed workout, he sat on the grass, canted back in a lawn chair, savoring the mild winter sun as he spoke fondly of Budhia. "He's like a son to me," he said before adding with a warm, self-derisive chuckle, "Well, more like a grandson."

I asked if he saw Budhia becoming a champion. He laughed. "Now is not the right time to say. Come back in 12 years and I'll tell you."

"But what kind of times is he running?"

The coach looked skyward for a moment, searching for the numbers. "For the 400," he said, "about two minutes."

Two-flat is good for a little kid; it would put Budhia in about the 85th percentile among 6-year-old American boys. Still, I was surprised. The stories I'd read suggested that, like Biranchi, Arun was driving Budhia toward world-class glory. (One headline read, "Budhia gets new coach, dreams for Olympics.") But now I got an inkling that Arun Das was like no other Budhia caretaker I'd met in all the days I'd spent rattling around Bhubaneswar in auto rickshaws. It seemed he might be playing a gentle trick on the Indian people—administering workouts, proffering photo ops, and gamely sustaining the illusion that Budhia was on the brink of greatness while simultaneously protecting the boy. He was, it struck me, letting Budhia be a kid in a society where a leisurely childhood is a luxury.

After a few minutes, Budhia trotted toward us, to high-five a sprinter standing nearby. I tried to ask him a question, but by the time my words had been translated, he was already running off toward the steeplechase pit for a game of tag with the soccer players. These girls lived with him, and it looked as though they cherished him as a mascot.

"I am playing," he squealed as I stepped toward him with a question. "Just let me play."

* * *

I saw Budhia just one more time, at his school, on a day his class was doing "magic painting." Again, the teacher came over to his desk to interpret. "Was it hard," I asked, "doing all that running for Biranchi?"

"No, I just did what I was asked."

"Was it stressful?" He shook his head: no.

"Was Biranchi nice to you?"

Now there was an awkward silence and I could hear the high, happy din of the other students larking about, unsupervised. Budhia stared at the floor, biting his lip. The question seemed to put him under enormous pressure.

Biranchi Das had helped deliver him to a new and wonderful place in his life. A peon's son destined to caste-bound misery, he was now standing in a cool, pleasant room filled with the nation's elite. He'd transcended social barriers in a way that few Americans can fathom, and he'd performed his own kid magic. He had survived all the craven adults fighting to control him.

There was something elegant and beautiful about this lean little kid whose smile, at times, bordered on beatific. Maybe, in time, this magic would prevail. Maybe Budhia would turn out all right. But maybe, too, he was scarred. He seemed brooding and insular now. He kept staring down. He said nothing.

"He is not able to express himself," said the teacher. "The question is difficult."

I stopped my interview. Budhia finished his painting (of a Christmas tree), and then the class streamed outside to do calisthenics in the red, dusty schoolyard. There were two parallel lines of kids, and the exercises were supposed to be done in unison. But of course they weren't. Every kid, including Budhia, flubbed the performance. The lines were a melee of children idly scuffing their feet and wiping their noses and scratching their legs. I stood there and thought about how all of these kids would carry their own quirks—and the history and traumas of their earliest childhoods—forward from here, all alone, ultimately, against the challenge of growing up in a world filled with tough questions.

Eventually, the teacher told the kids to sprint to the back of the playground. I watched for Budhia to stand out—to lope ahead like a sad, lone gazelle. But by now every single kid in the crowd was screaming with glee and sputtering and swerving along over the dirt, and I lost him in a swirl of dust.

The Challenger

Runner's World, *April 14, 2023*

Before he won the Boston Marathon, before he won New York, and long before he built his mother a new home, Evans Chebet rented a small one-room house for \$12 a month about 45 miles south of Kondabilet, the tiny mountain village in Kenya where he grew up. The home was sparsely furnished with a stool and an old table. Chebet cooked outdoors—usually *sukuma wiki* (similar to collard greens) and *ugali*, a traditional cornmeal porridge—and in the long hours between training sessions, he sat outside and stared at the red dirt and the evergreen forest of the Kenyan highlands, reflecting on his luck.

It was 2007. Chebet was a 19-year-old aspiring distance runner, and he'd come to seek his fortune. He was living outside Kaptagat, a town of about 2,500 people, hoping to work his way into Kenya's talent pipeline. Many Kenyans who race internationally, including marathon world record holder Eliud Kipchoge, live in spartan high-altitude training camps in Kenya's Great Rift Valley, sleeping in tiny unadorned rooms and sharing housekeeping chores and communal meals. Chebet was trying to gain entry to a camp run by Rosa & Associates, an Italian sports management company.

Although he grew up with few financial resources, he was now—thanks to an uncle's largesse—rubbing shoulders with running's greats. "I was so happy to be there," he says.

Chebet was hardly a shining prospect. He'd never raced on the track. Indeed, he'd scarcely raced at all, and he was resigned to waiting outside the Rosa camp, and tagging along on the athletes' brisk morning workouts. "I'd start out with the front runners, trying to show my talent," he says. "But I'd get dropped."

While Kenya has flourished economically over the last decade, more than 36 percent of the population lives below the poverty rate, according to World Bank data. There were—and still are—hundreds of impoverished young men and women who haunt the locked gates of Kenya's elite training camps, harboring a ragged dream of stardom and wealth. Few succeed or even get a chance, but in 2008, a young Italian coach with Rosa named Claudio Berardelli saw something in Chebet and invited him in. "He was young and not very strong," Berardelli says, "but I'd seen some improvement."

That scrawny kid at the gate is now 34. He won both the Boston and New York City marathons in 2022, and he'll face a stacked field this year when he lines up to defend his Boston title. On April 17, in its 127th running, the Beantown classic will play host to a sort of holy visitation. The esteemed 38-year-old Kipchoge—the two-time Olympic champion, the only human ever to go sub-2:00 for the marathon—will be making his first-ever appearance at the starting line in Hopkinton. Kipchoge has been characteristically succinct about his race strategy, telling reporters, "I see myself winning."

The field will include a total of seven sub-2:05 Kipchoge challengers. Is Chebet the quickest of all these would-be spoilers? "If you are betting on a man to mess things up for the impeccable grandmaster, it could be Evans who delivers," says Toby Tanser, author of *More Fire: How to Run the Kenyan Way*. Tanser lives in Kenya and is friendly with Chebet and other top harriers.

Chebet won last year's Boston Marathon with shrewdness and authority. Early on, he tucked into the lead pack of about 15 runners. At mile 20, he climbed with this group up Heartbreak Hill. Then—still looking fresh, with just six mostly downhill miles left—he threw down the hammer and wheeled through the 22nd mile in 4:27. His next two splits were 4:26. No one could touch him. In the end, he beat runner-up Lawrence Cherono, also Kenyan, by a full half-minute, clocking a time of 2:06:51.

Seven months later, Chebet held a nagging Achilles injury at bay and hung on to win the New York City Marathon in 2:08:41 on a weirdly sweltering November day. And the victory was no fluke. The man has run 27 marathons, 10 more than Kipchoge, and he's won five of the last six he's entered.

But it's unlikely that the name Evans Chebet rings a bell with many runners. Even though Kenyans have won 23 of the 31 Boston Marathons held since 1990, most American fans don't make the effort to distinguish one Kenyan from the next. We know Kipchoge, sure, but beyond that it's just "the Kenyans" and facile chatter about how fleetness is "in their genes."

And while many Kenyan winners speak English, Chebet's facility with the language is limited. At the press conference after he won New York, he answered questions in Swahili. The marathon did not have an interpreter on hand, and when officials crowdsourced for translation, Chebet's words were rendered so vaguely, so roughly, that the winner remained behind a sort of curtain. So when I found myself in Kenya for work last December, I saw an opportunity to unlock the enigma surrounding Chebet and humanize the man who might just topple a legend.

* * *

Eliud Kipchoge is so widely celebrated in Kenya (and the world) that he can make other runners seem invisible. Just minutes after I land in Eldoret, where many of the country's top athletes live, I encounter a huge billboard just outside the airport with a larger-than-life picture of Kipchoge and the words "Welcome to the City of Champions." Soon my driver, Cornelius Lagat, is telling me Kipchoge "is more protected than the president of Kenya."

Evans Chebet is, in contrast, quite the opposite. A couple of hours after I call his publicist to ask for an interview, a guard is ushering me into Chebet's training camp in Kapsabet, a city of more than 80,000 about an hour southwest of Eldoret, where Chebet and 19 other athletes live in small parallel bedrooms.

At five feet seven and 132 pounds, Chebet is a slight man, with bright brown eyes and a shaved head. He rolls into the interview a few minutes late, wearing a yellow camo hoodie and an easy grin, even though his Achilles is still sore after New York. With his marathon winnings, he just financed, two days ago, a huge wedding to the love of his life—the mother of his three children, 26-year-old Benedicta Serem. A thousand guests had been on hand for the nuptials. Chebet's family had helped feed the crowd by slaughtering two cows, three goats, and 10 chickens.

We sit on a couple of worn couches and then, smiling, bemused by my curiosity, Chebet spends two hours talking to me through an interpreter, his voice soft, his tone almost unrelentingly positive. "I never dreamed I'd be racing against Eliud Kipchoge in the Boston Marathon," he says.

Chebet is the eighth of nine children. As a kid in his mountain village, he spent hours trotting along poking a stick at a worn tire beside him to make it roll smoothly over the rubbly road. The family owned one bicycle, a single-speed black Hero Jet that for many years was too big for him; he crashed and cried as he learned to ride it. Now, he laughs at the memory. When he was about 8, he took to running a hilly loop of about nine miles whenever he felt like it. "I loved running so much," he says.

Chebet's father, Kipyesang, had been a distance runner, a 5,000- and 10,000-meter man, and had won many trophies. Only after I pressed him did Chebet note that his father died of cancer when he was a young boy. A photo of Kipyesang hung by the door of the family's two-room house. Evans has no memory of him, but the financial struggles that followed his father's death remain vivid. "We had enough to eat just two meals a day," he says, "and dinner wasn't much—just a little *githeri* [a mixture of corn and beans]. I always felt like I had to support my family."

When Chebet was about 10, he began working as a day laborer, harvesting corn on nearby farms. Sometimes he burned wood, to make charcoal to sell. Sometimes, too, he herded the seven cows his family owned. Sometimes, when the cattle strayed and got lost, his older brothers, being older brothers, hit him with sticks.

He dropped out of school at 14, unable to pay the tuition, and began working full-time. He pedaled his village on the Hero Jet, gathering maize from farmers until he had enough to take three or four 90-pound sacks of grain to Eldoret. He traveled there a couple times a week in a communal van, lashing the grain to the roof and paying 80 cents for his ride.

Lifting the giant sacks left his body in pain but also built his muscles. In his spare time, he kept running. A neighbor gifted him a pair of trainers, and he would work out with his older brother John. His mother, Wanjiro, beheld Evans's easy, flowing stride and would point to Kipyesang's photo and tell him, "Run like your father. He left the talent to you."

In 2011, Berardelli took Chebet to his first major race, the Gargnano Ten Miler, in Italy, where he finished second in 50:53. It was a promising start, but even as Chebet spent the next few years getting faster, he never seemed able to win. In 2014, he finished second at two lucrative marathons, in Prague and in Seoul. Over the following three years, he finished second in three more marathons—in Valencia, Spain, and again in both Prague and Seoul. "He was always the number two guy," says Berardelli. "Subconsciously, I think he'd accepted being a very good athlete rather than a real champion."

Meanwhile, Berardelli was facing a crisis. His most prominent athlete, Rita Jeptoo, a three-time Boston Marathon winner, tested positive for EPO, a banned substance, in 2014. In 2015, after two other athletes coached by Berardelli—marathoner Mathew Kisorio and 800-meter runner Agatha Jeruto—were caught doping, he parted ways with Rosa & Associates. At the time, the company's director, Federico Rosa, told reporters that while he didn't believe Berardelli was involved in the cheating, he felt he "was not able to pay enough attention to his own athletes."

The Kenyan government felt differently, though, and in 2016 charged Berardelli and two others for administering drugs to Jeptoo and conspiring to destroy her career. They were eventually acquitted, but the media coverage of Jeptoo's fall was nonstop.

There has never been any widespread speculation about whether Chebet himself has used banned substances, nor any actions against him by an anti-doping body, but Berardelli's travails caused a shift. In 2016, exiled from Rosa, Berardelli opened a new camp in Kapsabet where Chebet now lives.

But the relationship between athlete and coach had always been a bit strained; Berardelli spoke only limited Swahili, which made communication difficult. And there may have been a difference in perspective. "When Claudio was setting the camp up," Chebet says, "he was a little strict, like sometimes he wouldn't let us go home, except on the weekends. I wasn't used to that."

Berardelli concedes that he is demanding. "I want athletes to have the right attitude, the right behavior," he says.

In late 2018, Chebet parted ways with his longtime mentor. Without a coach, he began crafting his own training plans and would informally head out with elite training groups. Now that he had proved himself, he received a warm welcome—and he held his position at the front.

As I sat at the training camp with Chebet, observing his chill bonhomie, I knew I wasn't seeing the whole of him. No one wins the Boston Marathon without harboring a little fire in his belly. Tanser told me, "Evans's mental strength is upper-level. He's a modest and reflective man, but he's also a street fighter. He believes strongly in himself, and he truly believes he will win. You'll never find him needing a sports psychologist."

Where does this unbreakable spirit come from? "Whenever I'm in a big race, I remember what I went through as a kid," Chebet says. "I had to fight to survive." He tells me that, to understand his fortitude, I need to visit his childhood village.

* * *

Kondabilet sits high in the Cherangani Hills, which are regarded as a source of storms in Kenya. Its name means "eye of the thunder" in Kalenjin, a local dialect. I travel out there one morning with a tour guide, Amos Kimutai, who speculates on the Kipchoge-Chebet showdown in Boston. "Everyone is waiting for this race between Eliud and Evans," says Kimutai, who's run a 2:19 marathon himself. "But Boston is hard to predict. When it's rainy and cold and windy, American runners do very well. If it's sunny—well, the Kenyans will take it," he says. "Evans is more tactical than Eliud. If it comes down to a sprint, Evans is going to take Kipchoge."

Our driver, Cornelius Lagat, rejects this take, arguing that Kipchoge, who is older than Chebet, harbors superior wisdom and therefore the upper hand. "Kipchoge has the experience," he says. "He will win."

We turn off the highway onto a dirt road that twists steeply upward. In the center of Kondabilet, we pass Poa Place, a tiny restaurant run by Chebet's mother, Wanjiro, age 71. Soon after that, we encounter a man driving a team of donkeys up from the Silanga river, each animal bearing two battered 20-liter plastic jugs filled with drinking water; there are still no pipes in Kondabilet.

The Chebets' home is a mile uphill from the river. Evans is away at the camp, but Wanjiro is there to meet me. Wearing a tiered blouse and a pleated skirt in shades of pink and brown, she is accompanied by six family members. We sit in the large, airy house her son had built on his family's land with his marathon profits. (Just in winning Boston and New York last year, he garnered $250,000 in prize money.) There is almost no furniture outside the living room, and the walls are unadorned, save for a few small holes sprouting electrical cords. (Parts of the village have electricity, but there are still no power lines where the Chebets live.)

"No *mzungu* has ever visited here," Wanjiro says through an interpreter, using a Swahili word for white person, "except for missionaries and aid workers."

Wanjiro says she's never been interviewed by a reporter, and now what is there to say? Still, she wastes no time before launching into a proud retelling of her son's life and achievements. Evans had his own vegetable garden when he was small. He was highly skilled at guiding oxen to plow the fields. And he always loved to run. "When Evans was young, he was running all the time—up and down through the hills," she says. "And every time he came home, he was stretching." She mimics Evans stretching, twisting her torso as she sits on the couch, bicycling her legs for a second. "Oh, your children!" she says, laughing with delight, "they bring you blessings!"

I look around the room. There is a sizable crowd watching our exchange, and they all hang reverently on the matriarch's every word. She is the mother of nine children, and there is something solid and deeply stabilizing about her presence. I reflect now on something Evans had told me: "After my father's death, it was my mother who felt the challenge. She struggled to provide for the entire family, but she always told us, 'There will be better days ahead.'"

Even though her son was unproven, Wanjiro believed he could become a champion. She took Evans to the church services held each Sunday in Kondabilet's mud-walled schoolhouse, and there he prayed that his family would be well-off like his neighbors. ("They owned a tractor," he explained.)

Now, sitting in the living room, I feel the same force of hope at work. Wanjiro is strong. She's kept Evans afloat, and all the while she has been buoyed by the people in that room. Evans, too, depends on them. The guy carries a fire within him, sure, but it is the love of those he knows best that sustains and propels him.

Wanjiro explains that most locals will watch the Boston Marathon via livestream on their phones. "We will be watching right in this room," she says. "We will be praying. If Evans can beat Kipchoge, we will be very happy."

Eventually, we wander outside into the yard, passing the two-room house Evans grew up in. Wanjiro still sleeps there—her entire wardrobe hangs from a clothesline by her bed. "It is better for old people to be in an old building," her son William explains as we get ready to leave. "The walls hold the heat better."

Wanjiro nods, listening, and then looks at me warmly as I climb into the car. "Next time you come," she says, "we will slaughter a sheep for you."

Chebet's time away from Berardelli was defined by a certain solitude. He rented an apartment of his own. He moved about independently, training wherever he liked, and even as he battled injuries, he ran well. In 2019, uncoached, he won the Buenos Aires Marathon in 2:05:00. Still, he was accustomed to living among others—that's how he'd always thrived. "I was used to being part of a program," he says. "I'd had a coach since I started running, and now I was not connected." Late in 2019, he visited Berardelli at his Kenyan home.

During the separation, Berardelli had improved his Swahili and had also done some reflecting. "I realized I needed to step back a little bit," he says. "I needed to be a bit less demanding on some things." Reconciliation did not take long. "In about five minutes," the coach told me, "Evans and I decided to put the past behind us."

When Chebet returned to his old training group, he found a new synergy at work. Two of his longtime cohorts, Benson Kipruto and Amos Kipruto—not brothers but members of the same Nandi ethnic group—were pushing one another so much that in time they'd win major marathons in, respectively, Boston and London.

"Evans didn't want to be left behind," Berardelli says. "He found a new motivation."

He also found in the Kiprutos the kind of support that sustains him, that he has always gotten from his family. "We are like brothers living in the same house," Benson Kipruto says, speaking of Evans and Amos. "We live together, and we understand each other."

"When we have a problem, they encourage you," Chebet says. "We are there for each other."

At the 2020 Valencia Marathon, with less than 200 meters to go, Chebet was trailing his countryman, Lawrence Cherono, and seemed bound for yet another runner-up performance. But then suddenly he located another gear. He churned into the lead, and on the last straightaway he buried Cherono, winning by a full four seconds as he lowered his PR to 2:03:00.

When I was visiting Kenya just a month after Chebet's victory in New York, Berardelli was worried that maybe he'd never witness such magic again, for Chebet had spent weeks away from camp, planning his wedding. The Achilles injury was scuttling his training. Berardelli wondered if his athlete was still motivated. "Financially, he's stable," Berardelli says. "He has what he needs. Is it over?"

When I talked with Chebet over Zoom in March, though, he said he was pain free. With Benson Kipruto, who will also run Boston, he'd just done a workout designed to prepare them for Heartbreak Hill and what follows. They'd knocked out 10 repeats over a one-mile stretch of road that featured a hard climb flowing into a steep descent. Chebet told me that he was ready—and that he has a crucial prerace ritual that he has never once skipped.

"A week before I leave Kenya," he explained, "I go home to Kond-abilet. My family gives me their blessings. We pray. And then I meet with my mother, and always she tells me, 'You need to go and get your best because you know where you've come from.'"

As we were wrapping up this conversation, I asked Chebet if he had any questions for me.

His response was almost automatic. "I want to know about your family," he said. I began telling my story, and as I spoke, Chebet canted his head a notch closer to the camera. He listened, intent, it seemed, on locating some truth in my gestures, in the tone of my voice.

When I was done, the interpreter swiveled his laptop so that Chebet could address me directly. I watched him speak. The moment seemed peaceful and underlain by the most earnest goodwill. "He is saying," the interpreter said, "that he is very grateful that you took the time to visit his family and to know his mother."

Pre-destined

Runner's World, *August 2005*

"GALEN!"

The boy doesn't move: just lies there flat on the warm track, his arms limp and spread-eagled over his head as he gazes up at the big, blue New Mexico sky, gasping for breath. Watch him now. Watch him lying there, his bony ribs heaving under his aqua blue T-shirt, laboring to suck sustenance out of the thin, dry mountain air here in Albuquerque, 5,000 feet above sea level. Galen Rupp is 19 years old, with sandy blond hair, and acne, and soft blue eyes that dart away shyly whenever you speak to him. He is six feet tall and weighs 137 pounds. When he runs, gliding over the ground in a very upright manner, his lean hips floating forward and his hair flying about in the breeze, he has a way of making you feel almost pained. "Oh," you think, "oh, my vanished youth!"

Last year, just after he finished high school in Portland, Oregon, Rupp broke Gerry Lindgren's 40-year-old American junior record for the 5,000 meters, running 13:37.91. He also ran a mile in 4:01, the fastest high school mile in the country in 2004. His efforts reminded distance-running fans in Oregon of the state's last epic prodigy—the cocky, brash, unpredictable Steve Prefontaine. Pre became nationally known as a high schooler before going on to set NCAA records and then competing in the 1972 Munich Olympics, where his gutsy performance in the 5,000 left him just short of a medal. But if Pre was a glowering bad boy who would die at age 24, when he crashed his car along a rocky Oregon road, Rupp is primarily diligent. He's a well-mannered young man willing to do whatever it takes, no matter how mundane or servile, to excel in distance running. Last summer, he did a two-hour "run" on an underwater treadmill while strapped to a face mask that made his lungs work as though he was at 11,000 feet. Today, as a freshman at the University of Oregon (Pre's alma mater), he's been known to log more than 100 miles a week, emphasizing speedwork and sometimes hitting a 5:15-per-mile clip on his "easy" days. "He trains at a higher level than anyone I know," says Stuart Eagon, a promising University of Wisconsin runner who spent his high school years in Oregon, groping in vain to beat Rupp.

"I can't think of any young runner that excites me more than Galen Rupp," says Larry Eder, the publisher of *American Track & Field* magazine. "He has the tools—and the work ethic—to be an Olympic medalist."

Running on this late winter day with the Oregon Project, a Nike-sponsored program for elite runners, Rupp's just done the sort of workout that sends a runner's muscles into burning starvation for the oxygen that is so far away, down at sea level. In the session completed moments ago, he churned through eight quarters in 57.5, with but a minute's rest in between. It's nothing special for him but still roughly equivalent, comfort-wise, to being repeatedly jabbed by several hundred sewing needles at once. Earlier, Adam Goucher, an American middle-distance runner, summed up the mood here when he paused, bent over double, with a long cord of white spittle sticking like glue to his lip. "You can taste the blood," Goucher wheezed.

"Galen!" It's the voice again. And now Alberto Salazar, the one-time world marathon record holder, trots over toward Rupp, a couple of stopwatches swinging loosely on his neck. "Galen," he says, "just a couple miles now on the grass."

It's a basic cooldown instruction, an apt one for a young runner working his way back from a foot stress fracture—and it is also Galen Rupp's cue to rise. He gets up, loose as a rag doll, and strolls over to the bleachers and changes out of his spikes, into his trainers. Salazar, the 46-year-old coach of the Oregon Project, just watches as Rupp dances away over the grass.

* * *

Lately, it seems we've been fed a steady diet of fresh-faced young men billed as the Next Great American Distance Runner—the phenom who (just watch!) will finally catch the Ethiopians and Kenyans. Four years ago, it was Alan Webb, who went 3:53 in breaking Jim Ryun's 36-year-old high school mile record, but injuries and tactical errors have kept him from matching the early acclaim. Most recently 22-year-old Dathan Ritzenhein, the 2003 NCAA cross-country champion, seemed poised to fly at this year's World Cross-Country Championships. Instead, he placed 62nd.

Now, Galen Rupp—and here we go again. Using "next" and "great" and "Pre." And why should we get excited this time? Two words: Alberto Salazar.

In Salazar, Rupp has more than a coach. He has a mentor, a spiritual guide—someone who has fostered a bond that's almost magical. Salazar's supporters say that he knows exactly what it takes to make Rupp one of the world's best. He's been to the mountain himself, of course, but he's far more than an ex-jock turned coach. He's also a tireless student of running, forever consulting experts on altitude training and stride tactics and invoking new tools—like a computer program that monitors a runner's fatigue level. He's devoted to his runners, too. "He's involved," says Goucher, who moved to Portland from Boulder, Colorado, to train with Salazar. "When I pulled a hamstring one day, within two hours I was getting a massage. The next day I ran 12 miles, no problem."

But critics of the Rupp-Salazar union call it corrosive and cloying. They charge that Rupp is treated like a prima donna; that he's given unfair advantages; and that his coach may singe him with the very intensity that aborted his own career.

Rupp has never run for any coach but Salazar. who discovered the kid five years ago when he took over the reins of the then-dismal distance squad at Portland's Central Catholic High School. Rupp was, at that point, a very good soccer player, a freshman who played varsity. Salazar invited him to a cross-country practice, and then reveled in the boy's effortless stride and in his pedigree: In high school, Rupp's mother, Jamie, was twice an Oregon state cross-country champion.

Three months after that first practice, Salazar brought Rupp to the Junior Olympics National Cross-Country Championships; Rupp placed second. Later Rupp traveled to Barbados, Canada, and Italy to race. Along the way Salazar shared his strong Roman Catholic convictions with Rupp. He prayed with Galen before races; he brought Galen to Mass one or two Sundays each month. At times he offered up counsel, telling Galen, "All this running stuff may seem really important to you. But I've been there. This isn't ultimately what matters. The important thing is how we glorify Him. I want to help you become a better person, a more caring person." Already a practicing Catholic, Rupp enlisted Salazar as his confirmation sponsor. He became more devout than either his mother or father.

And in time the coach placed in Rupp the sort of long-term hope one harbors for a son or daughter. (Salazar has three athletic children of his own, but none are distance runners.) Now, he says, "There's no reason Galen can't go sub-13 for the 5,000. And, yes, we're hoping that he can make the Olympic team in 2008. People say to me, 'Why are you putting pressure on this kid?' Well, the problem is that in this country people don't have clearly definable goals. We have goals."

If Salazar sounds stern, he's not, exactly. As Eder, the magazine publisher, puts it, "He's Mr. Mean Coach and Big Warm Cuddly Bear all wrapped into one." At Central, where his cross-country squad won the state title in 2003, Salazar rarely raised his voice or hovered menacingly. Instead, he fretted over Rupp's aches. He massaged Galen's muscles after tough workouts. Once, he held Rupp out of a cross-country meet for fear that the boy might hurt himself on the course's steep, gravelly hills.

All the while, Salazar teased him with practical jokes. "Once for about a week and a half," Salazar says, "I had Galen believing that I'd fought in Vietnam and that I'd been a prisoner of war." Another time, on a flight to a race, Salazar convinced Rupp that he was authorized to fly Delta airplanes in emergencies. "I had the stewardess come back and say, 'Mr. Salazar, are you ready? The pilot is feeling a little sick.' Galen believed me. His eyes were as big as saucers."

Salazar grew close to Rupp in part because he's a kindred spirit—a fellow toiler. When Salazar was dominant in the early 1980s, running a

world record of 2:08:13 at the 1981 New York City Marathon and setting national records for the 5,000 and 10,000, it certainly wasn't because
his Creator endowed him with a flawless gait. No, Salazar moved with all
the smoothness of a commuter chasing after the bus. He shuffled, leaning
back, his skinny arms chopping awkward squares in front of his singlet.
And he prevailed mostly because he was determined, as he had been from
his earliest competitive days.

While still in high school in Wayland, Massachusetts, Salazar
joined the storied Greater Boston Track Club to run with the likes of
Bill Rodgers, occasionally defying his coaches and sneaking off to run
extra, unauthorized miles. At the University of Oregon, he was part of
an experiment where runners trained with a special oxygen-depleting
device strapped to their back and face. And, at the finish of one race, he
was administered last rites.

Then, suddenly, he burned out and faded.

Throughout 1983, Salazar was plagued by bronchitis-like colds, and
at the 1984 Olympic Marathon, he finished a devastating 15th. Over
the next decade, he was famously and confoundingly hobbled—afflicted
with insomnia, then a thyroid disorder. He took Prozac to quell anxiety.
His early greatness eluded him, though, and at times, he said in 1994, "I
hated running with a passion. I used to wish for a cataclysmic injury in
which I would lose one of my legs. Then I wouldn't have to torture myself
anymore."

As Salazar brooded, he also turned, gradually, to a new grail: resur-
recting American running. He started by coaching top athletes—Mary
Decker Slaney, for instance—for Nike in 1994, and in 2001 he helped
launch the Oregon Project, Nike's deluxe campaign to make a select few
of America's best even better, expenses be damned. The Project's runners
all lived, initially, in a retrofitted "altitude house" wherein oxygen filters
create the thin air found at 12,000 feet. Salazar expressed hope that, by
2003, he'd have a pack of runners capable of a 27:40 10K.

That pack never developed, though, and most of Salazar's runners—
including his best 10K man, Dan Browne, who's run 27:47—moved out
of the altitude house, seeking privacy. Still, Salazar saw promise. Starting
in 2002, Galen Rupp began taking advantage of the Oregon Project

perks and hung out at the altitude house evenings, playing video games. He began coming to Oregon Project workouts, so that he could train, as his coach had, with the luminaries of his day.

Salazar challenged the kid. One afternoon when Galen was 16, the coach had him do six one-mile repeats with national 5,000-meter record holder Bob Kennedy and Karl Keska, an Olympic marathoner. "Galen was really not liking it," Salazar remembers. "Everything was faster than anything he'd ever done. But when he finished, he was ecstatic. It was his best long workout ever. He started taking off his spikes. 'Don't,' I said. 'Now you're doing a 3-2-1 [a 1,200 followed by an 800 and a 400] all by yourself.' He was swearing under his breath, and I said, 'You can swear all you want, but you better be on the track in two minutes to do the next interval.'

"It's not my job to be his buddy," Salazar explained to me, "and sometimes Galen just needs a little jolt."

Rupp did the intervals as instructed that day, and it was not the only time that he pushed past exhaustion. "At all our hardest workouts," says Alec Wall, who trained with Rupp in high school, "at the end, Alberto would tell Galen, 'You have to run this last quarter under 60, or you're not going to win your next race.' Galen would be absolutely dead; he looked finished. But then Alberto would be running across the infield, to every corner of the track, yelling and screaming at Galen the whole way around, and Galen would do it. He'd run under 60. I just think he didn't want to let Alberto down. They have a special coach-athlete bond."

And so this April, after spending 10 months training full-time with the Oregon Project, Rupp enrolled at the University of Oregon, Salazar's alma mater—thereby prompting the NCAA to spend several weeks asking whether he was a college-eligible amateur or a Nike-sponsored pro. The NCAA didn't clear Rupp until his parents repaid $6,100 in travel and training expenses. But still, the most intriguing thing about Galen's college launch is that it came with a caveat: He insisted on bringing Salazar to school with him. Alberto is now Rupp's "personal trainer." Roughly three times a week—either in Portland or at the university, two hours to the south, in Eugene—Salazar oversees Rupp's workouts in person. On other days, Salazar tells Oregon's distance coach, Pat Tyson, what Galen should do.

Salazar isn't technically a coach, and Oregon says that he's complying with NCAA rules, which forbid him from overseeing Galen at workouts or races. And the university does not pay him. Instead, he gets $200 a month, plus expenses, from Rupp's parents. "It's not a professional thing," he says. "It's personal: I want to help Galen in every way I can to realize his dreams."

* * *

Galen Rupp can do more than run. At Central Catholic, his cumulative GPA was 4.33. Teachers adored him. "He was amazing from the get-go," says English teacher Tom Rhody. "His approach to academics was flat out." Spanish teacher Phillipe Kreiter recalls that in order to induce Rupp to ease back on his studies so he could pursue and enjoy other interests, "I once gave him extra credit for not finishing an assignment."

"Galen was driven from the very beginning," says his mother, Jamie, who's a nurse manager in Portland. "Everything was always a race for him." His father, Greg, a respiratory therapist, adds, "Even if it was a game of Monopoly, Galen was out to win." He became a serious athlete at age 10, when he joined an elite soccer team, FC Portland. Three times a week, his mom drove him 45 minutes each way for practices on the team's lush suburban facilities. By the time he was 12, he was sometimes doing two-hour solo practice sessions in his backyard, juggling his soccer ball and weaving through poly cones. He traveled to tournaments nationwide, picking up trophies along the way.

But when I met him in New Mexico, over lunch at a dimly lit restaurant, he didn't have the swaggering air of a winner. Instead, he seemed careful and professional, like a child movie actor. A Nike publicist monitored our conversation. At first, Rupp told me how he met Salazar. "He came to my high school," he said. "I didn't know who he was. I just knew he'd won a bunch of marathons, but my mom made me introduce myself."

Soon, Rupp learned of the late-career hardship Salazar had endured. "Maybe he didn't take enough time off at the end of each season," Rupp said. "Maybe he didn't rest enough when injured." All that's clear to Galen is that, through suffering, Salazar accrued wisdom—and a deeper religious faith. "He's taught me that there's a reason for everything," Rupp said. "Now I know that things don't happen by chance. I know God has a plan for us. And I don't get down on myself if I get hurt or something. I know that in the big scheme, running is minor: The world isn't going to come to an end if you don't run well."

It was an odd remark because Rupp is, of course, training as though the world's fate does hinge on his running. Right now, as well as logging close to 110 miles some weeks, he lifts weights daily and supplements every run with about 45 minutes of stretches and agility drills. A few top collegians may equal Rupp's mileage, but they don't quite get in as many fast training miles. Rupp does an inordinate amount of quarters and 600s on the track. His goal is to catch Africa's top juniors, who still elude him. At March's 8K Junior World Cross-Country Championships in France, in a race for runners 19 and younger, he placed 20th behind 19 Africans and Middle Easterners. He finished in 25:05, more than a minute behind the winner. "Those guys aren't unbeatable," he said. "They're human. They may end up beating you, but you just have to focus on getting closer and closer. And that doesn't happen in one big jump. You have to keep chipping away; you have to keep working.

"I work hard with Alberto. Sometimes he makes me do things I hate, like we'll do 10-mile tempo runs at a 5:06 pace, or we'll do 15 times one kilometer and I'll be dying. I'll want to stop at 12, and he'll just say, 'Suck it up!' He shows me how much harder I can push myself."

At times, Salazar has pushed too far. Last fall he embraced a new Nike shoe, the light and extremely flexible Free, which is designed to hone the sinew we use walking barefoot. Promotional material for the Free advises: "As for training, keep a low intensity and volume. Progression is key." But Salazar had Rupp running as much as three miles a day barefoot and in the Free—and the combination, Rupp says, led to a stress fracture. "Alberto realized that we probably went overboard on the barefoot stuff. He's able to learn from his mistakes, though. We cut back." (Later, Salazar told me, "You make mistakes. That was one that I made.")

But when one doctor recommended Rupp encase his fractured foot in a cast for six weeks, Salazar tried a different course. He had Rupp reduce his land mileage, to about 40 a week, while increasing his underwater treadmill time. Twelve weeks after the fracture emerged, Galen won the 8K junior race at the USA Cross-Country Championships, beating Stuart Eagon by eight seconds, and qualified for the World's—proof, he feels, of Salazar's mastery.

"Sometimes I think Alberto knows my body better than I do," Rupp told me. "I'm privileged to have one of the best coaches in the world. I can't imagine leaving him. If you look at running in other countries—in Africa, say—you see guys who've trained with the same coach since they were 10 or 12 years old. If you're successful with one coach, why should you change?"

At his hotel in New Mexico, Rupp was sleeping in a special tent in which the oxygen was thinned to simulate 14,000 feet. He was the only runner sleeping in such a tent, and when Rupp was not around, John Cook, 64, an assistant coach with the Oregon Project, got a little sarcastic. "Come on," he said to me. "If you've got a girlfriend, are you gonna put her in a tent like that? I mean, if I brought one of those things home, my wife would call for the moving van. I'm sure Goucher wouldn't sleep in anything like that. But Galen just does what he's told. It's Alberto who's the fanatic."

* * *

The truth is, there was not much to do there in New Mexico. The runners were staying on the outskirts of Santa Fe, far from downtown, right by I-40, in a hotel that abutted the giant parking lot of a strip mall. Inevitably, cabin fever set in—and the athletes started playing pranks. One evening, a steeplechaser named Steve Slatterly broke into Coach Cook's room and swaddled the toilet seat in Saran Wrap. He then set various alarms—on the clock, on the TV, on the phone—so that Cook would wake at 2:30 a.m., and then again at 3:30 and 4:30. Cook never confronted Slatterly. He merely crept out into the parking lot late one night and Superglued Slatterly's plastic gas cap onto his truck. "So long, Steve," he said the next morning, as Slatterly readied to drive home to Colorado. "It's going to be a long day."

Rupp stayed aloof from such pranks. He spent most of his free time playing a video game called "NBA Live" on an Xbox, apparently oblivious to what people are saying about his training regimen.

"I believe that high school kids should be allowed to live a normal American life," says Jim Archer, who coached Stuart Eagon at Beaverton High School, near Portland. "But Salazar doesn't seem to see it that way. He wants kids to make their whole life revolve around running."

Tom Derderian, the coach for the Greater Boston Track Club, likewise describes Salazar as "obsessive." A teammate of Salazar's in the 1970s, he argues that Alberto is "willing to do anything to win" and is driven by an inferiority complex. In high school, Derderian explains, "[Salazar] wanted to excel, and so he tried everything: He moved to Kenya for a while; he ran with that silly mask on his face. And now he has this kid sleeping in a tent. What's the point? Athletics should be about gamesmanship—about being strategic and clever. If you're gaining advantages when you're sleeping, that's not fair."

Salazar detractors also decry the strange route that Rupp took to the University of Oregon. Last winter, it appeared that Rupp might never be an NCAA runner—that he would ultimately just turn pro. "To run at a world-class level," Salazar told me, "you can't go to school six hours a day. It's impossible." The coach added that Rupp wouldn't even need a degree until age 30 or so because he'd be running professionally.

That tune changed, though, in March following a shakeup at the University of Oregon. On the day before the start of the outdoor season, longtime track coach Martin Smith suddenly resigned, explaining in a press release, "I have become increasingly concerned about the controversy and related publicity regarding the track program." Smith didn't specify which controversy, but it appeared he was alluding to the public discontent of several Oregon alums, most notably Salazar and Nike cofounder Phil Knight, who felt that the famed Oregon distance running program—the program that at one time brought huge crowds to historic Hayward Field to chant "Pre! Pre! Pre! Pre!"—was in decline under Smith.

Salazar made his anti-Smith views clear last December when he published in the *Eugene Register-Guard* a letter that concluded, "You have to stand for something. Oregon has always stood for distance running." He also pushed for the hiring of Pat Tyson, Prefontaine's one-time roommate at Oregon and the coach of the highly successful cross-country teams at Mead High School in Spokane. "Pat Tyson would be a great distance coach at the University of Oregon," he told *USA Today* in February.

Knight, meanwhile, spoke with his checkbook. In 2003, the Lame Ducks, a booster club that includes Knight and other former Oregon distance greats such as Salazar and Rudy Chapa, gave the track team $205,900; $96,000 of this sum came from Knight himself. In 2004, neither Knight nor the Lame Ducks gave anything to the program. "Phil didn't want to contribute until the distance-running problem was sorted out," explains Steve Bence, a Nike employee and former Oregon runner. "He didn't like the way Martin Smith was coaching." Knight would not comment to *Runner's World*, nor would Martin Smith. And when asked if Oregon let Nike dictate who coaches its track team, University spokesperson Dave Williford said, "The speculation will go on for years. It's not our desire to contribute to that speculation."

The aftermath of Smith's departure, though, was this: Tyson volunteered to coach the distance runners for the spring season, and a week later Rupp showed up on campus. Why the sudden enrollment? "When Smith resigned," says Salazar, "U of O said to Galen, 'It's okay for you to come down and bring Alberto as your coach.' College just became a good fit for Galen."

Predictably, the conspiracy theorists opened fire. Rupp "really should take his punk ass back to Portland," one correspondent wrote on the popular Internet forum letsrun.com in the midst of a discussion that depicted Galen as a Nike pawn. A more sober poster lamented, "I now see that [Salazar] was never about options or furthering distance running for our youth in America. [He's about] control, power, and ego to fulfill his personal agenda."

Strangely, Rupp's Oregon teammates aren't quite as hardwired—and after he helped lead the team to a Pac-10 title in May, they can't complain too much about any preferential treatment. As steeplechaser Brett

Holts puts it, "Some people think it's a little weird that Galen doesn't work out with us. But if Alberto's helping him run fast, well, that's good for us, too."

As for Salazar? He laughs at the accusations against him, calling the internet posting ridiculous. "These people don't know me, and it's like they're questioning my relationship with my own kids, my own family. What they don't understand is that I had enough glory in my career. And everything I do with Galen, it's because I care about him. I love that kid like a son."

* * *

I saw Rupp one more time—in the Oregon Twilight meet, at Hayward Field on a gray evening just before Mother's Day. He was racing the 10,000 that night, and Salazar wanted Galen to beat his personal best by 49 seconds and run 28:20—that is 4:32 a mile, or 68 seconds a lap. Rupp went out in 67.4, went through the half at 2:14, and finished the first mile at 4:32. He clocked two miles in 9:06. Midway through the race, at 5,000 meters, he was in second, on the shoulder of Kenyan Isaac Arusei, and his split was 14:17—a 4:34 pace.

"The American junior record for the 10,000," said the announcer, "is 28:32, set by Rudy Chapa in 1976."

"He ain't gonna do it," said the guy sitting next to me, a coach. "Five thousand meters is a long way to go by yourself as a freshman."

The next lap was 68.5. Then came 68.0, 67.5, 65.5, 68.0, 68.0. Salazar was sitting low down in the bleachers by the last curve and, Rupp would say later, "He was yelling at me every lap: 'Stay where you're at, stay relaxed.' With one and a half to go, he said, 'If you run 67s from here, you'll hit 28:15.'"

Sixty-six-oh, 68.0, 68.0. Arusei was a distant memory now, at least 100 yards back, and suddenly a light mist began falling, as if to remind us all that we were beholding something nearly as ancient as nature—a young colt flying along with absolute grace in the Oregon spring.

"Rupp! Rupp! Rupp! Rupp!" roared the crowd. The bleachers were shaking.

Sixty-seven-oh, 67.0, 67.5.

"Rupp! Rupp! Rupp! Rupp!"

In the end, the clock read 28:15.52, astoundingly 17 seconds better than Chapa's old record, and the postrace drama unfolded as if the ad writers for Nike had scripted it. Here was Galen standing on the track in his yellow Oregon singlet, beaming, his hands high in triumph. Here he was trotting through a victory lap, signing T-shirts and programs. And here he was bathed in the glow of TV lights, saying, "To win a race in an Oregon uniform, well, there's nothing like it. This is what I always hoped for—to be a Duck at Hayward Field."

It was easy to get swept up in the giddiness of it all, sure, but still, after all the other reporters left and it was just Galen there under the press tent—all alone, with a Breathe Right strip on his nose—I had to ask him what his life was like in Eugene. Was he having fun? Had he gone to any parties or anything?

"I can't really go out and party," he said, puzzled. "I'm training."

What's the greatest experience you've had here, outside of running?

"Just hanging out with my friends, I guess. I don't get to see them a lot."

Do you really think you can catch the Africans?

"I don't know," Rupp shrugged. "I've just got to see how it goes."

Earlier, Salazar had given me a far more interesting answer to the same question. "I don't think anyone believes for a moment that the Africans at that championship in France were true juniors," he said. "There were guys there with passports saying they were 15 and they looked 25. I've talked one on one to top Kenyan runners—I'm not going to mention names, but top Kenyan runners contracted with Nike—and they've told me that the best true 18- and 19-year-olds in Kenya are running the 5K in the mid-13:20s. Galen's not that far off."

Was Salazar right? It's impossible to know. But what mattered was that his assessment was laced with a little anger, a little bitter suspicion. It carried the sharp taint of old stings, and it had some soul, really. And maybe it's soul—and anger and relentlessness—that American runners have been lacking for two decades now; maybe that's what they need in order to catch the Kenyans and Ethiopians. Alberto Salazar thinks so, certainly. He's trying to teach Galen Rupp to run with all-out soul, with self-sacrifice and tenacity. But a huge question remains: Can Rupp come into his own, as all champions must, and go without his coach pushing all of the buttons?

No one knows yet, and the only thing clear at Hayward Field on this night was that Rupp would not be partaking of Steve Prefontaine's favorite postrace ritual: He would not be drinking beer straight from the pitcher.

As Hayward Field started to empty, Galen lingered in the company of his family. He hugged his grandmother; he made dinner plans with his parents. Eventually, Salazar came over and spoke gently to Galen's mother: "I'm going to need to give Galen a massage. And he'll need to warm down in a minute, or he's really going to stiffen up."

Rupp said goodbye to his aunt, singing out, "Happy Mother's Day." And then he shuffled away, into the dusk, and Alberto Salazar waited for him, by the fence on the edge of the track, watching him every step of the way.

Running to Remember

The Red Bulletin, *March 8, 2023*

DISTANCE RUNNER KU STEVENS GREW UP IN A SMALL HOUSE ON A POT-holed street on a tiny Indian reservation in Yerington, Nevada, a cowboy town of 3,200 where the main drag still feels very Old West, boasting a Rexall Drug, a steakhouse, and a dusty museum honoring local war veterans.

On Ku's street, the yards were piled high with the tailings from the nearby Anaconda copper mine, so that the soil was too poisoned to sustain much vegetation. When he was in fifth grade, Ku and his friends terrorized their neighbors, playing doorbell ditch and lighting off fireworks. Was petty thuggery his destiny? Possibly. "When you're a Native American kid," says Ku, an Indigenous Paiute who recently turned 19, "you're taught to lose. You're taught to look at bloody moments in history where your people got killed and think, 'That could have been me.'"

One hot July night during Ku's mischievous phase, the Yerington police heard exploding firecrackers in the neighborhood. When Ku arrived home after midnight, there were two cruisers waiting for him in the driveway. He says his mother grounded him for the rest of the summer.

Sequestered in his bedroom, Ku had time to think. He recognized the racial pain he felt, living in a town where white kids threw slurs at Native Americans and where he'd been socially pressured, in fourth grade, into cutting off his long black hair. He also thought about how sometimes he'd felt deeply rooted, being Native. He remembered sitting in his family's sweat lodge. He remembered foraging the high desert for buckberries and pine nuts with his father, Delmar, and watching his dad take part in a sun dance. Several times, Delmar fasted and went without water for four straight days, all the while dancing barefoot on the hot desert ground. He prayed, as Ku puts it, "for his people, for their health and well-being."

That summer, Ku told himself, "I'm never going to hang out with those kids again. I can be somebody."

* * *

It was a sober decision for a 10-year-old to make but also characteristic of Ku. "He's always been focused," says his mother, Misty Stevens. "Even when he was in elementary school, he was serious about homework. I think it's because he saw the neighbor down the street passed out with a bunch of empty bottles around him."

Ku refused to go down that road, for he had an athletic gift and also a staggering dedication to running. For two years in high school, Ku didn't have a coach. Or any teammates. The sole runner for Yerington, he ran alone on long, straight desert roads. Then in 2022, Ku broke the Nevada state record for the 3,200-meter run, clocking in at 8:54.83.

As he grew stronger, he also grew his hair long again. He began, as well, to think about racial justice, in part because when he was in eighth grade, two Black stepsisters at Yerington High, his friends Taylissa Marriott and Jayla Tolliver, were racially harassed at school—and then so ignored by administrators when they complained that they won a $160,000 settlement against the Lyon County School District. "There are blind racists out there," Ku thought, "people who don't even realize that this country was built on the blood and bones of my ancestors, and on misogyny and racism and slavery."

In May 2021, Ku learned that 215 unmarked graves of Indigenous children had just been discovered on the campus of an Indian boarding school in Canada. He knew then that it was time for him to speak out. With both his voice and his legs. Helped by his parents, he began organizing a singular athletic event to remember—and also expose—a dark passage in American history.

* * *

It's a chilly morning in August 2022. The sky is still dark, and 30 or so runners and walkers, many of them Native American, are gathered in Yerington, on a grassy lawn near Ku's home, to spend the next two days hoofing some 50 miles west through the Carson Desert.

As part of the second annual Remembrance Run, hosted by Ku and his parents, Delmar and Misty, the group gathered here will journey to the now-shuttered Stewart Indian School, where, from 1890 to the 1960s, Native American kids as young as 4 boarded year-round, forcibly removed from their parents, abused, beaten, belittled, and forbidden to speak their native languages. Stewart was, like so many of the 400-plus Indian boarding schools that once scattered the United States, a K–12 facility with a graveyard on campus.

The runners are traveling in reverse the very route that one Stewart student—Ku's great-grandfather, Frank Quinn—is believed to have taken to escape the school in the early 1900s, when he was about 8 years old. They're making this journey at a critical moment: Last May, the U.S. Department of the Interior released a report estimating that "thousands or tens of thousands" of Native children died at these boarding schools. Congresswoman Sharice Davids, a Kansas Democrat, is now pushing a bill that would establish a Truth and Healing Commission on Indian boarding schools. And last summer, Pope Francis toured Canada, apologizing for the Catholic Church's administration of many such schools and admitting the church was complicit in "genocide."

"We're not trying to make you feel bad about what your ancestors might have done," Ku says, explaining the run's purpose. "We're just letting you know why Native Americans suffer such immense historical trauma." His words are considered, his manner solemn. He exudes confidence and responsibility, and sometimes it's hard to remember that he's still a teenager. During one interview at his house, Ku decided, on his own initiative, to spend the afternoon weeding his family's gravel driveway. He wielded a rake in the bone-dry 95-degree heat as he explained how Donald Trump is simply an heir to the racism underlying the 19th-century ravaging of Indigenous America.

* * *

At sunrise, we gather in a circle and Paiute/Shoshone shaman Russell Abel, once a meth addict, now a fit, chiseled runner, prays for "every step we take." He prays, as well, for Ku, "who brought us together." Soon, another spiritual leader wanders among us, ritually smudging each participant, burning sage in a seashell, then guiding the smoke toward our torsos and legs by waving an eagle feather up and down. As Ku is smudged, he shakes out his legs, colt-like, loose; warming up, staying silent. He is intent, it seems, on imbibing all of the hope and the history contained in the smoke.

Then a moment later he is running, a gracefully lean young man with long black hair that sways with each footfall. Along with three other gazelle-thin harriers—32-year-old Lupe Cabada, who's coached Ku part-time since 2020, and two top-tier Nevada high schoolers—he's running at what for him is a snail's pace, seven minutes a mile. At this pace, he can chat about girls, about his love for playing Super Smash Bros. on his Nintendo Switch, or about his 2001 BMW 330 Ci, which he wrecked by hitting a pole a few months ago. He can crack inside jokes with his running cronies, but that's not really his style. There's a cool, composed air to Ku, and now, as he stares off into the vast blue Nevada sky, he looks like a very different person from that kid who played games of doorbell ditch in 2015.

These days, Ku is a movie star, too. For a year now, a film crew has been documenting his life—his races, his graduation, the minor tiffs with his parents—as they make a full-length nonfiction film zeroing in on the Remembrance Run. Director/producer Paige Bethmann, a 28-year-old Indigenous Haudenosaunee from upstate New York, moved to Reno for the project because she was taken with the story of "a young person running 50 miles across the desert to honor his ancestors. He's so articulate. He's so positive."

Ku is also a political operative. As he lopes west, Nevada's governor, Steve Sisolak, is planning to meet him at the Stewart School to address the boarding school issue. Catherine Cortez Masto, a U.S. senator representing Nevada, will be there too, as will Billy Mills, a Lakota runner who won the 10,000-meter race at the 1964 Olympics before becoming the eloquent leader of Running Strong for American Indian Youth, which funded this year's Remembrance Run with a $10,000 Dreamstarter Award.

Will Ku become the next Billy Mills? It could happen. A month after this run, he'll start his freshman year at the University of Oregon, becoming one of the first Native American harriers to join the nation's most storied track program. U of O is where Nike founder Phil Knight made the world's first waffle-soled shoes, and where '70s-era phenom Steve Prefontaine became distance running's icon of grit, gutting barrel-chested through 1,500- and 5,000-meter races as he minted brawny aphorisms such as "To give anything less than your best is to sacrifice the gift."

As Ku turns left onto a gravel road, I think to myself: Who here isn't rooting for this kid to shine? Hailing from a reservation afflicted by drug addiction and rampant suicide, he is a symbol of hope. It's Ku's picture that's emblazoned across all the T-shirts for this second annual Remembrance Run, and it's Ku who is posing with a ceremonial wooden staff in all the newspaper stories about the run. It's unlikely this journey would even have happened were it not for his star power, and as the sun climbs in the sky and the desert becomes a scorching, treeless oven, to a person, every single runner cites Ku as their inspiration.

"A lot of people think all Native Americans are dead," Amber Torres, the chair of the Walker River Paiute Tribe, tells me as she jogs along, "or that we're just angry or that we're drunks. In using his very powerful voice to focus on the boarding school issue, Ku's showing people why we're angry and why we're bitter. He's also showing people that we're still here—and that we can overcome hardship."

* * *

I'm riding alongside the runners on a gravel bicycle with drop handlebars and semiwide knobby tires. I ride thousands of miles a year, but when we turn, just a couple miles in, onto a steep footpath, I can't keep pace with Ku and his fleet entourage. The loose stones underfoot afford scant traction, and the land around me is a parched gray-brown expanse that gets but five inches of rain a year. I have to wonder: What did Frank Quinn do for water when he ran away from Stewart? Where did he find warmth when the sun set and the night cooled?

Unfortunately, Quinn never shared such details. The memory of the escape was too searing, but other reports make clear that Stewart runaways were risking their lives. In 1905, when four girls bolted from the school in winter, they were later found 200 miles away, in southern Nevada, "unconscious from cold and exhaustion," according to a newspaper account. "They were lying in the open under the trees with the thermometer 3 degrees below zero." In 1915, seven boys bolted, got caught after two days and were summarily whipped before spending three days in the dark, windowless school jail. Such treatment was normal; Stewart employed a full-time disciplinarian to ensure that this was so.

Nearly all the runners and walkers trailing Ku carry a memory of the disciplinarian in their bones. Still, the mood is often festive. When we arrive at the first rest station—they're set up every five miles—there are tunes blaring, and a shade tent with an Astroturf rug and comfortable lawn chairs beneath it. We sit there, savoring an ample supply of pickle juice and coconut water, and as the runners come in, each one gets a razzle-dazzle cheer.

At most endurance events, the vibe isn't quite this homey. A Lycra-inflected vanity often prevails, and never-quite-enunciated social codes dictate that elite athletes harbor more cachet—more voice—than the quitters and stragglers. But in Indian Country, being community-minded is paramount, and the Stevens family has taken pains to ensure that everyone present feels included and cared for, even if they're rest-station volunteers who never run a step. At least five times, Ku's dad, Delmar, asks me if I'm getting enough to eat.

Underlying all this hospitality is Frank Quinn, an ancestor Ku so admires that he scribed Frank's name into the side panel of his track spikes. As an adult, Frank was an alfalfa farmer and a worker at the Anaconda mine. But he's remembered most for his generosity. "Frank always took care of people when they came to his house," says Ku, who learned of his great-grandpa through family stories. "They went away with a full belly. He made sure they had firewood."

There's room here on this run for boarding school survivors to feel comfortable, to tell stories, and when I meet up with Stacey James, who is Washoe and Eastern Cherokee and limping along in a knee brace, she tells me of her uncle who attempted to escape Stewart three times and then joined the Navy before turning 18 to serve in the Korean War. "His children—my cousins—have always talked about how horrible their childhood was," James tells me. "He drank a lot. He was not a good father. He hit his wife. But now the stories from Stewart are coming to light—of beatings, of children being molested—and forgiveness is starting to happen. I'm very thankful that Ku is bringing this issue to light. I hope that more people start healing."

* * *

This run is a war of attrition. With every hill, there are more people walking or riding along in support vehicles. Fun is still in the air, though. The fourth rest stop, at 20 miles, has a rock 'n' roll theme and free temporary tattoos. Eager film-crew members stand in line for elaborate sponge-on tramp stamps.

Ku is a bit removed from the hoopla, though. He just sits in his lawn chair quietly, his skin glistening with sweat, his torso bare. It's 95 degrees out now, and he just knocked off the 20th mile in 5:30, a burst that left his running mates sucking dust. At this point, there are only two people who've run all 20 miles with a plan to continue—Ku and coach Lupe Cabada, a 2:28 marathoner. They're conserving their energy. Wisely, for the day's final five-mile segment is ugly. It's an 800-foot climb up a dirt road, and it's so rubbly that midway up I'm walking my bike. My heart is hammering, and I find myself asking whether I'll even make it to the top. And what about the people behind me?

Every ultra-long-distance run is like a prayer—a prayer that each runner involved can transcend their human frailty; a prayer that, by lacing up their shoes and flinging themselves at rocks and roots and mountains and streams, they can cover 26, 31, 50 miles—whatever—carried along by little more than sinew and stick-to-activeness. There is so much uncertainty involved, and so much hope.

But sometimes the prayer involved is deeper, more rooted in history and suffering. As we move through the desert, growing dehydrated, getting sunburnt, seizing with the odd muscle cramp, we're glimpsing the pain Frank Quinn must have felt escaping Stewart. And when we stop, 25 miles in, to camp amid a rare stand of pine trees, a solidarity bonds our mission. The sun sets. It grows cold, and then we gather once more in a circle, lit only by a couple of lanterns, and watch as Ku steps into the middle, encouraging each of the 45 people present to speak one by one and to share stories about the boarding schools if they'd like. "This is a safe space," he tells us. "If you don't want the documentary crew to film you, just let them know."

Our leader is 18 years old and his manner is so calm, so poised that he only deepens the tranquility we all feel sitting here. We've been drawn to the desert by Ku's cool sense of purpose, and now this gathering feels more like a solemn college send-off party. "Ku," says one elder, "you're a very powerful young man. College is your journey, but do come back. Come home."

Heavy? Awkward? For most teenagers it certainly would be, but Ku finds a way to elevate the moment. "A lot of people say I'm inspirational," he tells the circle, "but I want you all to think of yourselves as inspirational. Go out there and be the best person you can be."

We get up out of our chairs eventually and wander back to our tents to sleep under the stars.

* * *

The next morning I talk to Paige Bethmann, the film director, and she argues that Ku is part of a new generation of Natives who've "realized that they can be the caretakers of our elders' stories." Bethmann is also a fan of *Reservation Dogs*, a Native-written teen comedy, now heading into its third season on Hulu, that sympathetically follows a group of teenage pals as they commit, and also fight, crime. And as we speak, she's wearing a ball cap that reads "You are on Native land." It was made by Urban Native Era, an Indigenous-owned apparel company that last year partnered with REI. "Our generation is more removed from the trauma," says Bethmann, "and I think that makes us more free to speak out."

Our route today begins with a ladder-steep climb out of the campground before it segues to the cruel slopes of Sunrise Pass, elevation 7,096. At the first rest stop, I find Lupe Cabada pressing a vibrating massage gun into a spasm in his abdomen. Ku looks on impassively. "I'm not sore," he tells me. "I think I'll run 12 tomorrow." A few hours later, around mile 38 of our two-day odyssey, he belts out a 4:38 downhill mile.

There's a beautiful spirit at work on this journey: Almost no one is giving up. People sit out segments, sure, but then I see them out on the road again, briskly power walking or running with a shuffling, bent-back stride that's half-walk. If folks can't do a full leg, they cover a mile or two. The collective momentum is poignant and purposeful.

Eventually we all duck into a hole cut in a barbed-wire fence and find ourselves wading through a bend in the shallow, shin-high Carson River. I'm with Russell Abel, the shaman, now. As we carry our shoes, wading along through the sublimely cool water, no one is speaking. I hear only soft splashing, and the moment seems holy: So much intention, and now we've almost arrived.

When we reach the edge of the Stewart campus, Billy Mills, the gold medalist, is there waiting for us, a hale 84-year-old man sporting track warm-up pants. As he greets Ku, his smile is beneficent, his hopes vast. "It's not going to be what Ku achieves in sport that matters," he tells me in soft, meditative tones. "It will be the legacy that he leaves for creating justice. The footprints these runners traced today will create the America of tomorrow. They will heal the sacredness of the American democratic spirit."

A moment later, Remembrance runners and walkers march, en masse, behind Mills to the Stewart cemetery. Then Ku stands at the gate, addressing a crowd of 200 as TV cameramen clamber about them. "I'm just an 18-year-old," he says. "So how would something that happened 100 years ago affect me? But it does. I want all of you here to know that. It affects all of us Natives. But we're strong. All of you who made this journey, you're strong. Now let's go give our offerings to these kids."

Ku bows his head, and with Senator Cortez Masto at his side, he makes his way into the graveyard. He bends low to the tombstones and prays.

Two weeks later he's in Eugene, Oregon. He wears U of O Duck colors, green and gold, as he trains at Hayward Field, the site of the last four U.S. Olympic trials for track and field. He joins the Native American Student Union, and when the Native American Boarding School Healing Coalition holds a Zoom conference for 500 people, he delivers a speech while sitting cross-legged on the floor of his dorm room.

These days, Ku harbors a dream that involves Nike and its N7 Fund, which awards grants to Native American and Indigenous organizations to help youth lead "healthier, happier and successful lives," according to the company. Ku hopes one day to design shoes for the N7 Fund—running shoes that would bear Indigenous iconography. "A lot of kids can't accept being Native," he explains one afternoon, remembering his own experience. "These shoes would be empowering. If I had them when I was younger, I would have felt so much better about myself."

As he speaks, I'm somehow reminded of Ku's favorite shoes, the orange-and-white Nike track spikes he wore when he broke the state record for his 3,200-meter run. Back in Yerington, those shoes hung from the TV in his bedroom. Now he's brought them with him to college, and they're still decorated with the three words he scribed onto them one night, in pen, to sum up what propels him. Written into the swoosh, his small block letters read: FOR MY PEOPLE.

Henry II

Runner's World, *September 2007*

THE NIGHT BEFORE, NOLAN SHAHEED PLAYED JAZZ AT THE JOHN F. Kennedy Center, in Washington, DC. Hot, honking jazz trumpet up there on the big stage, beneath the soft, luscious lights, Shaheed looking natty in black trousers and a black button-down shirt as the rest of the Sweet Baby Blues Band—the trombonist, the clarinetist, the saxophone players, the fat guy on bass—wailed around him.

Shaheed stayed up until 1:30 a.m. that night, then snatched a two-hour catnap and caught an early-bird flight west, across the country to Oregon. By the time he arrived at the high school track in the Portland suburb of Canby, the 58-year-old should, by all rights, have been fried. But Shaheed is the nation's premier miler among runners 55 and older—a man who last year ran a 4:46.43. He was not tired. No, Shaheed had sufficient energy to sing, in a buoyant falsetto in the parking lot at Canby High, the Temptations' "My Girl" and then later the Beatles' "Come Together."

Shaheed was in Oregon that cool afternoon in May for the Fountain of Youth Masters Mile, and now he and his 13 opponents were all limbering up, stretching their lean, ropy calves, and then popping up suddenly to take a few high-kicking warmup strides down the straightaway. These were top age-group runners, mostly—graying men in their 30s, 40s, and 50s who arguably harbored more wisdom on aching quads and trick knees than the American Academy of Orthopaedic Surgeons. They'd seen faster days, sure, but still, as I sat watching up in the bleachers, they seemed vibrant, transcendent of time's gravitational pull.

Except, well, for one of them—the man I'd come to see. Fifty-five-year-old Henry Rono was far, far beefier than anyone else in the field, at five feet eight, 171 pounds, and he moved about gingerly, nursing a hamstring he'd tweaked two weeks before. In his black shorts and spikes, he seemed ungainly, like an Average Joe who'd been errantly summoned from a nearby neighborhood barbecue.

But Henry Rono was no interloper. In the late 1970s, after he emigrated from Kenya to attend Washington State University, Rono was perhaps the best distance runner on the planet. In a sport favoring specialists, he was a Renaissance champion. In March 1977, he outlasted American standout Steve Scott in a mile race on the track, then a few months later outkicked Boston Marathon winner Bill Rodgers in a half-marathon through the sticky torpor of Puerto Rico. In the spring and summer of 1978, he accomplished a feat unequaled before or since in track-and-field history. In a span of just 81 days, he broke four world records—in the 3,000 meters, the 3,000-meter steeplechase, the 5,000 meters, and the 10,000 meters.

He set those records a long time ago, when he was 26 and weighed 140 pounds—and still had Olympic dreams. Today, he's trying to spring back from the verge of alcoholic ruin, from decades of floating around the United States doing odd jobs—parking cars, washing cars, checking bags at an airport. He spent many nights hunched on a bar stool, drinking Budweiser, and his weight ballooned to 220 pounds. For the past year, though, he's been training, slimming down, trying to come back. His goal? Improbably, to break the age 55 to 59 world record for the mile: 4:40.4, set 30 years ago by Australian Jack Ryan.

I watched from up in the bleachers as Rono nudged himself among Shaheed and the other masters at the starting line. Around me were grade-schoolers—kids who had raced earlier that morning—horsing around, paying no heed to the elders. "Runners, take your mark," the starter was now saying. Rono crouched down, his arms cocked as he awaited the gun.

* * *

As I sat there looking down, I tried to remember the Henry Rono who'd shined for me as an idol when I was a distance runner in high school and college in the '80s. That was certainly long after Kenyan runners had emerged as world beaters, led by Kip Keino and his gold-medal performance in the 1,500 meters in the 1968 Olympics. But to me, a gangly, white, suburban kid, there was something about Rono that set him apart from his countryman. He seemed, in many ways, otherworldly.

Here was a Nandi tribesman whose two bottom teeth were wrenched out, ritually, when he was 10. Rono ran to school, barefoot, through the lush grasses and thick forests of Kenya's Rift Valley, and when it came to carb-loading, he eschewed the prerace pasta supper that my running cohorts and I held as sacrosanct. Instead, he opted for *ugali*, a traditional Kenyan corn-meal mush.

He was magical, and he was also theatrical. At one race, the 1978 NCAA steeplechase finals, he enacted a little performance art, sprinting the straightaways and jogging the turns as he flew on to victory. Later, even with a growing beer gut from the alcohol he was regularly consuming, Rono took on Alberto Salazar, the former University of Oregon great, in a 10,000-meter invitational. The two had competed often in college, and in a closely fought duel on Oregon turf—Hayward Field, in Eugene—Rono nipped Salazar at the tape by the breadth of his jiggling belly.

Steve Cram, the British middle-distance star, was one of the first elite runners to notice Rono's growing girth. In the spring of 1981, Cram spied him wheezing along a mountain road in Boulder, Colorado, "looking 20 to 30 pounds overweight." Cram trotted over to chat, and in earnest tones, Rono told him, "This summer, I'm going to break the world record for 5,000 meters." It was his own record, set three years earlier.

"It was a bit weird," Cram told me recently. Early that season Rono was predictably a very slow-moving vehicle. In one 5,000 race, he ran two minutes slower than his world record of 13:08.4. Still, he kept competing on the European circuit that summer. Finally, in September 1981 in Knarvik, Norway, Rono made good on his prediction. Running with no real competition, but after a night of heavy drinking, he eclipsed the record by more than two seconds, finishing in 13:06.2. "Thank God that track was round," he would later tell his one-time agent, Tracy Sundlun. "My head was spinning, and I was just trying to keep up with it."

Henry Rono's drinking, though, has never been that funny a topic, for it is rooted in a deep alienation. When he first came to the United States in 1976, to run for WSU and settle in arid, lily-white Pullman, Washington, there were few locals with whom Rono could chat in Kenyan Swahili. His fellow students were typically earnest, four-square Americans into football and deer hunting, and the high, rectilinear buildings seemed, he would later say, "unfriendly. I felt like a fish brought out of the ocean, into the desert, and the feeling of that fish is cold."

Rono developed an ulcer, worrying, feeling out of place. He drank. He drank to "feel warm, to face people. I would drink whenever I needed it. Beer became like food for me. I'd just drink until I was full—until the bars closed." Once, he crashed into a campus fence, and then sat in his dorm room, brooding as a policeman chastised him: "You have a problem with alcohol."

By 1983, Rono was living in Eugene and struggling to maintain his elite status. For a time in the mid-'80s, he did return to Kenya, living both in Nairobi and on a farm. Eventually, he moved back to the United States and, every so often, showed up at races. In 1986, he whipped himself into shape to run a 2:19:12 Chicago Marathon—good for 26th place. In 1991, seemingly out of the blue, he won a half-marathon in Austin, Texas, in 1:05:06, nipping Rodgers again.

In general, though, the arc of his life was tragic. Between 1986 and 1993, he cycled in and out of various rehab centers. He incensed many who cared for him, including Sundlun, who in 1987 told a reporter, "He is still a consuming alcoholic. He's just treading water. The situation is not going to resolve itself. You've got a shell of a former person." He lived in New York, Boston, Portland, Eugene, Las Vegas, and Albuquerque. At one point in the early '90s, Rono even spent six months living on the streets of Salt Lake City. "I wondered where all my friends were," he says. "I wondered, *Where were all my friends from when I was running?*"

When Rono resurfaced last year, talking about Jack Ryan's record, he finally seemed serious about plying the straight and narrow. He said he had not touched a drop of alcohol in five years, and he had a vision: He wanted to run. In June 2006, Rono left the middle school in Albuquerque, where he had been working with special-ed kids as a teacher's aide, and vowed to survive solely on running. He's now coaching a few gifted athletes, among them Solomon Kandie, a 29-year-old Kenyan who's clocked a 1:04 half-marathon. He trains with these youthful gazelles twice daily, logging as many as 80 miles a week—grueling endurance runs and hill repeats, mostly—in the brown, rocky Sandia Mountains northeast of Albuquerque. Meanwhile, he's flying around the country to races, at times financed by promoters hungry for his celebrity. He's looking for a shoe sponsor, and imminently AuthorHouse will release his autobiography, *Olympic Dreams*.

* * *

The book is anguished, and even its title is wistful. (Rono never competed in the Games. For political reasons, Kenya boycotted the two Olympiads that took place in his prime, in 1976 and 1980.) Still, in certain quarters of the running world, *Olympic Dreams* will stand as a seminal document. Rono has fans—nostalgic middle-aged men, mostly—and last year, when he began posting the details of his workouts on a popular message board on letsrun.com, the faithful logged in, hailing their man as a resurrected savior.

"You could be the touchy-feely new-age Frank Shorter and reinvent the running boom," a fellow going by Coleslaw in Victoria gushed recently in writing to Rono. "Your demographic will, of course, include none other than the swelling ranks of waddlers and staggerers who fill the streets of American marathons everywhere."

"Henry, many people care about you," wrote Tinman. "You also have some wisdom to share—much of it from years of experience—which gives us something to learn from. There are tidbits of truth in each line you type."

By far the longest thread in letsrun history is "Henry Rono training for masters mile record." When I first started following it, I thought the whole thing was a bit overwrought, for Rono was abysmally slow. Last December, for instance, he ran a 19:20 5K—very human by elite standards. But then in April, in Carlsbad, California, Rono ran a 17:48 over a flat, looping 5K course. It was nothing earth-shattering, but it was an impressive dash for an old man, and suddenly there was a glimmer of genuine hope. As I tracked his progress, I wondered if, in time, Rono really could break Jack Ryan's record. I also started making inquiries about interviewing him.

The problem was, Rono has always had a turbulent relationship with the press. English is his third language, after Nandi and Swahili, and miscommunications over the years have made Rono apprehensive with reporters. But I had a plan. I happen to live in Portland, so when I learned he was coming here for the Fountain of Youth race, I e-mailed him to request some time. To my surprise, he wrote back just two hours later. "Thanks, Bill. Looks great. See you then, Henry."

As it turned out, though, it wasn't that easy. The next day, I got a phone call, and on the other end of the staticky line was a man in a pique, his voice high and plaintive, his words thickly accented. "Why don't you pay me?" Henry Rono yelled from an airport somewhere, en route to a race. "Every time I do the interview, I get money!"

I explained that wouldn't be possible; reputable journalism didn't include payment for interviews. Rono persisted, changing his tactics— and demanding that I lean on Dave Clingan, the race director, to give him an appearance fee. Clingan was already paying Rono's airfare, personally, and he had no sponsorship for the race. I reasoned with Rono that masters' track lacks the sex appeal to lure big-money sponsors. "You can try calling Dave," I said, "but—"

Rono screamed something—I couldn't make it out. Then he hung up, and I just stood there, sad over how my hero had come to me, insisting on being paid, and remembering, too, what a hard life Henry Rono has led.

Rono's father died when Rono was 6. He was driving a tractor on a white man's farm when he came upon a snake. He leapt off in fright and landed on a spinning three-disc plough. He was killed instantly. Later, to pay for Henry's education, his mother began selling *jakaa* and *pusaa*, home-brewed alcoholic concoctions. When this didn't yield enough cash, Rono writes in *Olympic Dreams*, she married Rono's sister off to a military officer for a dowry of "five cows, five sheep, two goats, and 500 Kenyan shillings."

In time, after he began to shine as a competitive runner, Rono joined the Kenyan military, to attain a sanctuary for training. By 1974, he was Kenya's top prospect. The next year, he ran neck-and-neck with the world's premier miler, Filbert Bayi, of Tanzania. In 1976, the 24-year-old decided to move across the world to Pullman to join several other Kenyan stars being coached by John Chaplin at WSU.

Now retired, Chaplin is a coaching legend who's nurtured dozens of Olympic athletes. He's also an animated, sarcastic jokester who, in his day, maintained a rivalry with the University of Oregon that bordered, some believe, on the maniacal. At one track meet, as Rono closed in on a steeplechase world record, Chaplin suddenly burst onto the track, waving his jacket, forcing a crestfallen Rono to slow down and inducing a horde of disgruntled spectators to pour out of the stands, onto the field. "Those fans there in Eugene," Chaplin told me, "they didn't *deserve* a world record."

In his book, Rono describes Chaplin as controlling and abusive. "He was dismissive of my educational needs," Rono writes. "All he cared about was whether I passed my classes and was eligible to compete." Chaplin, Rono adds, "was aware of my drinking and, at times, even encouraging of it. . . . Chaplin would give me money in the evenings after every other workout, telling me, 'Go have fun for a while before you go to bed.'"

Chaplin vehemently denies abetting Rono's drinking. "I have no idea why Henry says that, none whatsoever," he told me, sounding wounded. "Henry is one of my kids. I brought him to this country, and he calls me whenever he needs to. I promise you—he'll call again."

Chaplin has been advising Rono for years. After Rono graduated from WSU, Chaplin told him, "Go home. There's nothing here for you— no support system. Go be with your family. Take care of them."

Rono had a wife in Kenya by this point. (He would eventually father three children, one of whom, Nixon, would die at age 3 or 4, of cancer.) But he did not follow Chaplin's advice. Instead, with a shoe deal from Nike, Rono moved to Eugene in 1983. He ran a bit. But mostly he drank.

The day before the race in Portland I called Rono on his cell phone. I reached him shortly after his flight had landed—his plane was still taxiing in, actually—and again he hung up on me. So I called his agent, Lynne Buchanan, who knew that Rono needed publicity to market his comeback. Five minutes later she rang me back, chiming, "Someone wants to talk to you."

An hour later I met Rono at Dave Clingan's house. Then he and I drove off for something to eat. As we wove through traffic, he was inaccessible, ensconced in a phone call to his lawyer. We parked and walked into a cheap Chinese restaurant, where the waitress, seeing my reporter's pad, raised a curious eyebrow.

"He used to be the greatest runner in the world," I said.

"Oh," she said, "let me tell you about the specials."

It was midafternoon. There were no other diners, and when Rono at last hung up, there was a silence and a stiff distance between us. He seemed weary, but when he finally started talking, he spoke with hope of an exercise program he developed last year for his middle-school students. "Instead of using prescription drugs, sitting on the couch," he said, "my idea was they could exercise after school. When kids are in physical condition, they are capable of doing their homework."

The program was never implemented, for lack of funding, but still, envisioning it, Rono got inspired to resume running himself. "At first," he said, "even an old lady could pass me."

We talked for a few minutes about his comeback—and then, without prompting, he spoke of his drinking. "The alcohol controlled me," he says. "I kept losing jobs, changing jobs. I was getting nervous. You reach a point when you are not stable. You don't know where you are going to have your next meal. You are financially bankrupt."

I asked Rono how he ended up homeless in Salt Lake. "I went to a race in Atlanta, the Peachtree," he said. "I did bad. Goming home on the plane, I started drinking. So when I got out in Salt Lake to change planes, I asked, 'Do they have a place around here for detox?' I went right into detox, that night. When I came out, I felt good. But I wanted a beer."

In 1996, Rono moved to Albuquerque. "After a while there," he said, "I wasn't drinking so much. You reach a point where every time you drive you get a DUI." Rono got three between 1996 and 1998, and after he curbed his drinking enough to get his teacher's aide job, he was, he said, "hostile in class, angry with the children. I was lucky not to be fired, and I thought, *I have to get alcohol out of my system.* Then I stopped drinking. I stopped."

Rono sat up straight now, and crisply said, "Even when I was wandering around homeless, I knew someday I was going to be somewhere." He was finished eating and, suddenly, finished talking. We left, with plans to talk more later on.

The race the next day had the vague trappings of a showdown, for a few months earlier this message had appeared on letsrun:

Hi Henry,

It's an honor chatting with you even if it's online. I'm Nolan Shaheed . . . and I am glad to hear that you are endeavoring to set the record in the mile. As you know, it's my endeavor, too. It would be great for us to go for the record in the same race at the same meet at the same time.

Shaheed is Muslim. He eats but one meal a day, right after his workout of roughly 12 miles, and once a week he fasts, subsisting simply on water. He is five feet nine, 122 pounds, and at the starting line, in his stylish indigo singlet, he bore a wizened intensity. The showdown was a foregone conclusion.

Shaheed whirred through the first lap in 67 seconds, tagging behind a clump of younger guys, and then slowed only slightly, hitting the half at 2:18 and the three-quarter mark at 3:29 before finishing eighth overall, in 4:42.7—an American age-group record and two seconds off Jack Ryan's world mark. Rono, meanwhile, was last from the get-go. He ran a plodding, evenly paced race that took him to the finish line in 5:45.8, almost a straightaway behind his nearest competitor. He was actually lapped by Tony Young, the race's 45-year-old winner.

Still, while Rono was bent over at the finish, gasping, Shaheed rushed toward him, lavish with praise. "You are one of the greatest runners of all time," he said. "You're an inspiration! Next time, man, it'll be *your* race!"

Later, leaning against the kitchen counter back at Clingan's house, Shaheed urged Rono to chat a bit with him in Swahili. Rono obliged, carefully pushing the words out between the gap in his teeth. *"Hujambo ndugu yangu?"* (How are you, my brother?)

"Hujambo ndugu yangu?" Shaheed repeated. Rono rolled his head back and laughed with delight.

But then I asked Rono a question myself, and the bonhomie vanished. Rono now became somber, almost woeful as he argued that he had nothing to gain by talking to me. "The media," he said, "they steal your energy. You know, it is because of the media that I became homeless.

"In 1989," he went on, "I was working at a chicken-soup factory [back] in Eugene. The first day, the media starts looking at me, and so at the end of eight hours, the boss says, 'Come to the office with me. How often does the media follow you?' I said, 'All the time,' and so then he says, 'Guess what? Here's a check for $40. Now don't come back here again.' I was victimized. When you feel like that, you drink. I was drinking because of the media."

* * *

There was an uneasy air when Rono and I said goodbye, so I wasn't surprised when, a few days later, he dissed me on letsrun. In an inspired morning riff that also attacked Clingan and a Nike rep who'd given him a few free pairs of shoes, Rono said of his Portland visit, "They set a [t]rap on me and [I had] no way to turn." He explained that, when he got to Clingan's house, the shoes were already there, waiting for him. "Did you want me to turn around and leave Dave?" Rono asked, and then took issue with my buying him dinner: "Meanwhile here is a reporter who will pay for your meals tonight. I have no money with me. Did you want me to sleep hungry at night? I had three people bending me down."

There is little doubt that Henry Rono is a character of disparate moods. Many people describe him as sweet and kind. Kris Houghton, whom Rono trains, told me how he and other runners gather each morning at Rono's tiny hillside apartment. "Henry lets us shower there," he said. "We eat there, and then we all take a nap. He's got little futons and blankets set up right there. He's very giving."

And by all accounts he always has been. Thomas Kennedy, a retired history professor at WSU, told me that, in the '70s and early '80s, when Kennedy served as Rono's host father, "Henry became an honorary member of our family. He won our hearts. The thing about Henry is people like him. At first, you think he's just withdrawn—a dull personality. But then he flashes a smile; you see his bright eyes. He has this persisting naiveté, you know."

Geoff Hollister, once the track-and-field director for Nike, likewise spoke of Rono in warm, familial tones. "In his first years here," Hollister said, "he was close to my son, Tracy. They'd play 'lion' up in our loft together. He was very playful, great around kids, and just very enjoyable."

When Hollister traveled with Rono to Kenya in 1978, Rono told him, "You've taken good care of me, and now that you're in my country, I'm going to take good care of you." As newspaper headlines screamed, "Where's Henry?" Rono protectively pulled Hollister along through adoring legions of fans.

But by the time Rono had first moved to Eugene in 1983, he was beyond such gallantry—and his drinking had become such a problem, according to Hollister, that it needed attention. With a Nike colleague, Hollister tried to force Rono to go back to Pullman where other Kenyans were training. "We went to pick him up," Hollister remembers, "and he was outraged. We told him, 'We're doing this as friends, for you.' And he said, 'You are not my friends.' He was in total denial. He refused to go."

Eventually, Rono's old rival, Alberto Salazar, tried to intervene. He invited Rono to live with him and his young family in Eugene. Rono did, but he kept drinking, and after a few months Salazar had no choice but to boot him. Henry Rono was suddenly alone in the world, and desperate.

"I got this call one Thanksgiving," Hollister says, "and it was Henry. He said, 'I'm just calling to see who my real friends are.'"

"Your real friend already tried to help you," Hollister replied, "and you didn't want it. Until you can start showing me that you're serious about this, I really don't expect to hear from you again. I want you to recover, but you've got to take the steps."

Last spring and into the summer, Rono kept running, to little effect. He slogged through Bay to Breakers, a 12K road race in San Francisco, at a 7:07 pace, and then, so hobbled by an injury that he was seen limping, he ran a 6:24.84 single mile in Nashville. Panic surged up on letsrun. "Henry," wrote one correspondent, "just take the next week off from running; get a lot of therapy for your injuries, and start eating nothing but chicken and vegetables and green tea."

"Henry," wrote NYC, "why don't you find a job, at least part-time? Everybody has to work, including you. That's what all of us do."

"NO! NO!" Rono replied. "I'm not a part-time person. I'm a full-time man." Later, he added, "Remember I can't train and teach—it is impossible. Being around kids, yelling and screaming takes all the strength of an athlete like me, who is humble to kids. I take in their feelings, and it hurts my nerves. After that, you just get home, eat a lot, sleep a lot, and you gain a lot [of] weight up to 225 pounds."

I called Rono one more time, but again he hung up on me—and I was resigned to monitoring his progress on letsrun. One day he did a 90-minute morning jaunt followed by an afternoon track workout—four 200-meter intervals—a combo that rendered his hamstring a "painful rock." Another day, he ran along a mountain trail—steeply up, and then down—for four hours and 36 minutes. "I had [to] bend down and drink running water, I was so thirst[y]," he wrote. Eventually, he pondered a new strategy—running downhill at speed. "This is [what] my running nature is asking for," he wrote.

For all the mileage, though, he was still overweight and still a long way from a world record. I groped to understand why he was working so hard.

The only answer I could come up with was something Rono told me in Portland as we sat there together in that Chinese restaurant. "Sometimes when I was homeless," he said, "I find a place where I can put my bags. I hide them, like behind a bush, and then I run a little—maybe half an hour, you know, just down the street. And then I feel good. I feel free. When I am running, I see the light."

Fixing Diane's Brain

Runner's World, *February 2011*

EVERY FEW SECONDS, THERE'S ANOTHER FLASH IN THE DARKNESS, AND for an instant you see them—the jubilant Chinese ultramarathon runners, lit up, posing for photographs. At 5 a.m. on this day last May, roughly 200 of them are gathered in the chill that envelops Juyongguan, China, where the ancient Great Wall lures millions of tourists annually from nearby Beijing. And never mind that the North Face 100, the exasperating 62-mile race that awaits them, offers some 2,100 feet of vertical climbing. Nearly all of them are spritzing around as though they're about to embark on a champagne cruise.

* * *

Everyone is taking digital photos of everyone else. One wizened 58-year-old racer, Bian Jinghai, is wearing an orange bandanna pirate-style and inexplicably shouting "Mao Zedong is up there, and I am down here" as he dances about like a prize-fighter poised to enter the ring. Another older runner vows to race barefoot, in homage to Mother Earth, and tiny, 92-pound Xu Yuan Shan, who claims to have once run a 2:45 marathon, is raging around Nixon-like, flashing the victory sign at myriad cameramen.

Amid this morning's starting-line mayhem, though, one athlete, an American, is almost totally still. Diane Van Deren is standing off to the side, by the shuttered Great Wall souvenir stands, wearing sunglasses and a fresh, glistening coat of sunscreen as her husband, Scott, holds her close, quietly offering counsel.

Van Deren is 50, and she's traveled from her Colorado home as an athlete sponsored by the North Face, the race organizer. In the days before the race, Van Deren has proven a sprightly and winning spokesperson for the outdoor apparel company. Five feet nine inches tall, and blond with blue eyes, she exudes a windblown good cheer and a certain renegade spark. She's promoted running in near religious terms. "When I run in the mountains, that's my medicine," she told the Chinese journalists during a press conference. "That's my heart." She's also told the story of how she once ran up 14,110-foot Pikes Peak in Colorado, and then hitched a ride down on the back of a stranger's Harley. She's a jaunty jock who travels nearly everywhere in pastel-bright running togs, and she's a sentimental mother of three 20-something kids. Back in Beijing, she brought a roomful of reporters to their feet by singing, a cappella, a song she'd written herself about her son, a Marine who until recently was driving a Humvee through the battlefields of Iraq.

Now, however, Van Deren is silent. Her face is impassive behind her wraparound shades. This race—every race—looms large for her. Her running career is the culmination of a long and trying saga.

For nearly 17 years, until she was 37, Van Deren suffered from epilepsy, enduring hundreds of seizures, sometimes as often as two or three times in a week. With each seizure, she lost consciousness for about a minute. Usually, her body just went limp as she stared off into space. But there were also the two dozen or so grand mal seizures she suffered, when her muscles radically contracted and her legs and arms flailed uncontrollably. With each seizure came the distinct chance that she could die. Rather than risk death, she did the next best thing: She let doctors drill a hole into her skull.

In 1997, Van Deren underwent a partial right temporal lobectomy. Doctors removed a portion of her brain that was the focal point of her seizures. The surgery ended her epilepsy; Van Deren hasn't seized once since the operation. But the surgeon's work created a blind spot in the upper left part of her vision. And there is also the residual neural damage from the seizures. She cannot track time well; she is always running late, and she has almost no sense of direction. Her memory is weak—she can't recall where, exactly, she took her honeymoon—and when she's confronted with excessive sensory noise, as she is now, at this clamorous starting line, she gets weary and irritable. Sometimes Van Deren needs to lie down and nap for hours.

She is an ultramarathoner with extraordinary limitations. In races she must cover hundreds of miles, and yet often has no idea how long she has been running—or where she is going.

Still, Van Deren's surgery may actually have aided her distance running. "The right side of the brain, where Diane had surgery, is involved in processing emotion," says one of her doctors, Don Gerber, a clinical neuropsychologist at Craig Hospital in Denver. "The surgery affected the way she processes her emotional reaction to pain. I'm not saying Diane doesn't feel pain, but pain is a complex process. You have a sensory input, and then the question is: How does the brain interpret that? Diane's brain interprets pain differently than yours or mine does."

Gerber's assessment is controversial among neurologists, and all that's certain, really, is that Van Deren has almost primordial gifts of endurance. In February 2008, in the Canadian Yukon, she won the Yukon Arctic Ultra, spending nearly eight days pulling a 50-pound supplies sled 300 miles and through temperatures that plunged to around 50 below. The next winter she covered 430 miles. And once, in Alaska, she trudged 85 miles through snow on a sprained ankle after stepping in a moose hole.

This race in China will be, relatively speaking, a cakewalk. Still, it begins by scrambling up about 1,000 steep steps carved into the Great Wall itself. "Dear runners," says the race starter, speaking in stiff, stilted English as she summons the runners to the line. "Dear runners."

When the race starts, the field erupts with hoots of applause. Van Deren moves forward, quietly, her head down.

Diane Van Deren first experienced brain trauma when she was 16 months old. Otherwise healthy, she came down one day with a high fever. She was rushed to a hospital near her childhood home in Omaha, Nebraska. Nurses packed her quivering body in ice, but still she trembled for almost an hour. The seizure was not extraordinary. About 5 percent of American children endure a fever-induced seizure before age 5. Most never seize again. For many years, it seemed Van Deren would end up in that lucky majority.

As a kid, she played catcher on a boys' baseball team, going by the name Dan and shoving her pigtails under her cap. As a teenager, she was a Colorado state champion in tennis and golf. She left high school early to spend four years touring the United States and Europe as a professional tennis player. She also ran a bit to keep fit. In 1982, at the age of 22 and on a whim, she entered a marathon in southwest Texas and won the women's division.

Her infantile seizure had scarred a small portion of her right brain, though, and the cells there were vulnerable to reinjury. In her 20s, without even being aware of it, Van Deren began having tiny seizures. They didn't manifest as convulsions, but rather as subtle perceptual shifts. Out on the tennis court, or while relaxing at home, she had what she calls "funny sensations. It was like a déjà vu feeling," she says, "like you're in a dream, and you're thinking, Oh, what's happening right now has happened to me before. You feel like you're floating; it's an out-of-body experience."

Lasting just seconds, these mini-seizures were "auras," in neurological parlance. Auras are the first stage of a full-blown epileptic attack. Dr. Mark Spitz, the University of Colorado neurologist who would later order Van Deren's surgery, describes them as an electrical phenomenon. The brain, he explains, consists of millions of cells that are "wired" to one another to transmit sensory, motor, and processing data. "When an aura occurs," he says, "it's like the beginning of a fire in the brain. That fire can grow so that the person is increasingly vulnerable to stronger seizures."

None of this was evident, though, when Diane and Scott Van Deren met in 1982. The two were recent college graduates, and he was taken by her larksome spirit and drive. At the time Diane was training for the Ironman World Championship. She was a novelty—Ironwomen were still rare then—and Scott was smitten. "She seemed spontaneous," he says. "She seemed fun."

The Van Derens married when they were both 23. A few years later Scott went to work for Mountain Steel & Supply, founded by Diane's father. Diane worked there herself, in sales, but lasted only six months—and never pursued another desk job. "Office work has never been my thing," she says. She taught aerobics instead, and kept running, sometimes five miles, sometimes 20, a day. When the mood struck, she entered a local triathlon.

By the time Diane was 28, she was pregnant with her third child. Her brain was at the mercy of hormonal shifts. One night, as he lay in bed, sleeping, Scott awoke to the sound of his wife having a grand mal seizure. "She was violently shaking," Scott says. "I'd never seen a [grand mal] before." Diane had been diagnosed with epilepsy due to an attack earlier in that pregnancy, and now, Scott says, "I thought to myself, *Here we go*. I knew that we were entering a new chapter in our lives. I moved a lamp, so she wouldn't knock it over, and then I called 911."

For years afterward, Scott would lie awake in bed, intently listening. "I got very in tune with Diane's breathing," he says. "Snoring was a good thing; it meant she was getting some peaceful rest." But there were more seizures, and when their children were small, says Scott, the household "revolved around how Diane was feeling. There was constant worry over when she'd have her next seizure." Each one crushed her. "I'd feel like I'd been run over by a truck," Diane recalls. Depending on the severity of the seizure, she'd take to bed for two or three days. Nannies were hired to drive the children and to clean the house.

Throughout all the trauma, though, Diane evolved a rare trick: She learned to abort her seizures by running.

She had noticed that her attacks usually occurred when she was resting—at the movie theater, say, or in a quiet restaurant. Her brain cells were "idle" then, as Dr. Spitz explains it, and as such more prone to "catch fire" when an abnormal seizure discharge occurred. What she needed to do was to activate brain cells quickly, the instant she felt an aura come on. Few people can do this, Spitz says, but Van Deren kept her running shoes by the door, and whenever that eerie déjà vu feeling settled upon her, she stood up and rushed toward those shoes. "I knew that I only had a few seconds," she says. "I had to get moving."

Dr. Spitz says Van Deren's seizures always began in her right hippocampus, a small sea horse-shaped ridge that sits deep within the brain, storing and retrieving memories. "Running," he says, "probably activated the part of the hippocampus where seizures started. When the cells there were active, they didn't accept the abnormal electrical activity, and the seizure fizzled out."

She laced up her shoes and started running—out her driveway and then over ranchers' tawny, fenced rangeland in the rural area outside of Denver. "I'd go right out into a forest," she says. "I'd be anxious, but there was a softness to being outdoors. I felt the pine needles underfoot on the trail, and listened to the birds. It calmed me. I kept running. The point was to just keep my mind going, my body moving. I'd run until I'd broken the cycle of the seizure. Sometimes I'd run for two or three hours."

* * *

After climbing up the Great Wall, the race course rolls onto back roads. Then, roughly 12 kilometers into the race, it climbs to its highest point, at 2,477 feet, offering a hazy view of Beijing 30 miles away. From the ridge top, it's a steep, pounding descent into Tiger Valley, where, near the 19K mark, race officials have festooned several desolate cliffs with 20-foot-high red and white banners.

Scott Van Deren and I are standing beside these banners, on the bank of a river, in the morning coolness, waiting. Van Deren is a big man—six feet four and quite fit, thanks to a weight-room regimen and a heavy cycling habit. His voice is deep, and his manner toward his wife protective and steady. In 1995, when Diane was suffering frequent seizures, he moved the family to their current home on a 35-acre windswept property in Sedalia, Colorado, in part so that Diane could be around horses. "There's something therapeutic about brushing horses," he says.

Scott now owns the family steel business. He has the confident air of a man accustomed to getting things done, but at this moment he can only peer with hope up the mountain path as the runners start trickling down toward us, their voices echoing in the narrow canyon. First comes a boyish-looking Chinese student, 23-year-old Yun Yan Qiao, bounding through in one hour, 39 minutes. The first woman—43-year-old Zhang Huiji—comes through at 1:57. More than 20 minutes later, Scott Van Deren is still waiting. "I expect her any moment," he says.

Scott has waited helplessly like this before. In 2008, at the North Face Ultra-Trail du Mont-Blanc, Diane started the 103-mile race with a fever and began shaking as she ran. Twice she stopped to sleep for an hour—something she'd never done before. It took her more than 40 hours to finish. Today, after two hours and 22 minutes, she finally comes through the 19K mark, in eighth place in the women's race, running at a 12-minute, 15-second pace. She's not far off from where she should be, really. By her standards this race is a sprint—it doesn't play to her strengths—and at 50, she's older than all but one woman beating her. Still, Scott is worried. "My instinct is this isn't her day," he says. "She looks tight."

Indeed, Van Deren's face is a tense mask, her stride slightly halting and choppy. She strained her Achilles a few months earlier during a predawn run. It's been stiff ever since. But it's impossible to discern if Van Deren's in pain, for she's dialed into the race. When she comes to the aid station at 26K, now in seventh place, Scott can only try to get through to her by delivering one clear message that he's carefully rehearsed in his mind. "Get your pace," he says. "You've got three big climbs ahead."

Scott isn't a coach. He's never been a runner. His advice isn't necessarily astute. It's chivalrous. For a few seconds he runs beside Diane. "You look great, babe," he shouts as she gulps down some water.

"I'm outta here," says Diane. She tosses the water bottle and then breaks into a trot.

* * *

When Van Deren first began having grand mal seizures in 1988, she refused to give in to them. Unable to drive, she walked to the supermarket, three miles away, pregnant, and pushing her two infant children in a stroller. Then she walked home, with the groceries in a backpack. Once her kids grew, she went downhill skiing—and wrapped her arms around the back of the chairlift each time she boarded, so she wouldn't fall out if she seized.

The auras kept coming, though, and sometimes Van Deren didn't grab her running shoes fast enough. She seized, and more cells in her brain died, and more rewired, and as a result her prelude-like auras shortened and shortened. "The seizures," she says, "overtook my body and my confidence. I tried to dig deep and hide my confusion. I didn't want my kids to feed off my fear."

Nonetheless, Michael Van Deren, the Marine, says that his mom's illness permeated his childhood. He remembers his mother once having a grand mal attack in the living room when he was 7 and his dad was away for the weekend. "It was full blown," says Michael, who is now 24. "She was clenching her teeth. I yelled at Robin and Matt"—his younger siblings—"to leave the room. I didn't want them to see that."

Scott Van Deren adds, "Diane's epilepsy absolutely dominated the relational pattern of the family. The second I walked in from work, I'd ask, 'How's Mom? What's she doing?' I couldn't rest." The next seizure was always a threat. Once, when Scott was treating customers to dinner at a restaurant in Vail, Diane seized at the table. "It was a casual meeting on a summer day," he says, "and we hadn't discussed Diane's epilepsy with those people."

But the seizure that pains Diane most, in hindsight, happened when her daughter, Robin, now 22, was in grade school. Diane was coaching Robin's basketball team, and at a game, before hundreds of spectators, Diane says, "I had this aura and the next thing I knew the other coach was standing over me, saying, 'Diane, is everything okay?'" The gym went silent. "I was out of control," Diane says, woefully re-creating the moment. "I couldn't control myself, and I hurt for my children: They had to see their mom having a grand mal seizure right on the gym floor."

Dr. Spitz wanted to send Van Deren to surgery, but he could operate only if he could identify the source of her seizures. To do so, he brought her into the hospital, deprived her of meds, and then attached electrodes to her scalp to measure electrical activity. She proceeded to have three seizures over the next four days. A videotape of one, a grand mal, shows Diane biting her tongue and then gurgling audibly on the bloody saliva in her throat.

Dr. Spitz isolated Diane's problems to her right hippocampus. She'd be seizure free, probably, if the damaged tissue there was excised. Spitz saw surgery as Van Deren's safest path. Without it, her seizures were likely to become more severe and more frequent, he explained, and she faced about a 10 percent chance of dying from a seizure over the next

10 years. The surgery, in contrast, delivered just a 3 percent chance of a stroke. "I was calling Spitz's office over and over, trying to get into surgery right away," says Diane. "I was in fear of dying of a seizure."

Scott was more measured. He insisted they seek a second opinion. Again, surgery was recommended. So in February 1997, in Denver, a neurological team operated on Diane's brain. Using a high-speed drill, the surgeon removed an outer section of bone from her skull. He cut deeper, into the brain's dura, or protective membrane, and then focused a microscope on the exposed temporal lobe. Using an aspirator, he excised part of the lobe along with the affected portion of the hippocampus.

A few hours after Van Deren awoke, she felt "horrific pain." And it seems that her innate stubbornness kicked in. There was a shunt lodged in her skull, to drain blood, and she tried to tear it out. According to Scott, "She tried to get out of the room. A doctor and two nurses had to strap her into the bed, and she tried to bite one of them. Then she kicked a nurse."

The doctors had to remove the partially dislodged shunt, exacerbating the pressure in Van Deren's head. "When I went in to see her," Scott says, "she was like a combative animal. She said, 'Get me out of here. Why are you letting them do this to me? I hate you.' She called me every name in the book—f---ing this, f---ing that."

"The brain is very personal," Diane would explain later. "It doesn't like to be messed with."

By the time Van Deren reaches the aid station at 32K, she remains in seventh place. She has blood on her arms and her shins. While running on rubbly dirt a few miles back, and staring downward in search of good footing, she couldn't see the low branches surrounding the narrow trail due to her poor peripheral vision. A couple of times she had tripped and fallen down. But she continued to press on. "I just listen to my feet when I run," she had told me earlier, "and I try to get a rhythm going. I breathe in two steps. I breathe out two steps."

At one point, Scott Van Deren and I ride in a van alongside Diane. We're so close to her that we can hear her footfalls. "Get mad," Scott yells out the window. "Get mad now!"

"You got any gels?" Diane asks. "Got any gels?"

We don't. There'll be nothing for her to eat until the 44K mark. She sucks at her energy drink and keeps running.

* * *

What Van Deren remembers most from the weeks following the surgery is the pain. "Every time I'd bend down, it hurt," she says. "Even tying my shoes, I felt like my head was going to explode from the pressure. I played golf, and when I put the tee in, my head just throbbed." She was eager to run again, however, and roughly a month after the operation, she did, covering 10 miles, gingerly. "I tried to hold my head as steady as possible," she says. Still, she kept running every day. "The mountains were my safe zone. I was at peace there."

* * *

Having worked with many patients who had undergone surgeries similar to Van Deren's, Dr. Spitz says the weeks, months, and even years after such an operation can be as emotionally challenging as they are physically. "You need to figure out what your future in this world is without having seizures," Spitz explains. "And that can be harder than you might think. I've seen many divorces take place after the surgery. In the years before her surgery, Diane had pretty much stopped competing because of the seizures. She had become very dependent on her family. Now she had to figure out what to do with her new life."

For a while, Van Deren seemed content to live in the moment. When she ran, her husband says, it wasn't about competing; it was about "being free and outside." Van Deren could cover 20 miles on the trails, and when she was done feel invigorated versus being exhausted. And then she would run a little farther.

Finally, in 2002, roughly five years after her surgery, she entered a low-key race—a 50-mile Colorado trail run in which there was only one other entrant. "The race director had to run along with them through the first few miles," Scott says, "to show them the route." Diane finished, in a tie with the other runner, and soon she was dreaming big. Later that year she signed up for the Hardrock 100, which climbs more than 30,000 feet in the Colorado Rockies. "If I could get through years of seizures and then brain surgery," she says, "I could take this baby on. I could do it."

Hardrock's race director stifled Van Deren's race plan, though—she needed to have previously finished at least one 100-mile ultra. Undeterred, she jumped into another 100-miler, this one starting in Leadville, Colorado, elevation 12,600 feet. She ran for about 70 miles, twisted her knee, and continued to hobble on. When Van Deren finally dropped out at the 72-mile mark, her desire to run, and to compete, had only intensified.

She began planning for her next 100-mile race, and Van Deren told a friend, Kathy Pidcock, "I expect to win it." Pidcock, who was then an elite ultrarunner, crafted for Van Deren a rugged training program—a 100-mile-per-week regimen heavy on high-altitude training and back-to-back 25-mile outings. "Whatever I told her to do, she did," says Pidcock. "She never questioned me, and she was so strong. I knew she would make it." She did. In June 2003, Van Deren completed the Bighorn Trail 100 Mile Run, in Wyoming, in 31 hours, 54 minutes, finishing sixth in the women's race. She figured, "I've done it. That's my last one."

Two days later, though, she talked to a roomful of grade-schoolers with epilepsy at a camp in Colorado. "These were kids who had 20 or 30 seizures a day," she says. "They were having seizures right in front of me, and one of them, a girl named Mandy, asked, 'Are you going to run another 100-mile race?'"

Van Deren's feet were still swollen; her shins were bruised from postholing in snowfields. But Mandy persisted: "Will you run your next 100-miler for me? I can't run. I have seizures."

"I felt guilty," Van Deren says. "I thought, If I could only give them a piece of what I've felt overcoming my epilepsy . . ."

Soon, Van Deren was the first woman finisher in the San Diego 100-Mile Endurance Run, placing second overall. Then in 2004, over a six-month period, she ran seven ultras, including three longer than 95 miles. In 2004, after finally being accepted into the race, she was the ninth-place woman at the Hardrock 100.

How did Van Deren rise so suddenly from obscurity? Granted, she'd already proven herself a world-class athlete, but that was in tennis, a very different sport. And she'd run some, sure. But what enabled her to knock off so many ultras, so speedily, with so little recovery time? Each year, thousands of Americans have epilepsy surgery. Can we expect some of them to start flourishing in endurance sports with new and magical pain tolerance?

Dr. Gerber credits her endurance in part to her brain limitations. He says runners who can better track time and map where they are can be distracted by the details. But Van Deren has a special facility for what he calls "flow" that lets her transcend the anguish of running long. "It's a mental state," Gerber says. "You become enmeshed in what you're doing. It's almost Zen. She can run for hours and not know how long she's been going."

But Dr. William Theodore, chief of the clinical epilepsy division at the National Institute of Health, says no evidence exists that epilepsy surgery will cause a change in pain tolerance. "Certain parts of the brain are related to pain, but they're very deep structures. They're almost never involved in epilepsy surgery."

Another expert, Dr. Jerome Engel, director of the UCLA Seizure Disorder Center, says the majority of epilepsy patients who undergo partial lobectomies do not experience either diminished brain function or changes in character. Still, Engel calls Van Deren an "atypical case." While he has never examined her, he's struck by reports of her unusual postsurgical cognitive problems—of her trouble with getting lost, for instance. To him, such symptoms suggest that her brain bears "bilateral damage"; in other words, her presurgical seizures could have scarred both lobes of her brain. If that is the case, Engel suggests, "it could affect her pain tolerance." He explains that the electrical shocks involved in a seizure cause the brain to release its own opioids, or pain relievers. When both sides of the brain have endured seizures, the opioids' effect is, Engel says, "more powerful."

One medical professional who worked directly with Van Deren thinks the equation is simpler. "Diane was a great athlete before surgery, and she's still a great athlete," says Mark Spitz, her original doctor. "The surgery didn't change that."

Van Deren herself disagrees, slightly. "The surgery helped," she says, "because it was painful. I learned how to endure pain. But I've always been superfocused and stubborn." Van Deren argues that her gift lies in keeping up the fight—in refusing to wallow in sadness, even amid the trials of epilepsy and her current impairments. During a recent 50-mile race, she says, "A guy knocked me off the trail in the first mile. I rolled my ankle all the way over and just kept running, for 49 miles more, even though a PT thought it was broken. Here's why I'm good: I don't give up."

At about 45K, the North Face 100 cuts through a small village, and the course markers are nowhere to be seen. Several runners get lost, and our guide—Sky Song, a young North Face marketing rep—gets a call: The top 10 runners are stalled at a country store. We begin flying toward them. En route, we see diminutive Xu Yuan Shan, the 2:45 marathoner, churning along, just off the lead pack. "Get in the van," Sky cries out the window. "You're lost!"

Xu climbs in, sweaty and winded, and then Song keeps rolling. The leaders elude him, though. Some, but not all, catch a ride back to the course from a policeman, and soon there's another snafu. When leader Yun Yan Qiao hits the 50K aid station, he looks for the drop bag he packed the night before with extra socks and snacks. Race organizers were supposed to bring each runner's bag to this station, but Yun's isn't here. In exasperation, he drops out. Later, when Van Deren learns that Yun quit, she's disgusted. "He could have finished," she hisses. "So many people in ultras lose it when one thing crumbles. You just can't do that."

Van Deren doesn't. In 2008, in the Yukon Arctic Ultra, her water bottles froze solid—for 20 miles, she ran without a drop. A few days later, she reached the Yukon River in 70-mile-per-hour winds and didn't know which way to go. As the wind tossed her to her knees, she began marking her way with red tape. She went in one direction for an hour. When it appeared that was the wrong way, she doubled back, patiently. She kept at it for four hours and eventually found her way.

Now, in China, Van Deren's caught in another long struggle. All day, there's been a phenom running ahead of her—a chipper young Chinese woman in navy knee-length pants, a red collared shirt, and cheap gray running sneakers. Zheng Rufang, 28, is primarily a cyclist. She trains with the Chinese national team, and she's dressed, she'll say later, to signal, "I am not a runner. I know nothing about running." About 75 kilometers into the race, her inexperience starts to show. Climbing a small mountain, up hundreds of concrete steps, past little Buddhist shrines carved into the cliffs of the Yinshan Pagoda Forest, she's worn out—dragging. There's another Chinese woman just ahead of her. And when Van Deren chugs up behind them, out of sight but closing, it's as though she can smell the roadkill.

"How far ahead are they?" she asks as she passes me on the stairs. Her cool reserve is gone now, more than 11 hours into the race. Her face is sunburned, and there's an edge of wild hunger to her voice.

"About three minutes," I say.

Van Deren cranes her neck skyward, looking for them.

* * *

For all her ambition, Diane Van Deren can seem very vulnerable. On a trip to Beijing in 2009, she got lost for two hours after leaving her hotel for a run. It was the sort of misadventure that could befall any tourist, but the incident still looms for Van Deren as terrifying: worrisome proof of her limitations. She remembers being on the verge of tears and desperately beseeching directions, in shouted English, from the white-gloved soldiers who stand on small pedestals all over Beijing, stock still, at attention. The Chinese businessman who eventually saved her, leading her by the hand for more than a mile, back to her hotel, still shines for her as a saint.

Van Deren's general disorientation could prove fatal in competition—what if she took a wrong turn in the Arctic?—but she insists that it is also an anguishing impediment at home, in day-to-day life. She forgets appointments, she says, and cannot remember people's faces. Once at a family gathering, when everyone was asked to name their favorite Christmas, she drew a blank. "So many emotions were packed into those 10 seconds," she says, "Sadness, frustration, embarrassment. You don't know how much pain these disabilities have brought me. It's challenged my relationships with my family and friends."

Donald Gerber, the neuropsychologist, has provided her counsel over the past six years. He meets informally with Van Deren before each of her races. He tries to anticipate the trouble she might encounter, given her brain injury, and then devises coping strategies. "You want to minimize distraction and dangers," he says, "and make everything as routine as possible."

It was Dr. Gerber who advised Van Deren to take red tape to the Arctic, so she could mark her path if she got lost. Before she ran the snowy course of Alaska's Iditarod on foot, he likewise advised her to stop if suddenly the snow underfoot seemed soft and untrammeled by dogs. "That could be a sign you're off the Iditarod Trail," he advised.

As Dr. Gerber himself admits, his tips are "not rocket science." But they give Van Deren a certain assurance. "When I go out to race," she says, "I feel confident. And that's because Don and I had put together a game plan. I'm prepared. I'm always prepared."

* * *

On Yinshan Mountain, Van Deren keeps climbing past the tree line, and on up to where the mountain is just a windswept exposed rock looking out onto a succession of other slabs of basalt speckled with small, green, scrubby trees. Then she guts past Zheng Rufang and the other Chinese woman. At the 90K checkpoint, she's intent on burying them. "That girl in red," she shouts to Scott, "she's on my ass."

Scott Van Deren is now riding in Sky Song's van. "Babe, she isn't on your ass," he shouts out the window, a bit wearily. It's been a long day for him, too, and in fact, neither Chinese woman is anywhere in sight now. They're fading.

"She's on my ass. Where is that girl? Is she walking behind me?"

Genially, Scott ignores the question. "You look good, honey," he says. The van revs away from Diane, and then, with a smirk, he says to me, "Sometimes you have to lie."

The course rolls onto a mostly flat paved road, and between 90K and 98K, Van Deren passes 14 men. At about the 99K mark, in the darkness,

Scott is anxious again as we sit in the idling van, by a fork in the road. "Wait here," he says to Sky Song. "She could miss this turn." She doesn't. Scott guides her in and she finishes in 13:16, good for fifth among 10 women.

* * *

From the finish area, we ride away in the van. Diane is in the back, with her feet up, resting her Achilles, which bears a swollen, grape-sized bulge. It's dark out. She's taken her sunglasses off, and it's as though all her armor has melted. She's woozy and mushy—happily delirious, like a society dowager high on martinis. "Sky," she calls out to our guide, "you've been so sweet. Let me buy you a glass of wine. Sky, come to Colorado. Bring your wife."

Scott fixes a jacket into a pillow for Diane. She moans a little, in pain. They are middle-aged warriors, both of them, and Diane, who hopes to write a memoir someday, has admitted she may be nearing the end. "When I finished the 430-miler in the Yukon," she told me, "I thought, *There's a great chapter for my book.* There comes a time and a place where the odds just get slimmer and slimmer."

The van swoops over hills, and through little villages. Eventually, we're on the outskirts of Beijing, rolling through traffic for a few minutes before cutting north, back to our hotel by the Wall. It's a warm Saturday night. People are out taking strolls and drinking at sidewalk tables outside cafés. Inside the van, there's tranquility: the deep satisfaction that comes after a long race.

At this stage in her life, Diane Van Deren says her days are happy, mostly. She is grateful for her surgery—"without it," she says, "I'd probably be dead." And her older son, Michael, has returned safely from Iraq and begun working at the family steel business. He calls his mother before races, wishing her well. "There's laughter in our house now," Diane says, "and there wasn't before."

Weeks after we return from China, though, I give her a call. During our conversation I ask what she remembers of her trip and of the 100K race, and for a second there's a weird silence. "I'm sitting here panicking a little," she says. "My heart's pounding. It's almost like I'm drawing a blank. I remember the big picture. I remember landing at the airport. I remember being on the Great Wall, and I can always remember things that are traumatic, like falling on the trail. But other things?" There's a long pause.

We soon hang up, and when we speak a couple of days later, she says, "You know, when I went running today, I was like, 'Okay, Diane, think. What do you really remember of China?'" She goes on to recite her memories. They are essentially the same memories she's already told me about, and soon she seems to recognize that once again a small part of her has been lost, irretrievably. For maybe half a second, there's a blue silence.

But then Van Deren muscles past it, and back into good cheer. "Hey, you know, I just went to the doctor's yesterday," she says, "and I got an MRI done on my Achilles. There's nothing wrong with it. It's just tender and swollen. I can keep training, which is good. The Hard Rock 100 is only four weeks away. Four weeks, baby. It's coming right up. I'm there."

The Last Naturalist

Outside, *December 15, 2017*

GREAT LIVES OFTEN BEGIN AMID TUMULT AND SUFFERING. SEVENTY years ago, long before Bernd Heinrich became one of history's fastest ultramarathoners, and ages before his scientific studies on ravens made him a leading naturalist, he was a skinny, impoverished kid living in a hut in the forest of Hahnheide, in Germany. Before World War II, his family had owned a vast agricultural estate roughly 400 miles east of there, in Poland, with foxes and storks and rolling fields of potatoes and sugar beets; but after the Eastern Front pushed west, they became refugees. Bernd's father shoveled manure to survive, and the family lived mostly off forage—nuts, berries, mushrooms, and also trout, which Bernd caught with his bare hands.

It was a confusing time. Bernd and his sister had no other playmates, and he spent long days exploring the forest on his own. His father, a top entomologist specializing in wasps, was marginalized in postwar Germany, and he could be tyrannical. Once when Bernd was 5 years old and collecting beetles, he found a prized rare specimen at the base of a stump, and his father confiscated the insect to punish him for being "overstimulated," as he put it, when the boy leaped for the bug. Real men, Gerd Heinrich believed, were unflappable, with nerves of steel.

Was it there in the Hahnheide that Bernd formed the spine to notch an American record for the 100 kilometers, running the distance at a 6:25-mile pace in a Chicago race in 1981? Did hardship form the writer whose classics *Bumblebee Economics* and *Ravens in Winter* offer readers both impassioned tales about animals and meticulous science?

No, a later, happier chapter made him who he is.

In 1951, when Bernd was 11, his family wrangled passage to the United States and landed in western Maine. They planned to grow potatoes. Instead, they were taken in for a summer by a kind family, the Adamses, whose ramshackle farm was a mess, a mélange of dogs and cows and chickens and broken tractor equipment. To Bernd, the place was paradise, as he writes in his 2007 memoir, *The Snoring Bird*, recalling the adventures he shared with the two eldest Adams kids, Jimmy and Billy. The boys built a raft out of barn wood and spent countless hours watching baby catfish and white-bellied dragonflies. The Adamses taught Bernd English. He killed a hummingbird with his slingshot. He ran around barefoot and shirtless.

Bernd Heinrich is now 77 years old and the author of 21 books. Vaunted biologist E. O. Wilson speaks of him as an equal, calling him "one of the most original and productive people I know" and "one of the best natural-history writers we have." Runners also revere him, for his speed and for his 2002 book, *Why We Run*. "He was the first person of scientific stature to say that ultramarathoning is a natural pursuit for humans," says Christopher McDougall, author of the 2009 bestseller *Born to Run*. "He did the research himself, in 100-plus-mile races."

But let's set aside the literary plumage for a moment. In many ways, Bernd remains the same inquisitive kid who found bliss in his first American summer. He still runs, though no farther than about 12 miles at a time. He still watches wildlife, intently, and he still climbs trees. Sometimes he even climbs trees in snowshoes. In old age, he is embracing the joys of youth anew.

And he has returned to the Maine woods, to a 640-acre plot about 15 miles from that old farmhouse where he spent the summer of 1951. He owns a pickup truck and drives without compunction, but he does not have running water, phone service, or a refrigerator. He heats solely with wood and relies on a small solar panel to power his laptop and Wi-Fi router. He sometimes goes two months without ever leaving the property.

Bernd is hardly a hermit. For the past three years, he has shared the homestead with his partner, 57-year-old Lynn Jennings, a nine-time U.S. cross-country champion and the 10,000-meter bronze medalist at the

1992 Barcelona Olympics. It's a happy and fruitful arrangement. Over the past five years, Bernd has staged a late-life creative tear that calls to mind Johnny Cash or Georgia O'Keeffe, churning out a steady stream of academic papers, columns for *Natural History* magazine, and four books, including *The Naturalist's Notebook*, a just-published guide cowritten with Nathaniel Wheelwright, as well as 2016's *One Wild Bird at a Time*, which renders certain jays and blackbirds on his property as unique individuals, as fully realized as Elaine and Kramer on *Seinfeld*.

When I began adding up Bernd's septuagenarian streak, I realized that here was a rare man—a throwback. We live in an age that affords little time and space for communing with nature. We're busy. Our days are fragmented. But Bernd has dug in his heels against this collective drift. He has recognized where he wants to be in old age and settled in, with purpose.

* * *

In recent years, my life has echoed Bernd Heinrich's to a degree. I, too, have reconnected with my own private Eden. In autumn 2014, after my only child left the nest, I moved from Portland, Oregon, to the countryside of New Hampshire with dreams of roughing it. I would heat with wood. I would spend winters without running water. The idea was to reinvent a rambling, 1790s-built summer home that has been in my family since 1905. My grandmother swam in the nearby lake as a child. I caught fireflies on the lawn when I was five. My new life there would be just like Walden, except with Wi-Fi.

One of my first moves came that fall when, for $400, I bought a used woodstove and hired two musclebound guys to hoist the squat, 300-pound iron box up over the door lip, around a corner, and into place beneath an ancient brick chimney. The air was warm that evening, but there was a gentle breeze and a dry rustling in the trees, and I shivered with the prospect that I would soon be ensconced in the cold, wintry brilliance of my adventure.

I was also anxious, for I harbored a secret so humbling that I was afraid to share it with anyone: I had never actually operated a woodstove. I'd seen other people build fires in stoves, but I had always watched from a distance, enviously, feeling helpless and pathetically urban. At 50, I was still a fire-building virgin, and now my survival hinged on a skill I lacked.

That September, I watched numerous instructional videos on You-Tube. Then I lit my first fire. The flames danced behind the glass of the firebox. The room filled, slowly and subtly, with a warmth that seeped into my bones, and the joy that I felt was primal: a campfire is home, especially when it warms a house like the one I was living in. The place has six bedrooms, an attached barn that has been gently tilting into the earth for over a century, and a scruffy 1.2-acre lawn denuded of trees. Not a single wall was insulated, so I had to shut down the plumbing and use the privy in the barn, lest the pipes burst.

Still, that first winter was grand. I holed up in a single sealed-off room, sustained by the fire. I chipped crusted snow to boil for dishwater and cross-country-skied every afternoon. I carried armloads of firewood in from the barn and wandered the cold house in old sweaters flecked with bark, a ragamuffin lord presiding over a new, untapped universe. No one had wintered there for nearly 80 years.

But I wouldn't say I was living in that house, exactly. The place was still owned by my mother, who was 84 and afflicted with Parkinson's. I was just camping there, fecklessly, experimentally. I'd never once used a chainsaw. The names of the animals ranging across the lawn remained a mystery to me. In order to ground myself, as I craved, I needed to go deeper. I needed to learn things—about living on the land and about aging with grace.

I had this vague notion that what I needed was a mentor, and I'd heard about Bernd. I'd read his book on running, and I'd seen a recent photo of him scything his own grass, shirtless, his senior-citizen sinews reminiscent of a Greek statue. In time, feeling slightly cowed, I wrote him an obsequious note. Generously, he invited me up to his cabin for a visit.

Bernd lives three hours northeast of me, a half mile off a country road and up a hill on a path that in winter can be negotiated only on snowshoes. He returned to western Maine in 1977, after earning his PhD in zoology at the University of California at Los Angeles and starting a job teaching at UC Berkeley. He bought a sliver of forest appointed with a battered shack that he lived in very part-time. He soon built a rough log cabin, felling the trees himself. He often stayed there four days a week, commuting east from the University of Vermont, where he began teaching biology in 1981. But after retiring in 2004, he and a stonemason friend reorganized a jumble of stones, the remnant of a vanished cabin's foundation, into the base for Bernd's new home.

I start climbing toward that home late on a winter afternoon, when the conifers are laced with new-fallen snow. I follow the path until it levels out, then I hook left and find myself in a clearing that contains, magically, all the sights I've read about in Bernd's books. Here is his older cabin, a muted brownish silver, at the edge of the woods. Here is the gleaming new cabin and, on one wall, the doughnut-size hole that a northern flicker, a star character in *One Wild Bird at a Time*, carved into it. Woodsmoke billows out of the chimney.

Bernd and Lynn step out onto the porch to greet me, each cradling a mason jar filled with beer.

"You made it!" says Bernd. "You're here!" says Lynn. There's a special-ness about arriving that would be absent had I simply stepped in from a parking lot.

Inside, the house is immaculate and sparsely appointed. The pine floors are lustrous, the books on the shelves upright, the interior woodpile absent of dust. A wooden chest that Bernd made in the eighth grade sits in the living room, and upstairs there's a battered thermometer screwed to an exposed beam. The clutter is so minimal that each little item seems almost holy: this ladder leading upstairs, this knotted rope hanging beside it.

In the fading light, Bernd is somehow of a piece with this unassum-ing decor. He is a humble man, withdrawn and shy, with a five-feet-eight frame and wispy white hair. I'd come expecting a crisp German accent, but no, he speaks with the down-home inflections of Maine, saying "remembah" for *remember* and invoking "wicked" as an all-purpose adjec-tive. There is nothing hifalutin about him.

But he exudes a quiet force, and he moves directly to the topics that matter. Within five minutes of my arrival, Bernd assures me that he will be buried on the property. "My afterlife will be here," he says. "My body will be here, in the trees, in the birds, in all living things."

He talks about the joys of hunting deer on his own property. "Anywhere else," he says, "it's just shooting."

He speaks with disdain for people who are overly pious in their regard for nature—who, for instance, are against wood-burning stoves or think that bird feeders are bad because they build up dependence. "I hate people who want to put a fence around nature," he says. "How can you be a part of nature if you don't interact with it?"

We drink and we eat, and in time Lynn throws open the door so the night cold sweeps in. Then she steps to the coolest corner of the cabin, the closest thing they have to a refrigerator, and scoops a squirrel carcass up off the floor. She flings it outside, onto the snow.

"Come here, owl!" she cries.

"Come here, owl!" Bernd cries. They cast their voices skyward, up toward a tree, where a barred owl is perched on a limb. This owl is an old friend of Bernd's. On many other evenings, it has swooped down to the snow, almost to the doorstep, to retrieve a tossed chunk of squirrel.

"Come here, owl!"

"Come here, owl!"

The owl levers its head slightly, watchful, but it does not heed commands. We are in a wild place.

* * *

The next morning, Bernd and I strap on snowshoes and go for a run. It's an unnerving enterprise. Long ago I was a decent runner, but I'm now a skier and cyclist. Before driving north, I'd read a 2015 article that described Bernd, then 75, finishing off a workout at a 6:05-mile pace. He can still run a 10K in about 47 minutes, and I'm worried: Is this old man going to smoke me?

He could, possibly, but he's merciful. He starts out at a gentle 12-minute-mile crawl, glancing back at me every so often, solicitously. "Is everything okay?"

Everything is okay. The packed snow has a fresh dusting on top, and we dip and climb through thick woods until we're standing on Hemp Hill, where long ago Bernd discovered a flourishing marijuana crop, cultivated by an unknown entrepreneur. I think of him hunkering down in the nearby blind, researching *Ravens in Winter*, his 1989 landmark work, and its 1999 follow-up, *Mind of the Raven*. He studied both wild ravens and birds he hand-raised from nestlings and kept in a huge 40,000-square-foot aviary before releasing them. Ravens can live more than 50 years in captivity, and over time Bernd apprehended a Shakespearean intricacy in their social lives. He noted the obeisance that lesser males displayed around Goliath, the alpha. And observing ravens calling loudly near a moose carcass, he wondered if they were being altruistic in summoning their friends to a feast. To find out, he hid in a blind made of balsam fir and spruce branches, playing recorded calls on a loudspeaker, and spent countless dawns watching ravens from the top of a tall spruce tree. Bernd went on to famously demonstrate that the calling ravens were actually motivated by self-interest. They were rootless juveniles, it turned out, who had discovered food in a mature raven's territory. By inviting other ravens to feed, they avoided being chased off themselves.

As we run, he tells me that in 2014, Goliath and his mate, Whitefeather, found themselves in conflict with a third. "For a couple days," he says, "I saw huge aerial displays involving three ravens"—the pair, most likely, and an interloper. "I'd see two birds displaying their feathers at once. I'd see one bird chasing another, trying to get rid of it." It was a love triangle, probably, but however it resolved, Bernd has not seen the pair since 2014, and he's left only with questions: "How long do ravens stay together? What about jealousy?" Even now, Bernd finds himself scanning the woods in vain.

We pass a river crusted in ice and stand on the shore as Bernd explains how, each summer, he and Lynn clear rocks from their chest-deep swimming hole. At one point, Bernd says, "That's where Lynn shot her first deer."

"I know the landscape," he tells me, "and so I notice when something's out of place—when the grass is bent, say. I didn't know what I was going to research when I started living here full-time. But now I'm open to whatever comes along. It's like being a kid again; I just go to nature and find the question."

A few years ago, Bernd saw some ruffed grouse diving under the snow. He started watching them and established, finally, that they did it not to sleep but, rather, to hide out in daylight from predators. He might have submitted his observations to *Nature* or *Science*, but instead he sent it, as he has sent 11 consecutive scientific papers since 2013, to *Northeastern Naturalist*, a journal that 56 years ago, when it was known as *Maine Field Naturalist*, published an article that later embarrassed Bernd.

"Weasels in Farmington" was Bernd's first published paper, and it was little more than a medley of simple, clipped sentences. "Rabbits were plentiful during both seasons," it reads, "and ruffed grouse seemingly scarce." When Bernd was in his 30s, teaching at Berkeley, he expunged the paper from his curriculum vitae and eschewed the title of naturalist, choosing instead a label that implied more scientific rigor: biochemical biologist. He was bowing to public opinion, he says, which held that "being a naturalist was being a sissy."

But over time, he says, he grew uneasy with the esoteric quality of the papers he read in scientific journals. He became so nostalgic for the simplicity of "Weasels in Farmington" that last year he gave a speech bearing the title. Meanwhile he resolved that going forward, he would only make observations from nature. "Popular thinking," he says, "holds that naturalists are not critical thinkers. They can't do 'hard science.' But a naturalist is someone who is a keen observer, and to do something original and true, you have to be an observer first. I consider myself a biologist, but I became one by being a naturalist first."

For me, what stands out about these papers is the curiosity Bernd brings to familiar turf. Nearly all of us spend our days as he does, plying the same paths, and for millennia—right into my grandparents' earliest days—we were obliged to notice subtle shifts in our local landscape, to ask whether it was time to bring in the wood or to harvest the acorns. Now our senses are dulled, our eyes fixed on the screen. Do we ever notice the natural world?

As Bernd and I run, we watch for wildlife. Beneath some old apple trees we find the tracks of wild turkeys that have been picking at rotten fruit in the snow. Nearby are the tracks of three coyotes, one of which appears skittish: its marks come right up to recent human footprints, then dart away. Bernd had observed this behavior, possibly this coyote, before. Now he bends to the snow to investigate.

* * *

Anyone can look at coyote tracks, of course. But when I see Bernd do it, I'm aware of a larger story—of a man who experienced the trauma of war as a child, then learned that peace lies in nature and decided to make his life about connecting to it and understanding it.

But Bernd's wartime experience exerts a natural force of its own; the pain lingers in his animal brain. In 2016, he traveled with Lynn back to the Hahnheide forest. He went to search for memories, for places that figured in his family's exile, and he located the exact spot where, seven decades earlier, he'd captured a rare wasp that he was able to trade back to his father for the beetle that was taken away.

"I saw that," he says. "I saw that and . . ." Now his head crumples into his hands, and he begins sobbing in a mix of anguish and joy. "I thought, *Look at how fortunate I am and look at what I came from: nothing.* We could have been stuck behind the Iron Curtain forever."

Soon, in discussing a recent trip to New York City and the endless gray expanse of buildings he passed on the outskirts, Bernd surprises me with another spasm of weeping—a flashback to a wartime horror. "All I could think about," he says, "was going through Hamburg with Papa. The city was rubble as far as the eye could see."

He talks about his life not as calcified fact but as a mystery he's still trying to make sense of, right now, as he's speaking. "I don't know how I happened to come back to this land," he tells me. "It was brewing in my subconscious for a long time. I always wanted a cabin, and I guess I was doing things in an unconscious way that were bringing me here." It was only after he'd begun construction that he found, through research, that long ago Jimmy Adams's father, Floyd, had lived in the house whose stones form the base of his new cabin.

* * *

As Bernd and I speak, Lynn is in the kitchen, washing the dishes. During her pro career, she was a warrior in the scrum of middle-distance contests, a fighter known for her merciless kick. Her brio has not dwindled. These days she's a competitive rower. She can ride her bike 100 miles in just over five hours, and she still runs a bit, sometimes with Bernd, with whom she enjoys a playful rivalry.

She applies most of her energy to homesteading, though. She rhapsodizes about the "moments of exertion" that come with dragging an 80-pound sled filled with groceries up the hill. To get the old newspapers they use to start fires, she dives headlong into the recycling bin at the local dump, invoking, she quips, a "Fosbury Flop combined with a half gainer."

Cabin living has been a lifelong dream for Lynn. In 1978, when *Runner's World* ran a story celebrating her early prowess, she said, "You know what I'd like to do someday? I'd like to homestead. It would be great. Build your own house, forget about telephones and television . . ."

"I remember reading that article," Bernd tells me. "I thought, 'That's the girl for me.'"

For a split second Lynn glowers at him, scandalized. "Bernd!" she says. "I was 18 and you were—what? Thirty-eight?"

Bernd shrugs, smirking slightly. But he says nothing, and I reckon he's savoring the fact that eventually he did meet his dream girl, in 2011, when Lynn invited him to speak to her running camp in Vermont. At that point he was single, in the wake of a divorce. (He's been married three times and has four grown children.) He invited her to visit the cabin.

"I got a quarter of the way up the hill," Lynn remembers, "and I knew this was where I was supposed to be."

Bernd writes about Lynn in *One Wild Bird at a Time*. As the couple sat around a winter bonfire at night, sipping red wine, he noticed that his beloved barred owl had shown up by surprise, and he regarded its arrival, equally appreciated by Lynn, as the most wonderful thing he could hope for. "In the moment of joy and mystery," he wrote, "I felt connected with all the moments of my past and now my prospects for the future."

* * *

A special place can contain all stories—all of the past and all of the future, all the beginnings and endings. In 2016, the summer before my mom died, I drove her up to New Hampshire for a final visit. By then she was heavily medicated, but when we crested the final hilltop, with its stunning view of the local pond, her eyes glimmered with delight.

Her reaction was rooted in long memory, and also in nature. She was a naturalist. So many of us are, in our way, and as Bernd sees it, this is a fine thing. Indeed, it could save us. "A naturalist," he e-mailed me, "is one who still has the habit of trying to see the connections of how the world works. She does not go by say-so, by faith, or by theory. So we don't get lost in harebrained dreams or computer programs taken for reality. We all want to be associated with something greater and more beautiful than ourselves, and nature is the ultimate. I just think it is the one thing we can all agree on."

Six months later, in January, my mom died and I begin to contemplate a new chapter for the house. When I ask Bernd for advice on how to attract wildlife, he becomes evangelical; he actually visits to advise me. He stops by with Lynn, after giving a talk to birders nearby. The moment they pull in, at 7:30 a.m., Bernd spots a bird—a dusty gray phoebe—bobbing over the lawn. He follows it: down the hill from the parking area, around a brick terrace, until there he is, my honored guest, standing under the barn, six feet away from the base of the privy. "It went in right there," he says, pointing.

I can't get enough of his accent. They-ah.

Soon he notes the abandoned start of a phoebe nest. It is graying and matted and set atop a support beam under the barn. It has been there for five or 10 years, Bernd guesses, but I never noticed it. I have no memory of anyone at our house ever remarking upon a single bird.

"You could open up that window there," he says pointing, "and then maybe you'd have barn swallows. I'd also have a clearing around your house," he continues. "But see this grass here?" On the steep slope to the brook, he means. "Just let it grow. Don't worry about it." Eventually, he says, bugs will settle amid the long stalks, then birds—indigo buntings, say, and chestnut-sided warblers—and then, finally, predators: mice, voles, shrews . . .

His advice is not revelatory; I've read his books. But his being there is something. This man is New England's avatar of wild living, and I want to develop what he has. I want the ability to hear a whole story coded into a single chirp from a bird's beak.

So in the weeks that follow, I open that window in the barn. I drag some brush out from the woods, to give juncos and chickadees a place to alight before fluttering toward the new feeders I've hung. And I watch this one bird I spotted with Bernd, a downy woodpecker perched high on the trunk of a maple, pecking away, a bright tuft of red at the nape of his neck. "He's building the nest," Bernd had told me.

I begin checking that tree every morning, and for weeks—nothing. I'm crestfallen, and I say as much one day, writing a friend. But seconds after I hit send, I look out the window and see something red: Mr. Woodpecker himself, pausing on the trunk, then plunging into his hole—nesting, likely siring his brood. Right there in my own yard. I feel almost paternal.

But then Bernd writes to say he's raising a clutch of baby crows and deepening his rapport with a resident swallow family. "I spend hours watching them every day," he says. He's been on hand, beside their feather-lined nest, for the birth of five babies, and he's been transfixed by something startling: the male is bringing in the feathers. "The usual avian sex roles are reversed," he writes, in a fever, "and it means much else is different, too. And so I need to know every nuance of behavior from beginning to end."

Attached to the note is a photo, taken by Lynn, of him sitting outside on the grass, in a chair, holding a white feather at arm's length. His body language seems stiff, frozen. It's a weird picture, I think. Until I see, frame left, the blue blur, the swallow, fluttering past tree branches and rocks and weeds, right toward Bernd Heinrich's waiting hand.

CYCLING

Nairo Quintana, Colombia's Cycling Hero

Vice, *July 3, 2015*

Nairo Quintana got his first bicycle when he was 15 years old. It was red, and it was heavy—an old steel mountain bike with fat tires. His father, Luis, bought it for him at a secondhand store for $70, which was a monumental expense for the family. Luis was a disabled campesino who farmed potatoes and ran a roadside grocery stand. From the time he was 6, Nairo had been helping his dad, whose pelvis had been crushed in a childhood car crash. Nairo delivered milk and lifted heavy boxes of produce. When the Quintanas went to markets in the neighboring villages, Nairo sometimes woke at 4 a.m. to help his father bake bread.

They lived in a village called Combita high in the Colombian Andes, in a verdant farm region known as Boyaca. Luis saved up a year to buy Nairo the bike. He bought it partly out of gratitude, and partly for practical reasons. The bus to Nairo's school, 10 miles away and 3,000 feet below their hilltop home in Combita, cost 25 cents each way.

In some ways, it was a miracle that Nairo was even alive. At age 2, he fell sick with a serious fever. His parents believed that someone who'd touched a dead person had, in turn, touched Nairo thereby infecting him with an illness. For a year, the boy had constant diarrhea; he vomited and could not sleep. No doctor could help him. The Quintanas went to Our Lady of Miracles, a gold-domed church in Boyaca's capital, Tunja, and prayed. Finally, they called in a faith healer who gave Quintana herbs. He recovered. He was a bone-thin kid, with a sharp, narrow nose and intent brown eyes, and he was never athletic. He hated gym class, but he milked the family cows; he fed the chickens. "I was happy to buy him the bike," says his dad.

On that first day with the bike, Nairo rode home from the thrift store in Tunja—12 or 13 miles, over a quiet back road that swooped through the green hills where potato farmers tilled the soil on steep slopes using plows drawn by horses. It was only the third or fourth time he'd ever been on a bike. "I fell a lot," he says. "I got bruises. There was blood on my shins."

Eventually, though, he got to the last stretch, which was lined with pine and eucalyptus trees, and for the last kilometer, was as steep as anything in the Tour de France. Quintana remembers standing up out of the saddle and sprinting the last bit to his parents' modest adobe home, 10,000 feet above sea level. He stepped into the house, winded, flushed, sweating. "He was so happy," his mother, Eloisa, says. "and I was proud of him."

Imagine how she feels now: Nairo Quintana, now 25 and still diminutive at five feet five, 130 pounds, is probably the top hill climber in professional cycling. And as many experts see it, he is the man to beat at this year's Tour de France, which starts in Utrecht, in The Netherlands, on July 4, and spends the next three weeks rolling over a particularly hilly and cobblestone-ridden course, even for the Tour. "Quintana's my favorite," says Jonathan Vaughters, the manager for Colorado-based Team Cannondale-Garmin. "A lot of people say he'll get crushed on the cobbles—that he's a little guy and he'll just bounce around. But he's relaxed on the bike; he knows how to use his body as a shock absorber. And he has no fear. When everyone's out there pushing and shoving and rubbing handlebars, he doesn't back down."

Quintana did not race last year's Tour de France. But in his rookie Tour in 2013, he finished second and dazzled in the race's last competitive stage, which ended with a steep seven-mile climb up a ski hill called Le Semnoz. With a kilometer to go, Quintana was in a lead pack of three, along with Joaquim Rodriguez and the Tour's eventual winner, Chris Froome.

Froome surged, building up a lead of maybe five yards. It seemed like the race might be over, but then Quintana found one last drop of gas in the tank. He reeled Froome in, bit by bit, fighting, like a man climbing a rope, and then he just kept driving, so that Froome could only waggle his head in stunned exhaustion as sweat dripped from his nose.

* * *

Who was this guy? Three months earlier, at a race through Spain's Basque country, one commentator, Steve Schlanger of Universal Sports, proclaimed Quintana a freak who "came out of nowhere." It was a stupid comment, and not merely because it carried baseless intimations that Quintana was doping. Colombia has a long and deep connection to cycling. It's boasted its own multistage tour, the Vuelta de Colombia, since 1951, and in the early days hundreds of thousands turned out to watch as the riders toiled over some of the world's hilliest terrain, through remote villages that had never once seen a car.

Soccer has surpassed cycling as Colombia's national sport. Still, in Bogota today, it's easy to find middle-aged men who grow almost weepy, reminiscing about how in 1985 Colombian rider Lucho Herrera crashed during the second stage of the Tour de France, then resumed pedaling and won the stage with blood streaming from his face. In 1987, Herrera captured the Vuelta de Espana, which is along with the Tour and the Giro d'Italia, one of the world's three biggest bike races.

But Colombia's golden age of cycling is long gone, and the memories are tinged with pain. Since the 1960s, a long-running civil war between the leftist guerrilla group FARC (which is one of the world's largest drug cartels) and the Colombian government along with paramilitary forces, has led to civil unrest and economic stagnation. Colombia's problems famously peaked in the late '80s and early '90s, with the rise of drug lord Pablo Escobar. There was still scant money to fund cycling teams, and Colombia's riders became almost invisible on the European circuit.

But then in 2010, Quintana emerged, making his first splash in France, where he won the Tour de L'Avenir, an under-23 stage race whose winners have 12 times gone on to prevail in the Tour de France. Colombian president Juan Manuel Santos received the cyclist at his palace in Bogota. He promised to give Quintana a new house and draped a medal around his neck before a swarm of TV helicopters and motorcycle police shadowed the cyclist home to Boyaca, two hours northeast of Bogota.

The victory came at a bright moment for Colombia. Santos was just beginning to negotiate a peace settlement with FARC, and to many Colombians, Quintana seemed a symbol of the new hope. "We saw him," says Ana Vivas, a spokesperson for the Colombian Cycling Federation, "as a phoenix rising from the ashes."

In 2013, Quintana's stage victory on Semnoz happened to fall on July 20, Colombia's independence day, and Alfredo Castro, the commentator for Bogota-based Caracol Radio, set aside all restraint as the race ended. "Let joyfulness sound and let my country burst with happiness," he said before addressing Quintana directly. "America lays at your feet. The world lays at your feet. Paris awaits you—the Champs-Élysées! You've come from the campos of Boyaca to the Champs-Élysées. Thank you, brother. Thank you, brother. Thank you, Nairo. Thank you, son of the land. Thank you, peasant. Thank you, Don Luis [Nairo's father] for giving us this son."

Last year, when Quintana won the Giro d'Italia and thereby earned a pink race jersey, the sales of pink ponchos skyrocketed in Colombia. And now, as the world's best cyclists make their way to Utrecht, Colombia stands at a troubling and pivotal juncture.

For the past 30 months, FARC and the Colombian government have been engaged in peace talks in Havana, hoping to build a postwar Colombia in which drug trade would cease as FARC lay down its arms and shared political power. A resolution seemed near last December, when FARC promised to maintain a unilateral ceasefire, but then in April FARC guerrillas broke that promise, attacking the Colombian military in a remote western Colombia village called La Esperanza, or Hope, and killing 10 soldiers.

President Santos responded by ordering aerial assaults and the fighting has sparked on ever since. FARC is now on a campaign to sabotage Colombia's oil and electricity infrastructure, and on June 29, FARC rebels bombed the Tansandino oil pipeline in southern Colombia, causing more than 10,000 barrels of crude to spill into rivers and streams and leaving 150,000 Colombians without water.

A recent headline on Foreign Policy's website blared, "Colombia's Peace Talks Are on the Brink of Failure." But still hope dies hard. "We are working on building a new Colombia," Santos wrote via e-mail. "We are working on opening a new, exciting chapter in our history. And if Nairo won the Tour de France, it would be a great triumph and a big celebration for us. What could be a better symbol of our hopeful future than having a Colombian athlete at the top of the podium in the world's most prestigious bicycle competition?"

* * *

Nairo Quintana now rides for Movistar, a Spanish team named after its sponsor, a Madrid-based cell phone company. He earns at least $1 million a year and resides part time in Monaco. Still, he lives very simply. He never inhabited the fancy home Santos gave him, opting instead for a series of unimpressive Tunja apartments, and friends say that his only remotely lavish possession is a late model Toyota 4 x 4. He does not endorse any products in Colombia and he has leveraged his celebrity only once—in 2013, when he voiced support for Colombia's farmers as they waged a nationwide strike, pressing a resistant Santos for aid. "When you bring a sack of potatoes to the market, you have to cry," he told reporters. "You won't even make the money you need to pay for transportation. My family lost some of our land years ago, so we had to leave the potato business."

Quintana's father still makes him milk the cows when he returns to Combita. He has had the same girlfriend for nine years, a neighbor named Paola Hernandez. They began dating when he was 16 and she was 13, and today Hernandez handles Quintana's finances and frequently trails him in the 4 x4 as he trains, making sure to buckle their infant daughter, Mariana, into her car seat. Hernandez, it is rumored, despises the media. "She hates how they say his family was poor," a childhood neighbor, Sandra Rojas, said recently. "She gets very mad."

In May 2014, when I started working on this story, it looked like access would be crimped. "For the moment he's not giving interviews," Movistar's press office wrote. It soon became clear that no one had ever interviewed Quintana at length. Colombia's premier newsweekly,

La Semana, was shut out in its attempts, and Spanish journalist Carlos Zumer says that when he reported his e-book, *Nairo*, last year, Quintana went quiet—and reneged his promise of an interview—when he learned that Zumer would earn royalties. ("A book to be sold for money!" Zumer says, recounting his rejection. "Unacceptable.")

In late 2014, though, Quintana relented, and sat for a long talk with *El Tejedor de Progreso*, the house organ of a cement and gravel company. He answered his interlocutor's softball questions with overweening sweetness:

Q: Are there any dishes from Boyaca that seduce you?

A: Anything that includes country chicken because it's an animal that has a really good flavor.

Q: What would be your message for your countrymen?

A: I want them to receive a very special message from Nairo. May they have a merry Christmas and a prosperous new year filled with peace and happiness.

In February, Quintana's Movistar publicist, Juan Pablo Molinero, was genial over the phone. "Just tell me," he said when I called. "What do you need?"

What my editors wanted was some glimpse of Quintana's spare idyll in Boyaca. Could he show me his cattle and his chickens and the long winding highway he rode to school every morning, racing the bus drivers? And could Molinero somehow convince Quintana to care about scoring stateside publicity?

No, he could not. Quintana did not care. He just blew off his publicist's e-mails, prompting Molinero to send me a bleak warning: "I am afraid you travel to Tunja and after 15 minutes of interview he says it is over."

* * *

I saw Quintana a few days later, though, at Colombia's national championships, which took place in the country's second city, Medellin. We crossed paths in the lobby of our hotel just before race time, when he emerged from the elevator wheeling a white bicycle, the top bar of which bore a little typed name tag reading NAIRO QUINTANA. Without saying anything, he bent to the carpet and spun the rear wheel, eyeballing it solemnly, checking for mechanical tics. His focus was total; he was a soldier going to war.

On the Movistar bus to the start line, Quintana was the team comedian, standing and wriggling his behind at one point, to demonstrate exactly why women love skinny cyclists. But when the talk turned to race strategy, his manner was grave. "If there are eight riders in the breakaway pack," he said, "we have to send just one ahead. We have to attack wisely."

His voice was surprisingly deep, throaty and whispery, and it struck me that he'd been serious about life for a long time—as a little kid at the grocery stand, and then later, at 15, when he first raced, on a cheap $150 road bike, in street clothes, against kids in full Lycra kits. He was good even then, remembers an early coach, Luis Fernando Saldarriaga. "He wouldn't win, but he'd finish second or fourth," Saldarriaga says. "He had strength, and also peace of mind, having been raised in the country with no distractions. And he knew just when to attack. That was instinct for him."

Before he turned 16, Quintana landed on a local team, Boyaca es Para Vivirla, who canvassed door to door for funds. Then, when he traveled to France for the Tour de l'Avenir in 2010, he was reportedly subject to racist attacks. "It was the first year Colombians were back in Europe," says Ignacio Velez, a Colombian businessman who coordinated the trip, "and the French team was very aggressive." They called the dark-skinned Quintana a "fucking Indian," Velez says, and shoved one of his teammates to the pavement, prompting the rider to remount, catch up, and slug the Frenchman in the face. "It was Nairo's first tour," Velez says, "but he didn't care. He was confident, and one night he came to my hotel room, very shy, and said, 'Coach, it is me who will win the Tour de l'Avenir.'"

Quintana has twice come close to dying on his bike. Once, when he was 16, he lost consciousness when a car struck him on the way to school. When he was 18 he was T-boned by a taxi in Tunja. He went into a coma for five days as his family gathered at Our Lady of Miracles, praying. After each crash, he resumed training as soon as he could walk.

At the national championships, after Quintana climbed out of the bus and onto his bike, admirers circled him so thickly that he could barely pedal. Police officers had to hold him aloft, clutching his shoulders, lest he fall over on his way to the start.

The race itself was a sacrifice mission, though. Quintana's younger brother, Dayer—22 and also a Movistar rider—led over much of the 117-mile course, and so Quintana stayed back, leading the peloton, restraining it, trying to facilitate Dayer's first big win. About 10 kilometers from the finish, just before Dayer was blitzed by a fast-moving pack, Nairo crashed. When he crashed again with just a few meters to go, he wounded his elbow. He didn't finish, and he appeared in public just once after the race. He stood in the aisle of the parked Movistar bus and moved toward the driver's wheel, so his white bandage was for a moment visible through the bus's black tinted windows. The crowds surged, chanting, "Nairo! Nairo! Nairo! Nairo!" He signed a few T-shirts shoved in through a slit in the window. Then over the next three days, he rode home to Boyaca, 450 miles over two spines of the Andes.

I went to Boyaca that same week and traveled first to Combita. Quintana's parents no longer run the grocery there, but they live beside it, in the same adobe house, now slightly expanded. As I arrived, his father, Luis, pulled up in a small silver Chevrolet Sprint packed with six people. "I can't talk now," he shouted. "I'm taking this woman to the hospital."

He was a short, blustery man with wild silver hair and a cragged, weather-beaten face, and he wore a gray poncho and high rubber boots, a getup that resonates machismo in the Boyaca countryside. He explained that his current gig was transporting locals to Tunja for 40 cents each way. "I'm in a hurry," he said. But he was smiling and he could not help but brag a little about his son as the car idled and the sick woman waited. "We raised him with discipline," he said. "Discipline! When he started doing sports, we made him do his training routine. We didn't allow him to leave the house at night."

"But did he ever sneak out?" I asked.

"Never, not once," said his mother, Eloisa. "Nairo always obeyed. He was a good boy." She sat in the front seat, dressed for church in a maroon pant suit. Her voice was very quiet, almost a murmur, and when she shook my hand, her fingers were limp in my palm.

After the car sped away, I lingered at the grocery store, which had been expanded thanks to Nairo's winnings. It is now an enclosed structure, with a concrete pad for parking out front. It is also a makeshift shrine to the cyclist. A pink banner welcomes visitors to "The House of Nairo Quintana" and features a cartoon drawing of Nairo carving a potato whose curling peel closely resembles the spiral-shaped Giro d'Italia trophy. In the parking area, beneath a small shelter made of dull pink two-by-fours, visitors can buy various Quintana souvenirs—keychains, for instance, and statuettes of white mules bearing pink terra-cotta baskets emblazoned "Nairo."

It was a sunny day, and the store's current manager, Sandra Rojas, sat outside, greeting neighbors, as they trundled toward the store, bearing fresh buckets of milk, which Rojas would in turn sell to a distributor. "Nairo still plays like a little kid," Rojas said. "When he came home last time, he was shooting us with a squirt gun."

Rojas's friend, Lucila Hernandez, came by and likewise remembered Quintana as a fun guy. "At the fruit stand," she said, "if he had a bad orange, he would throw it at you. But then he'd give you a good orange for free. I remember when he and Paola started out," Hernandez added, referring to Quintana's girlfriend, who is also her cousin. "They'd talk at the bus stop for an hour sometimes. Then after that they were always hiding behind walls. I could see them hugging and kissing. It was a romance."

* * *

Quintana's apartment sits on a quiet residential street beside a huge shopping mall in Tunja, which has a population of 180,000. I located the place when I landed, then spent the next several days wandering the city's streets, savoring the whitewashed colonial churches and the vast, slate-floored town square where a looming statue of Colombia's liberator, Simon Bolivar, sits amid a swirl of pigeons. Green hills loom in the near distance, and in winding alleyways vendors sell bootleg DVDs and *almo-jabanas*, which are fritters made from corn flour and cheese.

Finally I arranged an audience with Quintana himself. The plan was that I'd meet him outside his apartment one morning at 8 and then follow him in a car as he breezed through a light workout of 30-odd miles. I waited on the sidewalk with one of his training partners, a little-known pro named Nestor Garcia and a Tunja policeman who is tasked daily with escorting Quintana. ("If I don't go," the cop explained, "gawkers stop in the road. Traffic jams form around him.")

Quintana appeared at 8:30, wearing pink bicycle cleats. He laughed at the jokes I told in broken Spanish and insisted that we pose for a snap together. Then he rode, smooth as water flowing over the gentle hills of Highway 55, his slender hips swaying each time he rose to stand on the pedals.

When we got to a roadside café, the two riders sat down for coffee, and Quintana called me to join them. With regards to the farmers' strike, he said, "My family are peasants, and so am I, and in a strike like that, where the army and police are involved, fighting the farmers, there is sometimes internal conflict in families: Many of the people in the army are also the sons of peasants. My brother is in the army, you know."

He spoke of his father with great admiration. "My father had a traffic accident when he was seven years old," he said. "He broke his legs and his pelvis, and he had many surgeries after that. He was challenged to do his work, but nothing stopped him. He used to say to us kids, 'You guys are young. Why do you get tired? Why do you not do things well? Look at me. I'm limp. My body is all messed up, and I'm still working.' That has been an example of life for us."

I asked if he felt different from other cyclists, being a Colombian of indigenous descent. "No," he said, "I don't feel different in the peloton, or in cycling. All over the world, I am respected for what I have done. Wherever I go, I feel like a normal person, not less and not more than other people, and where I live in Monaco, there are more people from all over the world than there are people from that area.

"I'm losing my identity as a peasant from Boyaca. I know this; I'm traveling all over the world to races. But I have not forgotten the countryside. I have some cattle here and I have someone who takes care of them, and when I'm finished with competitive cycling I will return to my roots. This is my region. This is where I am from, and this is where I would like to be."

A few days later, I went back to Combita. Nairo's dad was away in Tunja, but his mother was there, carrying an empty steel bucket. She did not have much time, she said. The cows needed milking. "But I will answer your questions," she said. Her manner was polite and dutiful. She stood still and waited for me to talk. I was very aware that I was intruding. So I scrambled, and desperately, gracelessly, I read from a list in my notebook.

"What year did the bank take your land back?"

"Around 2002."

"How many surgeries did your husband have?"

"About 15, I think."

"Do you have any childhood photos of Nairo?"

"No, they were all stolen by the carpenters who renovated the house."

With every question and answer, I felt more depraved. I understood why Quintana avoids the press, and I realized that some stories cannot be reduced to fact. I left.

A couple days later, though, as I was riding along in the passenger seat of a car, I happened to pass Quintana out on Highway 55. We drew even to him on a slight downhill and I opened the window, so my hair whipped in the wind, and I shouted his name: "Nairo!"

Quintana smiled in recognition. Then we pulled ahead. I watched in the mirror as he rolled down into the trough of the hill and started to climb. He was light on the pedals, and small, and yet his body was powerful somehow, tensile. He stood up out of the saddle and danced up the next hill with ease, like it was nothing, like he could conquer the world.

The Bike Wanderer

Bicycling, *April 14, 2022*

We all need to get away sometimes, and Iohan Gueorguiev got, arguably, more escape time than perhaps any other cyclist on earth. The endearing, soft-spoken star of his own wildly popular YouTube channel, See the World, Iohan spent most of six years—2014 to 2020—tracing a circuitous path south from the frozen hinterlands of the Canadian Arctic toward, but never quite reaching, the southern tip of Argentina.

Calling himself the Bike Wanderer, he slithered over ice roads in the Arctic on a fat bike whose frame bags were laden with camping and camera gear. He communed with bison in Wyoming, got frisked by cops at the Mexican border, crossed the Darién Gap with his bike in a kayak, and then moved on toward the salt plains of Bolivia.

If Iohan were even a little bit aggro about the whole thing—if he were inclined toward neon-bright spandex and chest-thumping Strava posts—he surely would have stirred some jealousy and spite among his nearly 100,000 YouTube followers. But no, Iohan was humble. He was sweet. In nearly every one of the 40 episodes he released, there's a moment when he's plaintively cooing to a stray animal. One episode, set in northern Argentina, opens with footage of an aggrieved, braying donkey trotting out of high grass onto a dusty red road, spoiling to charge. Iohan throws up his palm. "No, no, no, no," he tells the donkey as we get our first look at the high red buttes surrounding him, and the wispy white clouds in the blue sky. "I come in peace!"

Iohan taught himself cinematography after studying the documentaries of German filmmaker Werner Herzog. His work is expert, involving strategically placed tripods, a thoroughly loved Mavic Mini drone, a GoPro 7, and a Sony superzoom bridge camera. His narration is understated and wry, so that when he finds himself chatting to an indifferent beef cow in rural Colombia, he tries to sell the animal on meat eating, saying, "Everybody loves burgers." But even in their funniest moments, his films never dissolve into lark, for Iohan was at heart a mystic intent on showing us that life is huge, the possibilities endless. When he visited the Puna de Atacama, an arid, high plateau in Argentina, he stayed up all night to track the arc of the stars across the dark night sky. He shot with such care that as you watch the time-lapse sequence, you can almost feel the cold stillness of the dry land in your bones.

Iohan kept a detailed blog, and a mantra he taped to his handlebar bag distills its essence. "See the world," it read. "Follow a map to its edges and keep going. Forgo the plans and trust my instincts. Let curiosity be my guide." He appeared to be simple and pure. His fans, most of whom were cubicle rats resigned to making do with the odd weekend gravel ride, regarded him as almost holy, his life a validation that freedom and happiness really can be found in shirking all responsibility and plans, to just live in the moment.

"Perhaps if more people did what Iohan did, this would be a better world," muses Jeffrey D. McPartland in a recent Facebook comment.

To the faithful, the Bike Wanderer was leading an optimal life. The reality was very different. Iohan's story is a testament to the need for balance—for a mix of bland routine and wild adventure. It's also an allegory about the pain of celebrity, loved by thousands but known by almost nobody.

*　*　*

Iohan Gueorguiev was always an outsider. He grew up in Bulgaria, an Ohio-sized former Soviet ally of seven million in eastern Europe, in a working-class neighborhood in the nation's capital, Sofia. His father was an immigrant from Vietnam. The details of his dad's story are now lost, but he was likely part of a wave of North Vietnamese émigrés who began trickling into Bulgaria in the late 1970s, most of them to take part in a guest worker program that saw the Vietnamese laboring, generally in construction, for very low wages.

By the mid-'90s, when Iohan was a little kid, the Bulgarian economy was in shambles, thanks to the breakup of the Soviet Union. Annual inflation sometimes topped 300 percent. Building construction all but ceased, and the Vietnamese, suddenly out of work, became key players in Sofia's black market. Vietnamese street gangs tangled with gangs of ethnic Bulgarians, and anti-Vietnamese prejudice was rampant. "They swear at us," one Vietnamese man told the *New York Times* in 1990, referencing the Bulgarians. "They accuse us of not wanting to work or of just wanting to steal things to sell them. They don't know our problems."

In elementary school, Iohan was reserved, but he was also a quick learner and gifted swimmer. He was likely the only Vietnamese child among roughly 1,000 students, and he was sometimes singled out in an uncomfortable way. Other students called him Yoshi, which they erroneously believed was a common Vietnamese name. "He didn't respond," says his close childhood friend, Ivo Georgiev. "In school he was quiet and kind. He never said anything nasty. But I'm sure that name bothered him."

Regardless, Iohan seemed disconnected from his Asian heritage. His father left home early, possibly before Iohan was even born. The boy took a Bulgarian surname, likely his mother's, but early on she, too, faded from his life. She may have suffered from mental health issues. "She screamed and cried a lot," Georgiev recalls. "She would get grumpy for no apparent reason. She dressed strange and was incoherent." When Iohan was small, she'd disappear for periods of time. She rarely appeared at school. It was her brother, a handsome, clean-cut computer programmer, who came to parent-teacher conferences.

Mostly, though, Iohan was raised by his grandparents in an eight-story concrete apartment building. The relationship was fraught. At their advanced age, they had trouble disciplining the teenage Iohan. "His grandmother wanted him home for meals at certain times," says Georgiev, "but she was too old to control him, and he had no respect for her. He yelled at her; he acted violent. He hated following rules."

Even back then, Iohan had artistic inclinations. He read and wrote poetry, but his friends never saw a word. He was better known for his love of video games. Without telling his grandparents, he'd sneak off to internet cafés to play *World of Warcraft* and Diablo for days on end. "He seemed depressed, very closed," says Georgiev. He went without sleep and skipped school until one of his teachers visited him, beseeching him to return.

Iohan's uncle emigrated to Toronto when the boy was about 11. Soon after, Iohan developed a fixation on all things Canadian. "He brought a catalog of Canadian bicycles to school and he wouldn't stop showing it to people," Georgiev remembers. "It was really annoying."

Bikes became Iohan's obsession. His grandparents bought him a cheap mountain bike on which he made regular rides to Vitosha, a 7,500-foot volcanic peak more than 30 miles from his apartment. He would take a ski lift to the top, and then ride down on hiking trails punctuated by boulders and steep dropoffs. There was snow on Vitosha deep into June sometimes, and Iohan liked to ride over it. And he kept riding farther from home. "At a certain point we grew apart because I didn't want to go with him," says Georgiev. "I didn't want to get in trouble."

* * *

From Toronto, though, Iohan's uncle was keeping tabs on him. He wanted Iohan to follow him to professional success, and in 2003, after both of Iohan's grandparents died, his uncle flew the 15-year-old boy to Toronto to live with him. "They ran into conflicts right off the bat," says Georgiev. "As soon as Iohan was 18, he moved out to live on his own. He worked a series of dead-end jobs, barely scraping by." On and off, he'd return to his uncle's place and float vague plans of becoming a civil engineer, a designer of bridges.

In 2013, at age 25, Iohan finally agreed to enroll in McMaster University, near Toronto. He was a spectral presence there. His housemate, Matt Vukovic, remembers Iohan as a nomadic type. "He was always on the move," says Vukovic. "It was difficult for him to build relationships that involved intimacy or sharing confidences." Iohan was fluent in the basics of engineering, Vukovic says. "But academics were a necessity to him. Mostly, he wanted to be on his bike."

On breaks from school, Iohan traveled to Alaska, the Yukon, and British Columbia, shooting the first YouTube episodes. In 2015, Blackburn Design, which makes fenders, racks, and other bike parts, named him a Blackburn Ranger, giving him a one-year stipend. Soon after signing with Blackburn, Iohan left McMaster. This irritated his uncle, and Iohan increasingly dodged their conflicts. "At one point he told me that he hadn't talked to his uncle in over a year. I told him this was disrespectful," says Georgiev, who by then was living not far from Iohan, in Detroit.

Iohan responded, "I don't want to talk about it."

"Whenever we communicated," Georgiev says, "he didn't give me much information."

When Blackburn released a promotional video starring Iohan, though, the three-and-a-half-minute film seemed to tell the Bike Wanderer's whole story—and it introduced to the cycling world a new, charming character. In the video, Iohan pedals along an ice road in winter as a caption announces the locale: "The frozen Mackenzie River, Northwest Territories."

A giant 18-wheeler rolls by, and the driver opens the window to ask Iohan, "Where did you come from?"

"Ontario," Iohan says, his English accented and redolent of his native land, "but I'm going to Argentina."

"On your bike?" says the trucker, astonished.

"Yeah!" Iohan shouts.

"Oh, man," says the trucker. "I love you!"

Love for Iohan soon went global. The ice road clip would garner nearly two million views, and when he launched a page on the fund-raising platform Patreon, more than 300 fans stepped forward to underwrite his world travels. Iohan Gueorguiev's full-time job, suddenly, was to follow maps to their edges—and to make poignant films about his adventures.

* * *

How do we make sense of those magical six years, that glory run during which Iohan pushed out one dazzling video after another as he seemed to transform himself from a sullen outsider into an adventurous, light-hearted explorer of the earth's enchantments? Was the whole gambit destined to unravel?

Yeah, probably. Like Jimi Hendrix or Kurt Cobain, Iohan was a complex and fragile virtuoso. But let's linger first on his achievement, which shines most in episode 30, during which he spends 10 days riding 250 miles across the rocky, treeless moonscape of Argentina's Puna de Atacama with a French Canadian companion named Sylvain St-Denis.

The cyclists meet at dusk outside a windblown stone hut sitting at 14,750 feet, and the film's stark grandeur only deepens from there as the two friends ford knee-deep raging rivers, cook in wind shelter caves with firewood (to save fuel), and lie in their tents at night, beside cliffs and beneath a full moon, as they listen to a mountain lion cry in the darkness. At one point, a white flamingo flies in slow motion as a song on the soundtrack extols "how rare and beautiful it is to even exist."

"Traveling with Iohan was like cooking with the greatest chef on the planet," says St-Denis. "He was always planning the next episode in his head, and he always found the best angle for filming his journey—and of capturing the landscape, the nature, the animal life. I told him many times that he was a poet. And he was a calm, patient, and respectful travel mate. He was always joking and staying optimistic. He was happy, and very strong mentally and physically. When things were tough, he helped me."

But as he traveled with St-Denis, Iohan was silently suffering. Six years earlier, in 2013, he'd told his friend Ivo Georgiev that he was experiencing severe insomnia. The affliction would only grow worse, and eventually, scarcely able to sleep, Iohan would receive the diagnosis of central sleep apnea, an uncommon disorder rooted in the nervous system and distinct from obstructive sleep apnea, which involves an upper airway blockage.

Very few people knew of Iohan's insomnia, but his videos suggest a certain vulnerability. In the first episode, he carries his loaded bike—a weight of at least 90 pounds—through untrodden new snow as he ascends a wind-scoured Arctic mountain. In a quiet voice-over, he asks, "Why am I doing this?"

Iohan was a bit like Christopher McCandless, the protagonist of Jon Krakauer's 1996 book *Into the Wild*: a restless soul in need of shelter from his own self-destructive impulses. And in April 2014, when he traveled to Canada's Northwest Territories with plans to camp out in subzero temperatures, locals worried about him and offered shelter. He ended up sleeping indoors night after night. A photo montage mid-episode pays homage to his various hosts.

Matt Bardeen, an American expat in Chile who hosted Iohan at his home several times over the years, says, "Iohan felt a little like a son to me, even though I'm only 15 years older than him. And when I talk to others who hosted him, they also say he was like a son. He took a lot of risks. You wanted to reach out and help him."

As Bardeen sees it, Iohan was not quite settled in the world. "He was catlike in nature," Bardeen says. "He would visit. He would be friendly to everybody, but he would never go deep, and you never knew if he really liked you. His support network was very compartmentalized. I never knew who his other friends were."

To Bardeen, Iohan appeared emotionally challenged at times. Once, when the two men were in the mountains, they met a group of hikers who were panicking because they'd just lost one of their party. Iohan's initial response was blasé. He just said, "Oh, okay," which led Bardeen to wonder about his capacity for empathy.

In February 2020, Bardeen and Iohan spent 10 days driving into and then hiking the Argentine Andes. When Iohan flew back to North America afterward, headed to Colorado to get bike parts, he expected just a quick respite from bikepacking. It didn't work out that way.

* * *

Iohan landed in Colorado Springs on March 17, 2020. By then, the streets of every city in the country were empty. News outlets would soon circulate ghoulish photographs of patients in crowded Italian hospitals, their straining faces encased in transparent plastic bubbles as they succumbed to COVID-19. In New York City, white medical tents dotted Central Park.

Most people were hunkering down at home. But Iohan didn't have a home. When one friend suggested he stay with his uncle, he said, "That isn't an option." He didn't have a romantic partner, and he'd been out of touch with his mother.

Somewhat randomly, Iohan found an Airbnb in Calgary, Alberta, and began isolating there. Returning from a long bike trip has its challenges, even in times of health. The sense of being unaccountable—free—becomes a memory as unpaid bills and petty interpersonal conflicts return to the fore. The pandemic dealt Iohan an additional worry: In a shuttered world, would he ever be able to resume the traveling that had afforded him both his livelihood and his raison d'être? He had doubts. "I look at everywhere I have been and everywhere I want to go," he wrote to his old traveling partner, Sylvain St-Denis. "I don't think it would be the same after COVID."

There at the Airbnb in Calgary, Iohan tried not to think. He played video games just as he had long ago in Bulgaria—addictively, for days at a stretch. As before, generous strangers came out of the woodwork, offering him help. This time, Iohan's saviors were a middle-aged couple based in Cranbrook, British Columbia, four hours from Calgary. Dan and Melanie Loseth "fell in love with Iohan watching his videos," says Melanie. "It was his mannerisms, his voice. He reminded me of our oldest boy."

Iohan moved into the Loseths' basement in June 2020, and at first he seemed comfortable. One evening, he treated them to a special meal of Bulgarian cabbage rolls. But by January 2021, Melanie said recently on the podcast *My Back 40*, "his mood had really changed. He was way more sleep-deprived, and he'd just stay in the basement. He would hardly ever eat meals with us. He'd just come up and grab some leftovers."

When Melanie gingerly stepped into his lair, she found him racked with self-doubt. "He said he couldn't concentrate," she remembers. "He couldn't stand the sound of his voice, so he couldn't put out a full-length video. He pointed to his computer screen and said, 'I'm not that Iohan anymore.'"

Iohan saw no hope of continuing as a filmmaker, and he was anxious about his future. "He didn't know what he could do," Dan says.

Meanwhile, Iohan's conscience gnawed at him. He was taking his fans' Patreon money and not producing any significant films in return. That didn't sit well with him, and he had deeper, seemingly baseless worries. "He told us he had a drinking problem," says Dan, "and for proof he showed us five beer cans that he'd emptied over two days. It was very unconvincing." In a note to Bardeen, he made vague reference to a "fall from grace." Had he actually done something heinous? The Loseths, aware of his comings and goings, saw nothing untoward.

In March 2021, Iohan returned to Calgary for three months. "When I picked him up there in June, he started crying," Dan Loseth says. "He told me, 'I did nothing but play video games and smoke pot and drink.'" Later, Iohan told the couple, "I went to Calgary to end my life."

Iohan was so depressed that whenever Melanie told him he just needed to get outside, even for 15 minutes, he refused. He promised he would not kill himself in their house, though. He also began to seek solutions. He visited a doctor and finally received the apnea diagnosis. As he tried to sleep, his brain wasn't sending the proper signals to the muscles that controlled his breathing. He woke up constantly, so on July 25, his doctor gave him a sleeping mask connected to a device to help maintain his airflow.

It was, it seemed, Iohan's first step toward healing. Soon, after months of longing for a companion, he bought a puppy, a border collie, and named him Shadow. On August 17, he mounted a Shadow-sized rack onto his handlebar. Encouraged, the Loseths felt they were safe to leave Iohan at home while they visited their son in Saskatchewan. "He seemed to be doing way better," says Melanie.

Iohan was still tortured by insomnia, though, even with the new breathing mask. He'd begun making middle-of-the-night trips to the emergency room to ask, in vain, for something to help him sleep.

On August 18, Iohan sent Dan a link to a song by the Woods, a country band. One of these days I'll fly to the moon, the lyrics go. One of these days I'll have nothing to prove. One of these days I'll get out of this place.

Receiving the text, Dan felt hopeful. "He would often ask for opinions on music," he says. Dan imagined that maybe Iohan had regained his creative energies and had considered using the song in a video.

A few hours after writing to Dan, Iohan rode through the darkness to the hospital to ask once more for pills. He was rejected. He rode his bike home and fed Shadow. Then at 6:30 that morning, he sent Dan Loseth one last text. "If you get this," it said, "call the police to get me from the garage. This has been too much. I think I can get some sleep when I'm dead."

* * *

As the news of Iohan's suicide spread, hundreds of people who never knew him were stricken. "My husband and I spent today, the second day of knowing, in tears, sorrow and heartbreak," a woman named Marie Schneider wrote on a Bike Wanderer Facebook page. "We fell in love with Iohan in 2014. Social media is such an odd thing that I could love him so much (like family) and feel such heartbreak."

Shadow has a stable home with friends of the Loseths. Iohan's internet presence will likely fade over time, however. As his story went to press, only 21 of the 40 episodes he made are still up on YouTube, and the library will likely dwindle.

But Sylvain St-Denis, the French Canadian cyclist, believes Iohan's legacy will flourish most off the screen, out in the world, where he'll continue to teach us how to live. "Just before our journey ended in Argentina," says St-Denis, "Iohan told me something very important. He said, 'Sometimes it is good to follow a road without knowing if you will make it to the other side. I think this is the most important thing in bikepacking and in life in general.'"

Iohan wandered, and for several years he found what he so desperately needed out on the road. "Amongst the empty spaces and the endless mountain ranges and amongst the clouds," he says near the end of one early episode, summing up Alaska, "I found a new home every day and every night."

The searching wasn't easy. In Alaska, it was "harsh and beautiful, unpredictable and infinite," Iohan tells us, and perhaps it was the searching that destroyed him—the hungry depth of it, the way it took him out to the edge of the map and rendered him alone in the world.

It is difficult to think about how Iohan ended his journey in a land of pain and sorrow. But in his wandering, he reminded us that we all need to inject some curiosity, some exploration and risk taking, into our lives. Our souls need it. For don't we all want to see the world?

Million Mile Man

Outside, *November 22, 2016*

Cyclist Danny Chew completed his first 200-mile day when he was 10 years old. It was 1972. He rode an orange Schwinn Stingray with high-rise handlebars and a banana seat. He rode for 23 and a half hours through the rolling hills near Lodi, Ohio, through daylight and darkness, then limped into his family's shag-lined Ford van, a small kid in cutoffs and sneakers. His back was sore but his heart singing. "I felt satisfied," he says modestly. "I knew that I'd done something pretty cool."

For many people, the thrill might have been a passing thing, an evanescent boyhood delight. But Chew has Asperger's syndrome, and even though he is now 54, his giddy, kid-like fervor has never waned. It has instead distilled into a bright, lifelong monomania. He is arguably the most focused cyclist in the world. When Chew was 21, he resolved that he would ride a million miles before he died. He started logging his rides, obsessively, in hardbound notebooks. He kept records on how many 1,000-mile weeks he rode, on his centuries and double centuries, as well as his streaks of 100-mile days. Graphs captured his yearly mileage, and number crunching revealed that between 1978 and 1982 he rode an average of 14,867 miles a year. Neatly penned notes recorded strange adventures—like the time he rode the long way from Pittsburgh to Cleveland, 182 miles, without drinking water or eating. He decided that he would never pursue a career, and that dating was not his cup of tea either. "It'd be nice to have a relationship," he thought, "but then I'd have to get a job. She'd want kids. My riding time would go down, and I'd end up resenting it."

Chew lived with his mom. He remained a virgin until he was 38. He became the world's greatest cheapskate, subsisting on little more than stale bread and expired jars of mustard, and he rode, fast. Chew completed the Race across America eight times and won it twice, in 1996 and 1999.

What Chew is most famous for, however, is an annual post-Thanksgiving bike ride that he helped launch on a snowy day in Pittsburgh in 1983 and has coordinated solo since 1986. The Dirty Dozen climbs 13 of greater Pittsburgh's steepest hills, with riders racing the ups and coasting the downs. Eleven-time winner Steve Cummings calls it a quintessentially "Chewish" event. "He picks the worst weekend to do it," Cummings explains, fondly. "The weather is horrible, and he never gets any permits—he just shows up and starts it."

The 34th Dirty Dozen, set for Saturday, November 26, will draw about 300 riders and will also, tragically, be a fundraiser for Chew. On September 5, he suffered a life-changing accident. While out for a ride in the green countryside in eastern Ohio, where he was visiting friends, he crested a gentle hill and then began descending at a ho-hum 20 or 22 miles per hour. It was a placid day—sunny, with no wind. He and his training partner, Cassie Schumacher, were chatting when suddenly Chew felt dizzy. "He veered left," Schumacher says, "into a ditch, a typical drainage ditch with high grass, and I never heard any screaming. He never lost consciousness, but he hit his head and he just lay there, face down, saying, 'I feel freaky. I can't feel my legs. Am I still part of the bike?'"

He was 783,000 miles into his million-mile quest.

* * *

It's early October now, and Chew is lying in his bed at the Rehabilitation Institute of Chicago, reckoning with the cold reality that he is now paralyzed from the waist down, with drastically decreased abdominal function and also a reduced ability to curl his fingers and grip. The accident broke his neck and irreparably bruised some of the roughly one trillion nerves in his spinal cord—nerves that simply don't regenerate with the vigor of other tissues.

"It's a good thing I don't have a loaded gun or Dr. Kevorkian with me," he says, his voice nasally and flat as I arrive for a three-day visit. "It's a lot to take—to give up that sense of freedom that comes with riding a bike."

Typically a dry-eyed stoic, Chew is now weeping whenever the Dirty Dozen comes up. "A lot of people have children," he says, "but the Dirty Dozen is my kid, and it's all grown up now, and I'm so proud. I've had people come up to me after the ride and say, 'Thanks for the greatest day of my life.' I give these people a goal—to finish every hill."

Still fresh from the accident, Chew is now almost wholly dependent on the rehab staff: moving him from the bed requires two caretakers, who wriggle him into a sling attached to a small crane that hoists him up before lowering him down into his wheelchair. Still, he has a new goal: he wants to complete his million-mile quest on a hand cycle. "If I could ride 200 miles a week, 10,000 miles a year," he says, "I could do it."

His physician, Elliott Roth, the chair of Physical Medicine and Rehab at RIC, has warmly embraced Chew's mission, saying, "I don't think it's impossible at all. Danny's got a lot of things working against him, but 50 percent of people's outcome is related to their own determination." Meanwhile, there are so many competitive hand cyclists with Chew's level of disability (technically speaking, he is afflicted with T1 quadriplegia) that an entire division, Class H2, is reserved for them in international Paralympic races. The H2 world champion—42-year-old former Team USA wheelchair rugby player Will Groulx—rides 180 or so miles a week.

On this crisp fall morning in Chicago, however, Chew doesn't even own a hand cycle yet. He is moving through the hallways in a large, clunky, high-backed wheelchair designed to be pushed from behind, and when his physical therapist steps into the room, asking him to self-propel that chair for six minutes, he is jittery, terrified. "Six minutes?" he says. "I'm going to be exhausted."

Chew's neck is still broken and braced. The shoulder muscles surrounding his broken neck are taut. His hands cannot grip very well and—worst—his newly paralyzed body is not effectively regulating his blood pressure. "Before," Roth says, "the muscles in his legs pumped blood up into his heart. Now that's not happening, and his body is adjusting to the change."

Chew begins pushing the wheelchair down the corridor, and it's a bit agonizing to watch. He is a world-class athlete; now he is moving with the weary doggedness of a 90-year-old in a nursing home. He is gritting his teeth and grimacing, and the wheels of his chair are not quite rolling, but rather eking forward in tiny, spasmodic lurches. The discrepancy between past and present is so profound, and so humbling, that it almost seems like giving up would be the most graceful course. But Danny Chew is used to racing through the night on three hours' sleep. He's crossed the plains of Arkansas at 2 a.m., riding into the wind with his neck aching and spittle on his face, and now he knows that only by resorting to his greatest strength—his focus—can he lift himself out of despair. He keeps pushing the wheelchair. Then, one minute and 50 seconds into the session, he stops. He is ashen and afraid that he will pass out. When the PT takes his blood pressure, it is 81 over 52. Later, after she bends to the floor with a tape measure, she announces that he has covered 46.9 feet.

"I'm really tired," he says. "I'm so tired right now that I could fall asleep." The PT rolls him back to his room. He's airlifted back into bed, and I stand over him as he nods off. His body is long and lean under the sheets—devoid of body fat, ripped. And now his legs do not operate. Listening to the rise and fall of his breath, I feel nothing but mournful.

* * *

Life is complex, though. Many times during my visit, Chew is all lit up—bright-eyed, zany, and on. My second day there, he subjects me to what he calls his "RTP" mode of conversation, short for "Random Thrust Process," asking me scores of questions—about my relationship history, my shoe size, my political views, my exercise regime—and scarcely ever awaiting an answer. He says he gets his eccentricity from his late father, Hal, a special-education PhD and a proud freak—a vegetarian, a yogi, a devotee of Transcendental Meditation, and a man whose shag-lined Ford van bore a handmade wooden trailer capable of towing 13 bicycles. Hal Chew, he says, was a sort of guru. He was beloved by every hitchhiker he picked up on road trips, and in his basement, hanging barbells from two-by-fours, he built a bare-bones gym that carried his two sons to cycling prowess. (Danny's older brother, Tom Chew, was a member of the U.S. Olympic development team in the 1980s.)

The talk turns to romance. Chew tells me that his first kiss came when he was 27—and that he bowled his date over. "She got down on her knees, this beautiful woman," he tells me, "and she says, 'Do you want to make love?' I said no—no way. I love being different from the masses, and being a virgin was just another way I could be different."

When Chew was 38, radio shock jock Howard Stern invited him on air. The segment was titled "Pick the Virgin." Stern shouted at Chew: "You'll never get a woman! You'll die a virgin!"

"That motivated me to spite him," Chew says. "Within four months, I was in Oregon, living on a houseboat with this woman, and it was really nice. Whenever I came back from a ride in the rain, she'd have put warm blankets out for me." The relationship was brief, and Chew doesn't linger on it, reverting, instead to RTP mode, delivering me advice about matrimony—"Never marry anyone before you've lived with them for three years!"—before segueing into personal finance.

"Never ever eat a meal in a restaurant!" he says, shaking his index finger at me. "If you leave a two-dollar tip—that's money that could be invested. And when it comes to cutting your hair, just buy a $20 clipper from Wal-Mart. How much talent does it take to shave your head bald?" The man is resolute about living life on his own terms.

* * *

Weeks pass. On Facebook, Chew's older sister, Carol Perezluha, a professor of math at Florida's Seminole State College, posts a video of her brother being rolled along a Chicago bike path looking out on Lake Michigan. He's elated in the clip, saying, "This is the furthest I've been out on the wheelchair since I was hospitalized." An accompanying photo shows him canting his feet skyward in his chair, lakeside, so he can regulate his low blood pressure. The blood pressure remains a concern. It is still erratic. "Sometimes it gets so low he blacks out," his sister tells me. Once it spiraled so high that a host of caregivers rushed toward his bed, hovering. He is also having trouble regulating his body temperature.

Sometimes, even after he asks aides to bring him four blankets, his teeth chatter as he shivers in his bed.

Pre-accident, Chew suffered from occasional lightheadedness. The undiagnosed condition caused his crash. Is he fated to have a worse case of orthostatic hypotension—poor blood pressure regulation—than most paralyzed people? Dr. Roth doesn't think so. "His problem is very common for patients with spinal injuries," Roth says. "It's something that over time he can manage, by wearing tight stockings, for instance, and abdominal binders."

Still, for Chew's family—a loving group who once spent summer weekends together, riding—the crash is a nightmare that has thrown his two siblings into a search for a wheelchair-accessible van, handicapped-friendly housing, and ongoing care. His sister tells me that their mother, now 84, has been in "an awful state" of late. "Every day, she tells me she wishes it didn't happen. She's become disoriented."

There are promising signals too, though, and when Chew phones me (the calls come in at odd hours: 6:48 a.m., 10:11 p.m.), his news breaks are triumphs: "I can transfer myself out of bed now," he says. "I rode my wheelchair nine laps through the hallways. It's 19 laps to the mile. I did the hand cycle for an hour."

On November 14, his physical therapist, Kate Drolet, tells me, "Danny's improved immensely. He's got a motorized wheelchair now and he's completely independent on it. He goes all over the floor by himself, and after the Cubs won the World Series, we went to the victory parade. Even in the crowds, he didn't need any help navigating. He is one of the most motivated patients I have ever seen. He is very intent on setting personal goals. He loves numbers."

A plan gels for his release. He's slated to leave RIC on December 5, and this winter he'll live with a friend in eastern Ohio. This friend, it so happens, owns a gym, and Chew is already looking forward to the track there—it's nine laps to the mile. Meanwhile, Pittsburgh firm Desmone Architects has stepped forward, offering to redesign the family's home to make it suitable for Danny and his aging mom. The construction will cost more than $100,000. "Between Danny's mind and Mom's body," Carol Perezluha says, "I think they can do it."

Dr. Roth predicts that Chew should be able to get out on the roads, on a hand cycle, roughly a year from now, and a Pittsburgh friend is standing by, ready to serve as Chew's coach. Attila Domos is a paraplegic. A 48-year-old onetime bodybuilder who fell from a ladder in 1993, Domos hand-cycled 407.7 miles inside 24 hours last August. When I call him, he is effusive with praise for Chew. "Danny trained me," he says. "He told me that when you're doing a 24-hour ride, the night goes on forever. And he was right."

Another of Domos's remarks lingers most, though. "Recovery has almost nothing to do with how hard you work," he tells me. "After my accident, I stood for three or four hours a day, hoping that feeling would come back to my legs. It never did."

What if Danny Chew doesn't recover enough to hand-cycle great distances? "That's not an option," Chew says. "I've already ridden the wheelchair half a mile, and Attila tells me that translates to three miles on a hand cycle. He said he hates wheelchairs—that he'll never do another marathon in a wheelchair. Look, I'm just at the beginning of my recovery. I'll get there."

Wheels of Life

Washington Post Magazine, *September 17, 2006*

WE CAME ALONG THE SEA COAST IN A TAXI, AWAY FROM THE AIRPORT, the windows open to the warm evening rain as a woman's voice sounded soft and sing-songy on the crackly radio. "And they will be bicycling all over the island," she was saying, "and, oh, yes, they will be climbing the very big hills."

The taxi rounded a turn, its engine groaning a bit as it ground up an incline. We came into a forest, and suddenly the world was green and lush, the narrow macadam road empty of cars and squiggling skyward like a lane in a storybook. The verdant beauty around us was beyond words.

But perhaps you have seen Dominica, a tiny island nation of 70,000 people that sits just north of Barbados and several hundred miles from the Dominican Republic. Dominica played backdrop to this summer's blockbuster, *Pirates of the Caribbean: Dead Man's Chest.* The movie is a mawkish lark, and its basic story line—Watch out, Jack Sparrow! Those Carib Indian cannibals are going to roast your pirate bones on a spit!—was offensive to many Dominicans. But as it lingers on the island's mist-shrouded hills, with drums pulsing ominously in the background, the film gets at the spirit of the place: Two-thirds of Dominica is still blanketed in coniferous old growth. There are 365 twisting mountain rivers here and a host of waterfalls cascading down into clear emerald pools. And the land is so cragged and steep that it's almost unfathomable.

Though it is only 29 miles long and 16 miles at its widest, Dominica is home to two peaks more than 4,500 feet. The rest of the island is essentially a range of smaller mountains and valleys, and the roads are murderous. There is one paved hill that rises for a steady mile at a 28 percent grade. The Tour de France, in contrast, rarely offers up grades steeper than 10 percent, and almost never goes steeper than 15 percent. Virtually no one travels to Dominica to ride a bicycle.

"And there are three cyclists, you know," the woman was saying now in melodious tones on the radio. "There is John Moorhouse, a very talented bicycle racer who lives in Florida. There is a photographer—his name is Peter—and there is a very famous writer."

John Moorhouse, who is 36, was sitting beside me. A Dominican by blood, he spent his teenage years on the island before moving, in 1993, to Orlando, where he's become a standout in 24-hour mountain bike races, which see competitors looping dirt paths for a full day and night without ceasing. He rides his bike 250 miles a week, and in races he has no qualms about chomping down a whole stick of butter, straight from the wrapper, as he whirs starved and bleary-eyed through the 3 a.m. darkness. Moorhouse works as the U.S. distributor for Scottoiler, a British company that makes bicycle lubrication systems, but he dreams of returning to Dominica one day to guide bike tours. He was now on a reconnaissance mission, and he'd alerted the media by sending out a press release saying that his expedition here was to "conquer" the hills. In an agrarian country aiming to promote ecotourism, his quest was national news.

Behind Moorhouse, photographer Peter McBride, 35, was oblivious to his new celebrity and chatting away on his cell phone. McBride is stocky and ripped, with the rugged bonhomie and tousled good looks of a Patagonia clothing model. Once a member of the U.S. developmental ski team, he now specializes in adventure assignments—in sea kayaking Croatia and backcountry skiing the Republic of Georgia, that sort of thing.

And the "very famous writer"? Well, I had plenty of time to ponder that phrase, since the ride away from the airport, in Melville Hall, to Dominica's capital city, Roseau, is long and winding and slow—marred by potholes so nasty that, at one point, I saw a small tree growing in a two-foot-deep chasm bitten out of the edge of the road.

The "very famous writer" was me.

* * *

I am 42 years old, and I ride my bike 100 or so miles a week. I ride almost everywhere—to the grocery store, to the dentist, the nine miles to my daughter's school, even when it's cold and raining outside. But this devotion to biking is a new thing for me, begun only a few months before my Dominica trip, and for two decades now, I've approached exercise with an anxiety that has at times neared an engulfing obsession.

Let me explain. I was an athlete once, too—a distance runner. In college, I could run five miles in just over 26 minutes; I once ran a half-marathon in 1:13. I was strictly mediocre by NCAA standards, but good enough to glimpse in running a delight, a feeling of mastery, that had eluded me as a bony and skittish kid relegated to the "challenged" section of gym class. I could enter an all-comers, all-ages 10K and place 10th or 12th in a field of 500 people, and I lived, as all devout geeks do, with numbers streaming through my skull. I could recite my splits and my finish times from memory, and I knew, to the second, the records set by running's great luminaries. I made sense of the world—and of where I stood in it—through numbers.

But when I was 21, I pulled some back muscles. A minor overuse injury, nothing much, but somehow I was filled with the fear that I would never recover, that I would be no one again. And, indeed, I did not recover. Regularly, throughout my 20s and 30s, I fell into these horrible, claustrophobic episodes, months long, that would begin with a simple muscle pull—a knot in my hamstring, say. I would worry about the pain and brace so stiffly against it that I became like a dry stick waiting to crack. Officially, I had myofascial pain syndrome. My muscles kept pulling, going deep into spasm. I became ensconced in a rictus of pain, and soon that rictus became who I was.

For 11 years, starting when I was 27, I was so afflicted that, if I sat down on a hard chair, my lower back would immediately sing with a hot, electric-like pain—a pain that would persist, after a minute of sitting, for days. Sometimes, with the slightest provocation, I experienced that same stinging pain in my forearms, in the inside of my thighs. I saw a dozen doctors. I was told, at one point, errantly, that I had a certain arthritis—ankylosing spondylitis—and that my lower vertebrae could fuse over time as my neck curled downward, like a question mark. I wrote standing up. I dined at restaurants standing up.

But one winter the sitting pain simply disappeared, leaving behind a constellation of intermittent and less keening muscle aches. I spent $60 on a used bike then, to see if I could ride a couple of miles day after day. I could, and over time I bought a new bike. I rode faster, and I found myself excavating a dusty and long-dormant version of myself that I'd almost forgotten.

I was there on Dominica as a reporter, sure, and all I had to do was follow John Moorhouse around for three days and 110 miles. No one was going to kill me if I rented a car. But there was no way I was going to do that—no way. As I sat in the taxi, I resolved to wrestle up every hill, even though my back problem had flared up again. My hip was in pain, injured a week earlier, while I was stretching. I had not ridden in almost a week.

* * *

Luckily, a minor crisis shook the halls of governance in Roseau: The airlines misplaced my bike while it was en route to Dominica; my bike was at large. Dominica's minister of tourism, Yvor Nassief, got on the phone at once, to hound American Eagle. "Mr. Donahue," he said to me in somber tones, peering across his expansive desk, "we apologize. This is inexcusable."

Secretly, I was delighted. I had a whole extra day to stretch out my hip, and so I did what I often do when I feel the muscle fibers inside me are screaming at one another: I wandered around on foot, alone, aimlessly, trying to wriggle out of the cage of self-consciousness and find peace. I followed the Roseau River downhill from our hotel, near the village of Wotten Waven, and then cut sharply right, uphill, onto a narrow, steep tree-shaded road. Then I consulted my map.

Even though Dominica was a British colony until it attained independence in 1978, the names of the villages all around me were French—Giraudel, Massacre, Fond Cani, Laudat—and the people in the hills nearby often spoke Creole at home. The French held Dominica briefly in the 1700s—and then stayed on, even after the British navy defeated them. They built churches and schools and, with the English, brought in ships full of African slaves to work on sugar plantations. But the Europeans never really vanquished Dominica. The land was too mountainous to cultivate easily. The plantations were fragmented; the slaves kept running off into the woods to cook up bloody rebellions.

Today, Dominica remains untamed. There is only one fast-food chain restaurant on the island, and the airlines have to corkscrew down into Melville Hall, cutting hard and circling low in small planes, so as to angle onto the short runway squeezed between mountains. Neither Club Med nor the Sheraton has, as yet, elected to subject its clients to the indignities of landing here, and even Lonely Planet, which has published guidebooks on 135 countries, has so far shied away from producing a Dominica book.

I was there on Dominica because it's still wild, and I was after a sort of animal joy that you cannot get in a gym on a StairMaster. I wanted to feel the ragged beat of my heart in a place that resounded with its own green vitality. So I kept climbing—and came, eventually, to a sign for Trafalgar Falls, three miles away. A driver stopped to offer me a lift, and I hopped in and rode up a couple of absurdly steep pitches as the car pulsed with house music. Then the guy reached his home, still far away from the falls, and I walked on until I found myself nearing a tall, dreadlocked man who held a machete loose in his hand. He was not wearing a shirt, and his pecs and abs rippled with a sinewy grace.

"You like Dominica, mon?" he asked.

I said I did. We strolled together to a small roadside shack. I bought him a beer, and we chatted a bit. Then I walked away. The air was steamy and the hills around me teeming with life—with mango, guava, and passion fruit growing wild—and I kept picking the guavas up off the ground and eating them.

In time, I went back to the hotel. My bike had arrived, express, and with an Allen wrench I put it together. I tested the brakes, adjusted the seat. And then, along with Peter and John, I went out for a warm-up: down the hill into Roseau, the crickets chirping in the night all around us.

* * *

The next morning, we floated through Roseau again, riding in a pack. We cut left along the coast, through the villages of Loubiere, Pointe Michele, and Sibouli, and drivers heralded us with their horns, having seen us on television. "Ah," said one woman, "you are the big cyclists!" We came around a bend, and John pointed inland at a rocky peak in the clouds. "See that?" he said. "That's where we're going." He spoke almost wistfully; we were retracing the routes of his earliest adventures.

Moorhouse grew up in the suburbs of Boston, but his mother is a native Dominican, and when he was 14 the family moved back to her homeland. His dad, a machinist, bought him a motorcycle, and he used it to ramble all over the island. "I remember going into the Syndicate area, up north, to ride on a network of paths that looked out onto the sea," he told me. "I went into remote mountain villages, and there was no electricity. The people spoke Creole. I got to know the island by riding my motorcycle."

Moorhouse had a BMX bicycle back then, too, and he rode without fear. When I stepped into a café in his old village, Paix Bouche, one man put down his rum, then demonstrated how, long ago, John would carefully stand up on his moving bicycle, placing one foot on the seat and one on the handlebars, so as to "cycle surf" down the street. "John Moorhouse," he said with thick admiration. "Madman! Professionnel!"

In 2002, Moorhouse did try to launch himself as a pro athlete. He quit his job at a bike shop and created a five-man pro squad, Team 24, but his income—$4,000 here for a race victory; $500 there for wearing an "Ellsworth Bikes" shirt in a magazine photo—was sporadic. "Unless you're Lance Armstrong," he said, "it's really hard." Until very recently, he was working a string of odd jobs—installing highway guard rails, for instance. In between gigs, he would spend seven to 12 hours each day crawling the web and posting ads—on eBay, pinkbike.com—for his Dominican cycling trips.

For Moorhouse, this trip was crucial. Our expedition needed to shine, and he rode—we all rode—with fervor. Once, John rampaged along with one tire high in the air for the length of a football field. Later, as I sailed downward toward the base of an approaching climb, he shouted encouragement—"Momentum is your friend!"—and then flailed past, standing up as he pumped on the pedals.

At the top of one hill on that first afternoon, I took my pulse. My heart was going at 192 beats per minute.

* * *

When the pain in my back was at its worst, I spent years exploring alternative medicine, visiting chiropractors, acupuncturists, and, at the nadir, an "energy worker" who beseeched me: "Breathe! Breathe! Deep belly breaths now." Always, I felt a certain tacit judgment coming down on my head: My inner Vince Lombardi, they agreed, was an aberration of postindustrial Western society—and it needed to be curbed, if not utterly purged.

I expected that Dominica would deliver me the same lesson. I knew, in any case, that it had some crucial lesson to impart. The people there are healthy. They subsist on fresh fish and homegrown vegetables, and they walk the hills. A myth prevails: Locals believe that they are the longest-lived people in the world. In fact, Dominica's premier advocate for centenarians, a publicist named Alex Bruno, claims that there are now at least 15 Dominican citizens more than 100 years old, and the whole island embraces a woman named Ma Pampo, who died in 2003 at the reported age of 128, as a sort of national saint.

Before I visited the island, a friend wrote to me, speculating on Dominican longevity. "I think there is something about the pace of life there," she said, having just visited, "about the lack of stress and the uncomplicated fishing communities. There's time for a slow beer in the afternoon. And it rains a lot, so you seek shelter and sit it out."

Biking the island, I saw that life in Dominica is often languid and calm. Once, for instance, I came heaving to the top of a pass and the first thing I encountered was a thin, 60ish man sitting on the ground, his back against a tree as a lone bony cow behind him picked at the grass at the edge of a cliff. The man acknowledged me with a subtle nod and then resumed staring off into the distance, saying nothing, a study in energy conservation.

But there is a hard edge to Dominica, too. The soft-spoken Rastafarians hustle as they hoist crates of bananas into their trucks, and when their tempers flare they sometimes draw out their machetes and duel. In the roadside cafés, where old men gather to play dominoes, they slam their tiles down onto the table, sharply, as an expression of manhood.

And when I had the chance to meet 100-year-old Louisa Benoit, she was sitting up in her living room, her hair and her wardrobe impeccable, as she sewed a child's dress for a festival. Benoit has been working steadily as a seamstress since the 1920s, and I told her that she seemed pretty tough. "You bet I'm tough," she growled. "I can't walk, but you get down on that floor right now and I'll fight you. I'll beat you right now."

As dusk fell on our first day of riding, we climbed into a high mountain village, Bellevue Chopin, in the rain—and then began swooping downhill. It was almost dark out, but I heard something beside me. Two kids, maybe 15 years old, were riding down with us on ancient BMX bikes. Unlike us, they had no helmets, no lights.

We kept descending, picking up speed. We were going 25 miles an hour, then 30, then 35. Then I heard a scraping and crunching sound at my side. Sparks danced from the asphalt, and I watched one boy belly slide over the wet, rubbly pavement as his bike rattled beside him. I figured that he had broken a leg, at least, so I stopped, seized by a parental concern.

But by now the kid was already standing. He'd gotten up instantly, as though doing that might erase his brief lapse of poise from the record. I could do nothing but offer a lame admonition. "You really, really have to be careful," I said.

The kid did not want to be hassled. "We live here, mon," he said. He resumed his descent, ahead of me, and it was only then that I realized that he had no brakes on his bike. He was slowing and stopping himself by pressing his sneaker down on the top of the rear tire. Later, I would learn that this was how all the kids braked in Dominica.

* * *

We rode on, along the south coast in the dark. We had been on the road several hours by now, shedding gallons of sweat, and Pete simply cracked.

His muscles seized with cramps because he was so depleted of salt. Suddenly, he was almost mincing on his pedals and lagging behind. He folded for the day; he hitched a ride from a fellow named Sam. And in the village of Petite Savane, there were only three people on the street— John, me, and an old man, seriously intoxicated, who came running out of a café, rum in hand, to chase after us and offer support as we started in on our expedition's most grisly ascent, Morne Paix Bouche, which rises at a grade averaging about 20 percent. "Original!" the drunken man bellowed, expressing homage in Creole. "Original, mon!"

I started climbing. At first, I was aware of Sam's SUV lurking on the road above me, the beam of its headlights pivoting as it wound through the switchbacks. Soon, though, I was aware only of the pavement around me, and the roadside bushes and grass illuminated by my small light. Then the world narrowed even more. Everything peripheral was annihilated, and I existed, for maybe 10 minutes, in a bliss of focus and pain. With each stroke, I felt my pedals pause and creak at the top of the crank, and I felt my front wheel kicking up, off the pavement, each time I got to a switchback and cut straight at the fall line. My spit was viscous and tasting of blood, and low down on the stem of my brain I felt a certain glimmering satisfaction. "I'm doing this," I thought. "My muscles are working."

I kept climbing—one switchback, then another. But then, maybe 70 percent of the way up the hill, I looked up for a split second and saw Sam's car two or three switchbacks above. The headlights seemed distant, like candles guttering in the high nook of a cliff, and I knew suddenly that there was no way. It was not merely a matter of will; I was simply not strong enough to pedal to the top of this mountain. I got off my bike, and John passed me, huffing "good work, good work." Then I walked on, secretly ecstatic. I was standing, I knew, on a sweet island in time. Soon enough—within the next decade of my life, certainly—I would need to reconcile with my body growing older and weaker and slightly more brittle. I would need to find music in going slow. But right now—for a moment, at least—that onus was on hold. I had just pushed myself harder than I had pushed in 20 years, and nothing had broken.

* * *

But our travails were not over. We kept butting up against a problem: John remembered the roads only hazily, and each time we arrived at the base of a hill, he tended toward optimism, saying things like, "This one really isn't that bad." Right out of the blocks on day two, we hit a hill that John described as "short." A mile later, we were still climbing, straight up in the breezeless humidity.

"How far to the top?" I asked a woman out taking a stroll.

"Continue like so," she said with warm cheer as she waved her hand vaguely, "and you will soon be reaching your destination."

A half mile later, another passerby: "You have almost arrived, my friend."

About a half mile after that, we neared a man who had dreadlocks and wore a red, green and yellow knit hat. "How much farther?" I asked.

The man took a long drag on what appeared to be a cigarette, and then spoke. "Yeah, mon," he said.

Later that afternoon, in the village of Rosalie, we got to the base of a hill that John described as "two or three miles long." It actually rolled upward for 5.4 miles, and when Pete arrived at the crest, lugging, as always, 40 pounds of camera gear, he was cramped up again, and he could speak only one word with conviction: "Taxi!"

John and I pressed on, up switchbacks through the villages of Gaulette and Salybia, and as evening fell John surged ahead. I was alone, and at two different turns in the road men began running up hill, after me, the instant they caught sight of my white skin and my shiny bike. "Money," one man implored.

I was now on the Carib Indian reservation, where the unemployment rate is about 70 percent, and I had no game plan for such appeals. I just pedaled hard, dodging anyone who might beseech me for cash, until I reached our hotel.

At the Carib Territory Guest House, I was hit with a strange, serendipitous surprise: The place would play host, that evening, to a series of four boxing matches. A ring had been set up on the patio outside the kitchen. There were ropes knotted to the patio's concrete columns, and around the columns, there were foam pads. The floor of the ring was terra-cotta underlain by concrete.

The matches would pit the Dominican National Team, a middling player in the boxing stronghold that is the Caribbean, against an underdog—the Kalinago boxing club, whose members all hailed from the Carib reservation, bearing a long history of oppression.

The tan-skinned, almond-eyed Caribs are the Indians Columbus encountered when he first reached the Caribbean in 1492. Once scattered throughout the archipelago, they now possess a single land reserve, where many live in simple one- or two-room huts.

The Kalinago boxing team does not train in a gym. Instead, the boxers steel themselves by lifting rocks pried out of the earth. They spar on concrete, usually without benefit of face masks or gum shields. And on the night I was with them, they had to wait for the national team, which was inexplicably an hour late. They stood by the roadside in tank tops, lithe and lean and mean as snakes.

I waited nearby and talked to the Kalinago coach, Augustine Frederick, who is 32 and the sole Carib on the Dominican team. Frederick is a tiny man, a featherweight, and he is stoic and quietly earnest. He said: "They gave me their word. They will come." He said: "This is the first time my fighters have ever competed, and the national team, they feel like they will walk all over us. But you watch: We have been training a full year for these fights. We have a surprise for them."

The national team arrived, finally, and the fighting began: a lurid blur beneath the hot white flood lights. The Caribs fought barefoot, and the first bout was an ungainly thing, with the boxers elbowing and shoving and tangling their arms. But the true drama happened outside the ring. There were 60-odd spectators—nearly all Caribs, and among them a guy who'd chased after me—and everyone was delirious as the proprietor of the guesthouse, Charles Williams, did the play-by-play over a staticky microphone. "Oh, yes!" he yelled, his words rolling into a jazz scat. "Oh, yes! Something's happening here! Something's happening here!"

Williams, 56, is the chief of the Caribs and a controversial firebrand. Last year, he divided his tribal council when he noisily decried *Dead Man's Chest*, whose directors hired hundreds of Caribs to play scantily clad cannibals. He noted that there's no archeological evidence proving that his ancestors were cannibals, and he lambasted every Carib who took $95 a day for film extra work. "Shame on us," he said in a press release excerpted by many U.S. newspapers, "that for a few dollars we are betraying our flesh and blood."

As emcee, Williams did not hide his loyalties. He rejoiced when the first fight went, on decision, to the Caribs and then again when the next Carib fighter victoriously split the lip of his opponent. All night he kept crowing: "Go Carib boy! Go Carib boy!" Spare and agile himself, he kept dancing into the crowd and handing the mike to his friends, and they echoed his banter—albeit, with less poetic aplomb. "Very good," one man intoned, "very good, well done."

The referee called the third fight a draw, and then the fourth fight began—a stocky Carib bruiser, Julien Valmond, against a much taller, rail-thin boy with jet-black skin, a kid so delicate looking that I winced as he stepped into the ring. Within 30 seconds, Valmond had the kid on the ropes. At the back of the patio, he was efficiently pummeling the boy's face. The boy crumpled to the concrete. He stayed down for the count. And then the crowd flew into a frenzy, released, it seemed, from 500 years of hard luck. People leapt high into the air, their arms stretched above them in victory. They toppled white plastic deck chairs and danced. They chanted—"Julien! Julien! Julien!" Frederick, the coach, stood nearby, calmly beaming as he said, "I knew they would do their best," and Williams spouted a stream of unintelligible euphoria into the mike. Listening, I remembered what one old woman had told me as we set off on our journey: "You will have a fine time," she said without elaborating. "This is an open country."

Now I understood what she meant. Dominica is open-hearted: An unrehearsed humanity prevails. Restraint and tense hesitation and the walls between people all dissolve in the sweltering heat.

I wasn't used to life being so freewheeling, so loose-limbed. Generosity exists here in the United States certainly, and it can flash out at the most random moments—when you're stuck by the side of the road with a flat tire, say, and some stranger comes along with a jack. But still so much of daily life feels corporatized, digitized: Minute to minute, we are awash in phrases such as, "May I be of further assistance to you?" and "Press 1 for more options." We are never too far from a Mini Mart whose sterile fluorescent lights burn all through the night.

It can be cold and alienating to live in such a landscape, and an uncertain person can find myriad reasons to retreat, to go inside his shell. And that is what I did often when the muscles in my body were knifed by pain. I functioned so that there was not much perceptibly wrong with me, and nominally, gingerly, I stayed in shape, taking walks, swimming laps in a pool. But I conceived of myself as broken. Quite often I refrained from the most basic activities—climbing down a few flights of stairs, say—in fear that I would spiral down into worse, more intractable muscle inflammation and pain. I held the pain around me like a case, a shield, and I cultivated a hurt contempt for the world as the pain fed on itself and worsened.

Now, ringside, I felt the chanting shake through me: "Julien! Julien! Julien!" Eventually, someone kicked on the stereo, so it blasted loud reggae, and then we all flowed outside and milled about on the grass, chatting, saying nothing of substance, as we lingered out there in the dark.

* * *

The last day of riding was easy. We all made it, gliding, ultimately, down a winding eight-mile hill through groves of banana plants, and then over a rare stretch of flats, through the rain, into Roseau. We had drinks at a bar there, and then the next day Pete and I set off on one last adventure. We took a cab across the island to Paix Bouche, to take in a festival.

There are no hotels in Paix Bouche, and Pete showed up there with his bike disassembled, contained in a box. Awkwardly, he began traipsing around town with the huge, heavy box, begging for lodgings.

Within 20 minutes, he befriended the proprietor of the village store, Gerard Honoré, who secured us the run of the church hall. "We'll make sure you have whatever you need," Honoré said as he set a couple aging mattresses onto the floor for us. "If you need me"—he gestured toward his small house—"just knock on my window."

Soon darkness fell, and, on the blacktop up at the school, a reggae and soca band, the Nature Boyz, began playing on a raised wooden stage before a crowd of 300 or so, locals all.

The Nature Boyz starred Honoré's daughter Theona and her boyfriend, Bryson Williams, as singers. All of the band members wore indigo glow tubes for necklaces, and they danced with a synchronized, high-stepping syncopation that carried the fresh, juicy verve of the Jackson Five, circa 1974. In between songs, though, Williams was homey. He talked up the prizes the local school was offering that night, as part of a raffle. The grand prize was a farm animal, a goat. "Someone's gonna go home with a goat tonight," he said without irony. "Someone here is going to bring home a goat!"

I drank beer and danced—tentatively at first, and then, in time, into the sweaty swirl of the crowd, my arms swinging wildly, until I was lost in the beat. Soon, I was paged.

"Where's the white man?" Williams said from the stage. "We want the white man to come up here and dance."

He meant me, and for a couple seconds, as the crowd went quiet, casting about in the dark for my pale skin, I felt a little unnerved. This kid was mocking my cramped, arrhythmic middle-aged shuffle—I was certain of that. But there was a sweetness to his plea, too, a curiosity and a warmth, so I climbed the stairs up onto the stage, and for maybe 30 seconds, I danced—all out, in front of the band, beneath the glare of the lights.

"Yes!" Williams sang out. "Do the white man dance!" He mimicked my wheeling, back-bent maniac skank, and at once the crowd picked it up, too. The schoolyard was a sea of wide-whirling arms. "Do the white man dance!" everyone shouted, rolling into a chant. "Do the white man dance!"

The chant was still going when I stepped back out onto the blacktop, and a swarm of people surged toward me, clapping me on the back. A guy came along with a bottle of rum and, laughing, handed it to me. I took a hard slug.

After a while, I walked down the hill. The music faded until the night was silent, and for a minute or so I stood outside the church hall, looking up at the stars. Then I went inside and fell asleep.

Team Amani Sees the Future

Bicycling, *June 4, 2023*

THIS WEEKEND, FOR THE FIRST TIME EVER, A TRIO OF AFRICAN PROS will line up for gravel's most prestigious, most intensely fought race. Unbound Gravel takes riders through the Flint Hills of eastern Kansas, along winding prairie roads littered with sharp rocks and steep climbs. Kenya-based Team Amani has sent John Kariuki, a 26-year-old Kenyan, along with two Ugandan teammates, Charles Kagimu, 24, and Jordan Schleck, 20, to face off against the world's top gravel racers on the 200-mile course.

There will be a gaping hole in the Amani lineup, though. The team's founder and captain, Sule Kangangi, will not be in Kansas.

Sule was a visionary and a leader in African cycling. He'd had an inauspicious early childhood; neither of his parents were a meaningful presence in his life after age 11. He essentially raised himself. His sister went to live with their grandparents while he stayed behind in Kapsuswa, a poor neighborhood on the outskirts of Eldoret. He was old enough to find work, the thinking went, old enough to contribute financially to the family.

So Sule sold secondhand clothes. He swept the veranda at a local shop. He herded cattle. School wasn't an option—he couldn't afford the tuition—and Kapsuswa was in the process of being demolished on account of crime, which forced Sule to couch surf, moving from the home of one alcoholic uncle to another. Sometimes he had a mattress; sometimes his mattress got stolen.

Every few days, Sule would visit his grandparents. His grandfather had been a janitor; the steady work had granted him financial security. He was old by the time Sule was a teen and would get around slowly on a black upright single-speed bicycle—a Black Mamba, as such workhorses are called in East Africa. From his grandfather, Sule got a sense of what a happy, stable life looked like, and he wanted to create something similar for himself. He worked in a print shop and a convenience store. He took his grandfather's bike and put a seat on the back, to transport paying customers around Eldoret.

Then in 2007, Sule pieced together a road bike. He stepped up his training until he was often doing 150-mile rides, and he started to race. In 2016, a pro team, Kenyan Riders, recruited him. He raced in China, the United Arab Emirates, and Australia. He taught himself English, zeroing in on one new word a day: "exertion," for example, and "exhaustion."

Meanwhile, as Sule married and started a family, he tried to grow bike culture in East Africa. He coordinated a Black Mamba racing series. He pushed to attain better prize money for African riders at races—and grew leery of elite road racing, in which riders climb the ranks via an arcane points system that awards them for competing in races that are almost invariably held in Europe. When he launched Team Amani in 2018, his goal was to empower East African cyclists, both male and female, as they vie for dominance in gravel and mountain bike racing.

In August 2022, Sule traveled to the United States with Kariuki and Schleck, aiming to compete in three major stateside races—the Leadville 100, SBT GRVL, and finally the Vermont Overland, a roughly 59-mile ordeal that climbs about 7,500 feet through small towns and forests around Windsor, Vermont.

More than 1,100 riders lined up for the race on a cool, cloudless late-summer day. I was one of them, fighting to a 211th-place finish among men. In the beer line later, I found myself chatting with a fellow racer. Casually ignorant, I asked him how he did.

"I won the race," he proclaimed.

It was John Kariuki. No Black rider had ever won a major American gravel race, and Kariuki's teammate Jordan Schleck had sweetened the moment by finishing third.

But Sule never made it to the finish line. Two hours into the race, Kevin Bouchard-Hall, a physical therapist riding just behind him, found him lying beside a tree in a fetal position with blood coming from his mouth. "The fork on his bike had snapped off," says Bouchard-Hall.

Bouchard-Hall suspects that Sule hit the tree, but no one will ever know precisely what happened. Sule died on the way to the hospital. He was 33 years old. His teammates, who had gotten news of the crash and assumed it meant a fracture at worst, were stunned. "We were crying," Schleck says. "We couldn't seriously believe this had happened."

Suddenly Sule's three young children had no father, his wife became a widow, and his dream of launching East Africa as a power in gravel racing was shrouded in question marks.

* * *

"More coffee, sir?" The waiter's voice is tentative—it's a delicate moment. Sule's widow, Hellen Wahu, is sitting at the Goshen Inn in Eldoret, crying a little as she remembers her husband. "Sule taught people to believe in themselves. That's what he did, and he helped so many people," she says. Wahu explains how Sule often visited an orphanage and how, later in his life, he informally helped support nine widows in Eldoret, visiting each woman monthly to deliver provisions like cornmeal and soap. His biggest contribution, though, involved teaching other African cyclists how to flourish. "Sule showed them it's not about what a sponsor can give you," Wahu says. "It's about what you can do for yourself right now. He had so much hope."

I've come here to Kenya to gauge whether Sule's hopes for Team Amani can outlive him. In some ways, it seems like the answer is a certain yes. There's the team's 1–3 finish at last summer's Overland. And a few months before that, while Sule was still alive, Meta, the parent company of Facebook, shot a high-action, minute-long ad that featured Amani riders swooping through both the Kenyan highlands and Zwift-like virtual realms as it suggested that technology can bring equality in cycling.

Still, when it came to shaping a vision for the team's future, Team Amani had been almost 100 percent Sule. The idea took root in 2018 when Sule began talking to an American human rights lawyer and amateur cyclist, Mikel Delagrange, who co-owns Lola Bikes & Coffee, a café in The Hague, Netherlands, where he worked for the International Criminal Court.

For years, the shop had sponsored African road cyclists, and the two men had conversations about whether road racing was a good fit for African riders. Africa has been home to road squads like Team Africa Rising and Bike Aid for well over a decade, and although they've attained a few shining moments—Eritrean rider Biniam Girmay won a stage of the 2022 Giro d'Italia while fellow Eritrean Daniel Teklehaimanot held the polka-dot jersey for four consecutive stages in the 2015 Tour de France—success has been sparse. At Delagrange's suggestion, Sule began looking into whether gravel might be a better fit.

Still, Delagrange was hesitant to get involved. Having spent a decade working in Africa, he'd become disenchanted with international development projects. "They just reinforce the power dynamics of the colonial period. I didn't want to be another American with a project in Africa," says Delagrange, who now lives in Switzerland and works for the United Nations.

Delagrange's take is hardly new. Critics of aid to Africa point out that while the World Bank has spent billions to foster development there, more than 50 percent of its projects—such as wells, schools, roads, and dams—have failed amid local chaos and corruption. Meanwhile, in Kenya, a nation renowned for its world-dominating distance runners, organized athletics still seems tied to European colonialism. Many elite Kenyan runners live and train in camps owned by companies based in Europe. And these camps have hardly engendered stability. Currently more than 70 Kenyan runners are banned from competing because World Athletics suspects them of doping. And the 2021 murder of world-class Kenyan runner Agnes Tirop by her husband and coach, Ibrahim Rotich, also Kenyan, has brought new attention to a troubling dynamic: Female athletes in Kenya are so vulnerable to attack by money-hungry men that a group, Tirop's Angels, has formed to combat the problem.

Many argue that what's needed in Africa are not boutique projects—bike teams, say, or fair-trade coffee schemes—but rather economic and political stability that's built slowly, over decades.

But Sule's visions for a gravel team were infectious. "They weren't focused on the Tour de France," Delagrange says. So he resolved that he'd be in the "back seat," raising funds and helping with logistics, while Sule split his time between riding and masterminding Amani's rise.

Between 2019 and 2022, as Delagrange landed sponsorship deals with Wahoo and Factor Bikes, among others, he made 20 visits to Kenya. In 2021, he and Sule headed up the inaugural four-day Migration Gravel Race, which saw top Europeans racing locals on the rubbly red dirt roads of the Maasai Mara, a Kenyan national reserve. (Sule finished second, beaten only by Dutch legend Laurens ten Dam, and then won the race in 2022.) They got East Africans entry into elite Zwift races and began planning a home for Team Amani.

Iten, population 42,000, is a mountain town in Kenya's Great Rift Valley, where it sits an hour northeast of Sule's native city, Eldoret, and plays host to numerous elite running camps. Sule and Delagrange planned to build a world-class cycling facility for the team. Called Amani House, it includes athletes' quarters, replete with nine tiny parallel bedrooms and two bunkrooms. Next to the house, they envisioned a pump track to entice local kids into cycling, and a clubhouse containing a performance center full of Wahoo Kickrs and a bike-themed café that could lure tourists who might want to hire an Amani rider to guide them through the surrounding farmland and forests.

The Amani project seems viable, even to those acquainted with the challenges of growing cycling in Africa. "Other teams, they're looking for shortcuts," says David Kinjah, who's been coaching with Safari Simbaz, a Kenyan development group, for two decades. "They think they can just turn Kenyan runners into cyclists, but there aren't shortcuts. You have to build a culture, like they've done with running here, like they've done with cycling in Italy."

Amani is working on that, Kinjah believes, with the pump track and with plans to give bikes to local kids and host weekly races. "They're being smart," he says. "They're not wasting lots of money on travel. They're doing virtual races. They're letting their riders stay home and face the world."

Delagrange attributes Team Amani's savvy to Sule, whose early life demanded resourcefulness. "He listened. He observed. He studied everything—course routes, nutrition plans," Delagrange says. "He brought intelligence to everything he did. Nobody can fill his shoes."

Last September, after Team Amani buried Sule in Iten, Delagrange spent four hours with the riders, equivocating over whether the Amani project should continue. "I told them, 'I don't want to do this alone,'" he says. "I asked them, 'Can each of you pick up a piece of Sule's mantle?' And they said yes. It was the silver lining to a bottomless pit of sorrow."

By the time I visit in December, Team Amani is still in a transition phase. The pump track is finished, a jet-black ribbon of asphalt swooping across the red earth. Groundbreaking for the athletes' house is slightly delayed. And the team is still without an official captain. "Sule's absence is forcing others to lead," Delagrange says. But the group is widely dispersed. Several of the 11 riders live in Iten, but Olympic mountain bike hopeful Nancy Akinyi is in Nairobi, six hours away, and others are in Uganda and Rwanda. It's impossible to discern whether one of them is quietly leading or whether there's a power vacuum steeped in sadness.

* * *

In many ways, Iten is a typical Kenyan market town. Women sit on the ground downtown, selling socks and underwear and used T-shirts as motorbikes weave amid trucks spewing black clouds from their tailpipes. But Western tourists are everywhere, nearly all of them runners on pilgrimage to their sport's holy land. You see them out on the chaotic streets, doing errands or sipping cappuccino at the High Altitude Training Centre, an athlete-focused retreat founded by world champion runner Lornah Kiplagat. The hills and forests are nearby, sometimes enchantingly blanketed in fog.

John Kariuki, last summer's Overland winner, lives and trains in Iten, and when he and I meet for dinner, his manner is suave, nonchalant. A slight, wiry man, deep-voiced with a bushy beard, he begins by telling me he's a country music aficionado, a fan of Johnny Cash and Dolly Parton. At the U.S. race just before Overland—SBT, in Steamboat Springs, Colorado—he persuaded Delagrange to buy him a cowboy hat at a Western apparel shop. Then his eyes alighted on a pair of leather boots. "If you buy me those boots," he told Delagrange, "I'll win Vermont Overland." Delagrange acquiesced, and, about 20 miles into Overland, Kariuki thought of the boots as he surged into the lead. *Pay the boots!* he said to himself. *Pay the boots!* The words danced in his mind like a mantra as he rattled over roots and rocks, never once getting passed, until he finished with a four-minute lead over runner-up Adam Roberge, a Canadian.

In the wake of that victory, Delagrange began to see Kariuki as Sule's heir apparent. "He has a quiet confidence," he says.

Kariuki grew up in Nakuru, a city of 421,000 situated about 100 miles southeast of Iten, where, he tells me, shrugging, his earliest years were "average, not rich, not poor. I had shoes. Most of the kids around me couldn't afford them."

Kariuki left school in 10th grade and then landed an apprenticeship with an auto mechanic. He commuted to work on a battered mountain bike. One day in 2015, as he was riding along, a roadie zipped by him—a Black rider, all kitted up. "I'd never seen a road bike, and I couldn't believe that someone was going faster than me," says Kariuki, then an avid soccer player. He chased the guy up a hill, and after they reached the top, nearly even, both gasping, the roadie suggested Kariuki join Kenyan Riders. "That's when I started training full time," Kariuki says. "It was a tough decision to quit my mechanic job, because I didn't know if cycling could pay the bills."

I ask him if he thinks East African cyclists can accrue superstar status and become visible in the bike world. "At most races," Kariuki says, "we're the only Black riders out there. I think people will pay attention. I hope they will."

* * *

I spend a week in Iten meeting other Amani riders, each with a story. Twenty-year-old Joel Kyaviro came of age amid civil war in Congo. "In 2012, when I was 10, a bomb fell into our home and killed one of my brothers," he says. "Every time fighting broke out, we ran into the bush and hid."

Salim Kipkemboi, 24, is from the countryside just outside Iten. When he was 10 years old, he had to quit school. He began selling firewood by the roadside. He cut trees down with a handsaw, chopped the wood and then, when he had enough wood to sell, made four or five trips a day out to the road two kilometers away with a large sack of it on his back. His life was so focused on survival that, he says, "I didn't even know Nairobi existed." His muscles were honed, though, and Kenyan Riders discovered him when he was 13. He has now raced in more than 20 countries.

* * *

It's early December, and the Amani riders are tapering in preparation for the first Kenya National Gravel championships, set for December 18. The event is hosted jointly by Amani and the Kenya Cycling Federation, a controversial—and, some argue, tradition-bound—group that has had the same chair, Julius Mwangi, for more than 30 years.

The 63-mile race is open to all comers, with an entry fee set at 500 Kenyan shillings (around $4) to welcome the masses. It seems likely that a large contingent of European and American expats will show.

* * *

What do I have to lose? I sign up, and soon Kariuki is handicapping my chances as he sizes up my hunched 50-something physique. "You'll definitely beat all the other *mzungus*," he says, invoking the Swahili word for white person. "They only train on the weekends."

Generously, the Amani guys let me tag along on a few rides. It's sunny most days. We're almost on the equator, but we're also up above 7,000 feet, so the temperatures are pleasant, around 65 degrees. Most of the children we pass as they walk to school are dressed in uniform-issue V-neck sweaters. Some wear parkas as well. Other kids, upon seeing our little peloton, sprint to the roadside to hail us. Kariuki revels in this heroes' welcome. "Yeah, yeah!" he shouts to our small admirers in Swahili. "You guys are running fast!" When we encounter a group of children splashing about in a river, he shouts, "How's the water?"

There's an ease to these rides that's refreshing. Back home, there's always some goober pushing the pace or hyperfocused on gear or tire pressure. Here the focus is on the riding rather than on who has what component. Amani's athletes all race on quality Factor bikes, sure, but when a part breaks, it might take three weeks for a new one to come. One morning, as I ride with Geoffrey Langat, once a top inline-skate racer and now an ultradistance specialist on Team Amani, the rear wheel on his disc-brake bike is out of commission. He's replaced it temporarily with an old rim-brake wheel, the disc-brake calipers taped to his frame. "I just have to be a little careful on the hills," laughs Langat, who'll race the 350-mile Unbound Gravel XL in Kansas.

Later we pedal into the Bugar Forest, just outside Iten, as shafts of morning sunlight filter down through the conifers onto a narrow, winding dirt path.

As the race date approaches, I book a hotel room near the start line. Then one morning I get disappointing news: Kenya's gravel championship race has been cancelled. The pandemic is in check. Why has this happened? I write to Delagrange. "Sule's absence," he responds, "has never been more acutely felt."

Eventually I learn that negotiations between Amani and the Federation have been less than harmonious. Delagrange assumed that Amani's riders were ironing things out, as Sule once did. He sends the Amani riders a rueful WhatsApp message apologizing for the cancellation. He writes, "It seems my efforts at delegation have failed." The note appeases no one; it just irks the riders.

"It was last minute, just four days before the race," Geoffrey Langat says one afternoon as we're standing by the pump track. "People were already driving there. Mikel wants riders to have more responsibility, and we're willing. But we've never done this before. Someone has to teach us."

The riders' discontent will diminish in a few days, like a lover's temper cooling after a quarrel. But in this moment, it's a very real part of the ambitious, stressful Amani juggernaut. "Sule was good at politics, at dealing with the Federation," John Kariuki says. "But it wasn't easy for him. Sometimes he had to train at night. Gravel racing in East Africa is a new thing. It's like a baby. It needs special care."

I ask Kariuki if he spoke at the long meeting after Sule's burial. "Yes," he tells me, "I said that we have to show the world that this is not the end of this team."

* * *

Later that month, Overland race director Ansel Dickey sends out an 800-word e-mail meant to stoke enthusiasm for the 2023 race. The note quotes the ancient philosopher Marcus Aurelius but does not mention Sule's death. Kevin Bouchard-Hall, who spent seven lonely minutes sitting with Sule post-crash, is stunned. "There wasn't even a mention," he says. "Not a word."

"I can see why Kevin responded as he did," says Dickey, when I reach out for comment. Sule's death, he says, was a "new and terrifying experience for me, and I'm still trying to decide what's the best thing to do."

When I speak to Mikel Delagrange, he makes Team Amani's stance clear: "We don't hold Vermont Overland responsible for Sule's death." He notes that after last year's race, Dickey, who is primarily a filmmaker, released a poignant 16-minute film, *Amani in America*, that lingers on the triumph of the team's stateside journey, delivering, for instance, a slo-mo take of Kariuki getting splashed with champagne at the Overland finish line. Delagrange calls it "a beautiful tribute to Sule."

Delagrange is more focused on Amani's future. He says he's going to stop pressuring the riders to assume the tasks Sule handled. He says he wants "everyone to bring to the project the gifts that they have. They have a world of capacity."

Hellen Wahu, Sule's widow, has computer skills. She honed them long ago, after Sule helped her land a job at a print shop, and in March she relocates from Eldoret to Iten so she can work part time for Team Amani, coordinating the construction of its new buildings. Her kids are enrolled in Iten schools now. One morning, she sends me a video of her oldest child—Lance, 11—ripping it up on the pump track.

The athletes' quarters are now built and slated to open in June. Delagrange is seeking $200,000 in corporate funding for the performance center. He's hired support in Kenya to assist with team management, a nutritionist from Harvard University is volunteering time, and the team is in talks with several coaches. Meanwhile, as I call Delagrange every few days, he keeps talking about a new visionary, a young cyclist named Jean Hubert, who was born in Rwanda during the country's 1994 genocide, in which more than 800,000 people, mostly from the Tutsi ethnic minority, were killed by Hutu militias. University-educated and bike-crazy, although not a racer himself, Hubert, 29, still lives in Rwanda and runs a startup that makes apps.

Along with Delagrange, Hubert is intent on giving Sub-Saharan cyclists autonomy. "Most of these riders, they've never finished high school," he says. "Their lives have been difficult." In his nation's capital, Kigali, under the auspices of Team Amani, he's just opened Spoke Academy, which will see a few Rwandan cyclists spending six months learning communication skills—how to send e-mails, for instance, and how to network with sponsors. Eventually Amani hopes to have 30 teen riders studying at the Academy. "We don't want to just look to *mzungus* for our future," he says, explaining the focus on education.

Hubert is now on Amani's board of directors, and he plans to replicate Spoke Academy in Kenya. "Sule was my friend," he explains. "We're indebted to him. We have to make sure we finish what he started."

Still, I have to wonder: Will the team ever completely shrug off the scars of its founder's death? Can it eventually sail smoothly along as it endeavors to carry young Africans beyond the pain and fragmentation wrought by colonialism?

One morning I have a long conversation with Hubert. He shares that he lost his father in the genocide and that his schoolmates, many of them orphaned, turned to drugs and alcohol. I come away feeling that I've been misguided in looking for Team Amani to transcend Sule's death. The pain and the fragmentation that shrouds this team may last in some form forever. What's meaningful is the struggle away from it, no matter how lurching, no matter how flawed and how human.

"We will keep asking riders to take the lead," Hubert says. "We want to build citizens that have confidence in themselves, and that's hard to do—the donor mind-set is very rooted. Unrooting it will take a long time. But it will happen. Trust me. It will."

EXPLORATION

Breaking up the Boys Club
Outside, *October 2, 2019*

THE MAP OF SOUTHWEST TASMANIA IS AN UNBROKEN EXPANSE OF FOR-est green. There are no towns and no roads on this remote section of Australia's largest island. There's nothing save for a few sharply creased mountains and an array of lakes and streams. In many pockets of the rainforest, an endemic tree, the slow-growing horizontal scrub, sprouts a noxious tangle of drooping branches that spawn vertical shoots and crosshatching suckers until the woods are all but impenetrable. In 1822, when the Brits ran penal colonies in Tasmania, a group of escaped con-victs ate one another while attempting a getaway through this forest.

Last year, though, a Swiss explorer, 47-year-old Sarah Marquis, set out on a three-month, south-to-north solo traverse of Tasmania that included a long push through this thick rainforest. Moving forward at roughly two miles a day, carrying a 75-pound pack in the constant rain, Marquis hacked through the vinelike woody snares with a machete. She clambered at times to the top of the thicket, where she was frequently forced to trample on tree limbs 15 feet above the forest floor. She could have died stepping on a rotten branch.

But what got her was a steep ravine roughly 500 yards across at its top. On the second day of thrashing her way down through the first side of the ravine's waterlogged, vine-snared V, the muddy soil gave way beneath her, and she was swept, along with a cascade of rocks and ferns and trees, into a cold river. She blacked out, and when she awoke, she was facedown in the water. Her left arm screamed in pain. Her sat phone was useless at the shadowed base of the canyon. Was she just going to die down there?

Marquis had certainly been in tight spots before. She's a hiking specialist who spends months, sometimes even years, walking across scarcely traveled swaths of earth. From 2010 to 2013, she trekked 10,000 miles from Siberia to the Gobi Desert, then (after 13 days on a cargo ship) across Australia. In 2015, on another visit to Oz, she spent three months subsisting almost entirely on roots and grubs that she caught and fish that she snared. She has camped in minus-30-degree cold and endured blizzards, sandstorms, mudslides, dengue fever, and an almost fatal tooth infection.

Marquis is a modern-day explorer—but though anguish and suffering are as part and parcel of her expeditions as they were to early polar explorers like Robert Peary and Roald Amundsen, her goals are different. A hundred and ten years ago, the objectives of exploration were clear: you pointed yourself at some blank spot on the map and then muscled toward it and planted your flag. Today, however, nearly all terra incognita on the planet is gone. Conquering is a dead art.

"We've moved away from focusing on exploration for exploration's sake," says Cheryl Zook, director of the Explorers Program at the National Geographic Society. The program now funds filmmakers and oceanographers, anthropologists and crime investigators. It also funds Marquis, who's been a National Geographic Explorer since 2015 and is the author of seven French-language books about her expeditions.

Okay, there are still a few superstrivers who chase after clearly delineated iconic goals—American Colin O'Brady, for instance, who in 2018 became the first person to cross all 932 miles of the Antarctic landmass solo, unaided and unsupported, a feat he accomplished in 54 days while pulling a 300-pound sled. Arguably, though, the new soul of exploration lies in less harried and more imaginative quadrants, where a disparate constellation of world wanderers is dreaming up new ways to draw meaningful lines on our thoroughly traveled globe. Think here of Paul Salopek, a Pulitzer Prize–winning journalist now on a multiyear, 21,000-mile global walk that is retracing the paths of the first human migrants to disperse from Africa in the Stone Age. Salopek's cross-cultural journey is of a piece with an earlier feat of new-school exploration, swimmer Lynne Cox's 2.7-mile traverse of the Bering Strait between Alaska and Russia in 1987. In 44-degree waters, in the shadow of the Cold War, Cox was trying to forge détente between the United States and the Soviet Union.

Modern exploration isn't necessarily steeped in geopolitical themes. It's about probing new depths on old turf with an inventive flourish and passion. In June 2019, on Strava, recently retired Tour de France cyclist Ted King posted a 182-mile, nine-plus-hour Vermont–New Hampshire back-roads ramble, captioning it, "I rode to see my dad to wish him a Happy Father's Day."

Yes, I thought, pressing the "kudos" button within the app. The man's an explorer.

Sometimes the new-school explorer travels inward, searching for forgotten zones of the human psyche. Marquis says she travels—and crawls through deserts and rivers and mud—to "rediscover the lost language between humans and the animal kingdom." She aims, always, for an unmitigated one-on-one communion with nature. She wants to prove that, even amid the abstracted digital fog of our 21st-century lives, a human being can still sit alone by a campfire and feel primitive, like an animal.

Marquis's goal is entirely her own invention—she is, if nothing else, a free woman—and in chasing after that goal, she has been catcalled and harassed in most of the earth's major languages. She has not flinched, perhaps because she's been too focused on evading the other crazy perils that pervade all great adventure.

Down in the ravine, it turned out, Marquis had snapped the top of her humerus, the big, upper bone in her arm. She considered downing an emergency dose of Tramadol, a painkilling opiate. But she couldn't afford to numb her senses. There were scores of black snakes in the underbrush, and her sat phone wouldn't work down there, amid the thick vegetation. She would need to hike out for three days to find reception and a clearing big enough for a helicopter landing.

So she did. Off-balance, thanks to her pack and her gimp arm, she fell, over and over. Each crash sent a crescendo of pain into her shoulder.

She met the copter, and then, two weeks later, against doctor's orders, returned to her hiking route. She had to skip the last section of dense bush, but she spent three weeks completing a modified, easier version of her intended hike, walking mostly on flat, treeless paths, wincing each time her pack jostled her shoulder.

* * *

It's January now, nearly a year after the completion of Marquis's Tasmanian expedition, and I'm visiting her in Switzerland, in her tiny, 400-square-foot, '70s-era chalet, which sits a half mile off the nearest all-season road in the Swiss Alps. It's cold outside, and she's wearing a black fleece, black sweatpants, and beige Uggs as she sits on a stool in her kitchen. Her long blond hair is in disarray. We're watching snow fall in the sparse forest outside, down onto the boughs of the evergreens. There are houses nearby, but they are snow-caked summer houses, and the world is so quiet that I think I hear the snow falling.

Marquis bought this house, the long-neglected summer abode of a distinguished Geneva family, in 2017. Trash cluttered the home's warren of mini bedrooms at closing; there was a desiccated crow in the chimney. Still, Marquis envisioned the place a "quiet writer's cave." In an e-mail, she told me, "I've been waiting all my life for such a place."

In the past, she's tapped out her books in a mountain bungalow in Thailand, on a windblown crag in the Swiss Alps, and deep in the Spanish countryside. Now she's pinioned at home, nursing a broken rib, this injury sustained in a prosaic tumble down a snowy Swiss staircase. She's writing a book about her Tasmanian travels, and taped to a picture window, on Post-it Notes, are hand-scrawled ideas for her first draft. I feel like I've stepped into her mind, into her dream. I remember what she wrote to me earlier, discussing the cabin: "I will spend the harsh winter of the Swiss Alps here, with no vehicle access. I'll move with a canoe in summer and on foot in winter."

I've come here to imbibe Marquis's idyllic cabin life and also to meditate on a question that I often ask myself, being a journalist who's reported stories on six continents: How does a restless person find a still spot in the world? How can a nomad make a home that is at once sustaining and invigorating, not boring?

I want Marquis to tell me that she's going to learn the names of all the plants and birds outside her door. I want her to tell me that she'll live in this house until she dies, that she's already 800 pages into writing a book about the place. But now, as she cooks us some organic vegan whole-wheat pasta, she's backpedaling from her florid e-mail. "This is just a base camp for me," she says. "That's all. It's a place to store my fancy clothes. This is not my type of bush here. I belong to the Australian bush. I know every bird there, every tree, and I'd take a eucalyptus over a pine any day. And no"—she laughs, rolling her eyes before dissing me in her Australian-tinged English—"I don't think of dying here. I don't even have a bloody idea what I'm doing next week."

Jeezum, did I fly all the way across the Atlantic to get tacks thrown into my path like this? I can already sense a certain tension: I'm a man, here to write about a woman who's prevailed in life because she's kicked back against men who sought to write her script.

On the steppes of Mongolia, drunken nomads on horseback galloped out to Marquis's tent night after night and surrounded her, taunting her, just for fun. Marquis, in turn, terrorized two such antagonists after they charged at her with their horses. "I throw myself toward them all at once, arms in the air and screaming like a madwoman," she writes in *Wild by Nature*, the only book of hers that has been translated into English. She's intent on "scaring them and throwing them off balance," and she succeeds. "They glare angrily, understanding that I'm not afraid," she writes. "They depart without another word."

During my four-day stay, Marquis will be nothing but gracious, buying me one Swiss chocolate bar after another. But throughout, her message remains clear: men need to reframe how they think about women in exploration.

Marquis and I travel one afternoon to the nearby village of Chandolin, to visit the onetime home of her childhood idol, legendary 20th-century Swiss explorer and writer Ella Maillart. Maillart competed in the 1924 Olympics as a sailor and then went on to lead an all-women's sailing mission to Crete and travel across the Takla Makan Desert from Beijing to India with journalist Peter Fleming. Marquis becomes incensed when we discover that the town's only Maillart museum is a single, unattended room arrayed with a few dusty photographs. "This is bullshit," she says. "If Ella Maillart was a man, there'd be a brand-new museum here, with videos and sound effects."

In time I'll learn of how Marquis slept in pink leggings every night in the Mongolian desert, just to feel feminine as she towed a bulky cart through the dirt. I'll discover her Martha Stewart side, when she gives me a copy of her coffee-table book *La nature dans ma vie* (*Nature in My Life*), which gives readers tips on how they can be just like her, supported by 40 photos of the author—Marquis sitting lotus style, her flowing tresses exquisitely coiffed, her makeup just so; Marquis communing winsomely with a wicker basket of garden-fresh carrots; and so on.

Sarah Marquis is reframing what an explorer can do and be. So can't I reframe my own understanding of how her life works?

Maybe I'll have to, for she has never fit neatly into anyone else's story line.

* * *

Marquis grew up on a farm in Switzerland's rainy north country, surrounded by ducks and chicken and sheep, in a village so remote that she didn't see a movie in a theater until she was 15. She and her brother, Joel, who's two years younger, named each of the towering beech trees near their home. They climbed into the crowns of the trees, balancing on narrow branches 60 feet up as they swayed in the wind.

Starting when Marquis was five, her mother took her into the forest to hunt for mushrooms and medicinal plants. "I was learning everything about survival," says Marquis.

As a teenager, she left home for a railway job that involved traveling all over Switzerland, managing the operations of trains. Her coworkers, older men mostly, harassed her. (According to a *New York Times Magazine* profile of Marquis, on her first day, one colleague proclaimed that he could smell when she was on her period.) She took such taunts as a challenge. At age 17, alone, she rode a horse across Turkey. Then, in her 20s, she worked as a waitress at a ski resort and ventured, often, on brave expeditions that tested her still meager outdoor skills. She ventured into the bush of New Zealand's South Island, for example, endeavoring to live for a month only on fish that she speared. She lost 15 pounds.

Eventually, when she was 29, Marquis conceived her first grand expedition—an 8,700-mile loop around the interior of Australia. She was still a waitress; major sponsorship was a pipe dream. But Joel, by then an accomplished engineer and windsurfer who traveled the world in search of waves, was in her corner—and he was lucky. One day Joel bought a two-dollar lottery ticket and found, scratching it, three miniature TV icons in a row. He'd earned a hard-to-come-by invite onto a Swiss game show.

Before a live audience, Joel won $25,000. He used the funds to launch his sister's expedition. "Nobody thought she could make it," he explained to me, "but I knew she could. When we climbed those trees, she was steady and strong." Joel flew to Australia so he could serve as expedition coordinator, and the siblings collaborated with an ease and a fluidity that at times transcended language. "There wasn't any need to explain things," Marquis says. "We were in a desert, without landmarks or trees, and he'd leave a food drop, and I'd know where it was."

Marquis's first book, *L'aventurière des sables* (*The Adventurer of the Sands*), published in 2004, recounted that Australia trip. She self-published it, at the age of 32. Then she visited every bookstore in French-speaking Switzerland and genially, over coffee, cajoled dozens of store owners to buy the book on her own special terms—money up front, no returns. She spoke at more than 100 schools, accompanied by her dog and her brother, who punctuated her stories by riffing on his didgeridoo. Video snippets of her Australian adventure began showing up on Swiss television.

In 2006, Marquis spent eight months on a solo hike through the Andes, battling altitude sickness as she made her way to Machu Picchu. In 2010, she began her trek from Siberia to Australia. Gradually, and quite casually, Marquis became a household name in French-speaking Switzerland. A loyal contingent of fans bought every book that she wrote, and her fame seeped into France. The French edition of her 2014 book,

Wild by Nature, sold 180,000 copies, and in 2018, the French sports magazine *L'Equipe* put her on the cover.

Marquis is now sponsored by Icebreaker (an underwear brand), the North Face, Sportiva boots, Tissot watches, and Debiopharm, a Swiss pharmaceutical company. But she says she gets no salary. "They just fund an expedition if they like it," she says of her sponsors. "I have to fight for the money every time. I still work my ass off."

Marquis's publisher, Elsa Lafon, says that the explorer is popular because there's really nothing transcendent or superhuman about her. "Sarah has no background as an Olympian, and she's not an extreme skier or snowboarder," explains Lafon. "She's walking, and walking is something everyone can do. It's also a spiritual activity. People want to live as she does, and when I was with her in Switzerland, everyone stopped her to take pictures."

Like so many celebrities, Marquis is torn about her status as a public figure. In a way, she loves it. When we're at a restaurant one afternoon, she begins snapping photos of our food. "You can't even imagine how many young women follow me on Instagram," she explains happily. "There's a whole new wave of single women out there traveling alone now. They're not waiting for the perfect partner to do the journey." Marquis knows she's their role model. "I'm not attached to some magical guy who's paying for everything," she says. "And you'll never see me doing a photo shoot in a bikini. I could have played that game. I didn't."

But if Marquis loves inspiring young acolytes, she still likes her privacy. We're sitting in a remote booth at the restaurant, to avoid gawkers, and now she tells me that her highest ideal is "pure exploration. I want to be in nature until I become nature," she explains, "until it doesn't matter whether I'm a man or a woman and I arrive at the core of things."

* * *

When Marquis bought the chalet, it should have been razed. Starting afresh—building a brand-new cabin—would have been easier than breathing new life into a ruin, but the local Swiss zoning regulations forbid teardowns.

Marquis turned to her brother for assistance—that was a given. No one in her life (save perhaps her mother) has been more unwaveringly supportive. When Sarah and I meet Joel one afternoon at a café, I note that sister and brother share the same tilt to their heads, the same glinting smile. Joel is more settled now. He and his partner have two kids, and he has a lucrative gig as a Swiss Alps tour guide. He's always up for a challenge, though, so he and Sarah spent a month filling two dumpsters with garbage as they meditated on an architectural challenge: How do you transform a moldy, claustrophobic bunkhouse into a stylish writer's hermitage?

Their scheme came together jaggedly, with nothing written on paper. "We came up with a new plan every day," says Sarah, "and then we changed our minds."

The process, more intuitive than logical, is of a piece with the strategies Marquis deploys to survive in the wilds. She prepares meticulously, drying and vacuum-sealing all her own food, but out in the field she's guided quite often by her gut. Once, when she was camping beneath a cliff in China, she had a premonition that there'd be an avalanche. She moved her tent. Ten minutes later, according to Sarah, the rocks buried her earlier campsite. In Australia in 2015, she says, she evolved a Spidey sense as to which creeks contained crocodiles and which didn't. ("I became a crocodile," she says.) She claims to carry an internal compass, so that she can tell which way is north, without even consulting the stars.

"Women have more of an animal sense," she says. "We're made to bear a child. We're hormonal creatures, and we are able to feel our bodies and the earth. And surviving in the wild isn't just about strength. You need to have an understanding of the landscape. Women have that, and they can use that to survive."

Even though she's intent on liberating women everywhere, there's still a bit of the old-world explorer about Sarah Marquis. In the tradition of travel writers such as Paul Theroux and V. S. Naipaul, she is unafraid to be dismissive of the people she meets in the field. *Wild by Nature* sees her lampooning some of the Mongolians she encounters as "fat" and as "idiots" as she gripes about how they "pee right next to me" and frequent a bar that "smells of musty oldness mixed with vomit." In fairness, she also reports on the generosity of local women who help her out. In reviewing the book, *Publisher's Weekly* complained about her "long diatribes," saying they "sometimes border on the culturally insensitive."

When I ask her about that review, she's not pleased with me. "Americans," she says, "have no idea of how the world works. What is that reviewer saying? That it's okay for me to be attacked every night? So I'm culturally insensitive? I bloody don't care. That's your problem!"

I'm not sure if she means me or the reviewer, and I'm a little afraid to ask. But I guess I'm not shocked that her rough travel experiences have leavened her romantic streak with a sliver of grim, Hobbesian skepticism about human nature. "Look," she says, still dwelling on her Mongolian attackers, "it's complicated. On that trip, I learned empathy. I became a better person. But we are all animals at the base. Everyone's got their own world, and sometimes you are not welcome in that world. I wasn't welcome there."

So she keeps coming home, back to the mountains of Switzerland, where she has now finally built a house of her own, through arduous labor.

In the end, Marquis tore out most of the chalet's walls and folded the kitchen around a new wood-burning stove that feeds to the chimney. There are still distinct rooms, but there are no doors on the office or the dining nook, and light pours in through the glass entry door. The white pine decor, meanwhile, is buoyantly bright.

For me, though, what leaps out is that this chalet is shaped to house a single creative person—a second resident would be a stretch. In *Wild by Nature*, Marquis covers her romantic life glancingly, alluding to "hairy, bare chests where I rested my head for an instant," and in another book she mentions a breakup that "left me as scarred as if I'd fallen from a five-story building." At one point she tells me, "I love everything about men. There is nothing so exciting as a man who knows his strengths, his inner beauty."

But she still seems likely to keep inhabiting her tiny home by her lonesome. "I've had long relationships," she tells me, "but always, after some time, the man wants more, and I'm like, More of what? What they want more of is me, and I will not compromise who I am to be with a man."

Marquis gazes out the window, contemplating, then continues. "But I don't know," she says. "Love has everything to do with freedom—with deep communication, with allowing your partner to do what they want. But I've never met a man who's understood me completely." She rises up from her chair now. "Oh!" she says, throwing her arms up in faux exasperation. "Let's go for a walk."

* * *

We step out of the chalet, Marquis coughing a bit each time the frayed edge of her rib tickles her lungs, and we stroll along a cross-country ski trail, chatting about the guises she assumes out on expedition. "I dress like a man," she says, "for safety, and if I need to talk to somebody, I'm like this." She drops her shoulders now, so her arms hang, apelike and foreboding, by her sides as she continues in a low, gravelly voice. "'Where's water?' If they say something," she continues, "I jump right in. I don't give them any time to think." Her voice goes gravelly again. "'Is it a good stream? How far?'"

We keep walking. She tells me about the training she does in the six-month lead-up to each expedition. On a typical day, she says, she might run for an hour, then do a three-hour hike to a peak carrying a 65-pound backpack before swimming two or three miles. "By six at night," she says, "I am dead."

We pass a lone skier poling along, and then Marquis shares a trick she learned years ago, studying karate. It involves watching one's opponent closely, waiting for his focus to ebb, and then moving in for a flash strike. To my surprise, she demonstrates, suddenly jabbing her arm toward my chest, so I stagger backward a step. "It's useful," she says of the move.

When we reach the village and come to the garage where she parks her car, she opens the back to load some stuff in, and then, wanting to be of help, I press down on the hatch, trying to close it. The thing does not budge, not at all, so then, instinctively, I just reef on that hatch. I push down on it, hard, until I hear Marquis beside me, shuddering in distress. "Don't," she says. "Don't! It's hydraulic!"

"Oh," I say. "Sorry."

As we wind down out of the mountains, switchbacking, gazing at the roofs of the houses below, I apologize again. But then, when we're in a parking lot with the hatch open, I forget. I find myself muscling down on the damned thing again.

"Bill, Bill, Bill!" Marquis says, copping a feigned scolding tone. She's laughing, but still I have to wonder why I'm doing this. I'm a spacehead—that's part of it. But do I also feel the need to demonstrate my strength? I have to admit, I do. I feel intimidated by Marquis. She's blended her feminine qualities and raw physical strength to become a force on her own terms, an athlete and explorer I'll never match.

It's easy for men to say they champion the end of sexism in the out-doors, but when women start thrashing us or even marginalizing us? That takes a little recalibration. Speaking plainly, it's hard on the fragile male ego. It stings sometimes. I'm not condoning the drunken Mongolian nomads or the Swiss dingleberries who threw Ella Maillart's life history into a closet-size dustbin, but I do understand their mind-set—and also how pathetic it is.

* * *

I'm staying in the village, in a sunlit hillside condo. I can't tell you the name of the burg (I promised), but there are a few hundred people here and a post office and a café in which the village's most distinguished female residents gather each morning at 8:30 to chat. The *supermarché* carries only one small rack of books, all of them by Sarah Marquis, but when fans show up, seeking an audience with the author, the store's clerks throw them off the scent.

The realtor across the street from the store is also protective of Sarah who, before buying the chalet, lived in the village on and off for years in a succession of rentals. Françoise is 70-something, and petite, and inclined to wear black leather trousers à la Joan Jett. It is she who sold Sarah her house. "Other people were interested," she tells me, "but I said, 'No, it is not for sale.'"

Françoise, I think, felt a kinship with Sarah. She's done some explor-ing herself—in 1980, she flew around the world on the Concorde—and the two women are friends. When I meet with them for coffee one morning, they sit side by side and regard one another with a glimmering affection, reveling, it seems, in the knowledge that they are both free spirits and fierce.

Still, when I'm invited one evening to celebrate Françoise's birthday at the café, Sarah isn't there. The fondue party goes on without her. And Françoise, speaking precisely, suggests that the absence carries a certain rightness.

"She is part of the village, and she is not," Françoise says. "As she wishes."

* * *

"So," I ask, "where are you going for your next expedition?" Marquis is taking me to the train station. "Antarctica?"

"That's for the boys. They love to gear up and go fast. They love that physical challenge." I scribe these words into my notebook and, watching me as she swoops through the switchbacks, Marquis becomes irked. "Come on," she says. "I know you're going to use that quote out of context."

I change the subject. "Okay," I say. "But what's, like, your system for determining where you're going to go?"

Do I really expect there to be an intricate mathematical process? Or that she'll let me in on the secret? She tells me she looks for signs. Earlier she showed me a picture of a dragon's blood tree on Yemen's arid Socotra Island. It was at once Seussian and soulful, a giant, mushroom-shaped thing with knotted brown branches and palmlike green needles. "One day," she says, "I'd like to go there." When Yemen's civil war ends, she means.

We wind pass the church spire in a lower village. "But how long do you think you'll keep doing expeditions?" I ask.

"I don't know," Sarah says sharply. "I don't think the way you do." A moment later, she softens. "I'm going to be an awesome old woman," she says. "My face will be a topo map of all the places I've been. I'll be a little dry apple, but I will never get old."

When we reach the train station, I remember the hydraulic thing as I retrieve my suitcase from the back of the car. Sarah walks me out onto the platform. Per Swiss tradition, she kisses me three times on the cheeks—right, then left, then right. And then she walks away, and I watch the woman who can go anywhere in the world climb into her car and start back up the switchbacks toward her chalet in the snow.

Kindergarten Can Wait

Backpacker, *June 10, 2015*

WE SWOOP AROUND ANOTHER TURN IN THE MOUNTAINS. THE ROAD gets a bit steeper, and in the January rain, a gray tendril of mist drifts over the green woods. The engine churns as our car labors uphill. Beside me, the little boy in a car seat stares out the window. Christian Thomas is 5 years old and reed-thin with rosy, cherubic cheeks, and by now he has eaten about half of the chocolate donut holes contained in the 14-ounce Walmart box in his lap. What's on his mind? Is he dreading the hike planned for today? Plenty of adults would be anxious about a 15-mile trek in a chilly downpour, hoofing it up and down on the Appalachian Trail as it rolls through Shenandoah National Park. Or is he just mesmerized by the fat raindrops lashing at the windows?

Quiet, quiet, quiet. There are crinkled paper bags wadded on the floor of the car, a thrashed 1996 Jeep Cherokee, and dirty laundry is strewn everywhere. Yet somehow amid the chaos, this kid is tranquil, composed—put together. His brown hair is neatly parted. His manner is genial, and when he speaks he exudes the incongruous panache of a TV reporter delivering the news from outside a low-rent apartment complex. "I like fog," he says in a high, fluty voice. "It's cool! When you see a person, it's like, wow, he magicked here."

Christian giggles, charmed by his own wit. Then he keeps eating donut holes, and his mother turns around to peer back at him. Andrea Rego is 26, with long brunette pigtails. In her most recent job, she did office work at a construction company on Long Island. She can be feisty. Like a moment ago, frustrated, she said, "I'm gonna burn this car when this trip is done!" Now, in a sweet baby voice, she tells her son, "You can have as many of those as you want, bud. Eat up." She turns to me and adds, "I'd be happy if he ate the whole box. He needs the calories."

Maybe he does: It's early 2014 and Christian is hiking the entire Appalachian Trail, all 2,180 miles, with his mom and stepdad (well, technically his mom's boyfriend), Dion Pagonis, 29. Christian—now best known by his trail name, Buddy Backpacker—started eight months ago, in Harper's Ferry, West Virginia, and he's trudged through snow in North Carolina and black flies in Maine. He's slept with his Pooh Bear every night and he's out-hiked his mom. She stopped after just 400 miles, electing to chauffeur, which improved their resupply logistics and enabled Buddy and Dion to walk without heavy packs. In a week, after hiking numerous trail sections out of sequence, the trio will return to Harper's Ferry. Christian will become the youngest person in history to complete the AT. After that, the family plans to hike the Pacific Crest Trail (2,650 miles) and the Continental Divide Trail (3,100 miles).

At the moment, Christian weighs just 46 pounds. So he keeps eating donut holes, and then, after a while, he groans. "I don't feel too good, Mommy," he says. "My stomach hurts."

"You'll feel better when you start hiking, Bud," Andrea says, again in the baby voice. "You always do."

Dion says nothing. Almost always, Dion is silent.

We park at the trailhead, and when we climb out of the car the wind is ripping. When Andrea pulls a transparent rain poncho over Christian's jacket, it rattles in the gale. No other hikers are out. There are hardly any cars in the whole park, and it's still pouring. Being a parent myself, I think, "Now's when it happens. Now is when the kid throws a tantrum in protest."

But Christian is placid. His bellyache is gone or forgotten, and he's skipping around in the parking lot and enlisting me as a straight man for his pranks. (I'm still a novelty, having just arrived to hike with him for three days.) "Knock knock," he says.

"Who's there?"

"Car go."

"Car go who?"

"Car go beep beep." He throws his head back and laughs, so the parking lot fills for a moment with bright peals of joy.

"How many miles can you hike in a day?" he asks me as we start hiking.

"I don't know. About 20."

"That's nothing! I did 22 miles one day and I wasn't even tired."

* * *

How far is too far? How much toil and suffering should a kid take—and what for? A generation ago, back when children roamed the streets freely, pedaling their banana seat bikes in a time before helmets, no one fretted over such questions. When a six-year-old boy named Michael Cogswell thru-hiked the entire Appalachian Trail with his parents in 1980, there was nothing but feel-good rhetoric surrounding his hike. Newspapers made light of how the little boy crashed constantly, weighted by his pack, and this magazine ran a celebratory story in which the author, Michael's stepdad Jeffrey Cogswell, waxed poetic about the trailside flora—"red trillium, violets, purple ironweed"—and lionized the little boy's perseverance as a photo showed a wonderstruck Michael drinking from an ice-skimmed mountain creek.

Now, though, childrearing is a science, and sniping at other people's parenting techniques may be our favorite contact sport. When journalist Lenore Skenazy decided in 2008 to let her nine-year-old son ride the New York subway alone, she received thousands of hate letters and was called "America's Worst Mom." (Her response: freerangekids.com.) Similar skepticism has surrounded two Texas sisters who run half-marathons. When the *New York Times* profiled Kaytlynn Welsch, 12, and Heather Welsch, 10, in 2012, the headline asked, "Too Fast Too Soon?" One reader responded, "This is child abuse."

Any parent who loves the outdoors can find him- or herself pushing the envelope, sometimes unwittingly. I will confess that when my own daughter, now 20, was in preschool, I took her on a kayak trip during which our inflatable boat sprung a leak. Our tent and sleeping bags slipped out into the rapids, and I spent a frigid, sleepless night chastising myself for being selfish and negligent. But that was just a weekend. To thru-hike the AT, Christian has had to climb over rocks and roots almost every day for nine months, overcoming challenges that defeat plenty of adults, even as his young sinew and bones are still growing. Naturally, his parents have critics. In one recent post on a Facebook page, a hiker named Yvonne called Andrea out. "If BB's mother is still on here and viewing these posts, I want to challenge you!" she wrote. "I challenge you to take a moment, step back and ask yourself who this Appalachian Trail hike adventure and experience is all about . . . if it truly is about Buddy . . . allow him to explore, allow him stop and love the mountain views."

An AT stalwart calling himself GreyWolf took a harder line, alleging that Dion and Andrea brought Buddy hiking in unsafe conditions. "The temperature never got above the 20s and was in the teens at night. Should I call social services?" he railed.

But the family's Facebook pictures from Christian's journey on the AT voice a strong rejoinder to skeptics. Here's the boy standing atop Katahdin, his arms raised in triumph. Here he is catching snowflakes on his tongue on Christmas Eve in the Smokies. As I scroll through the images, I can't help but marvel at how Christian has experienced so much delight at such a young age. And part of me wonders: Should we really be asking if Andrea Rego is a bad mom for setting her son on such an arduous task? Is the correct question, in fact, Is she the best mother ever?

* * *

Certainly, she started from a rough spot.

When Andrea got pregnant with Christian in 2008, she was in her second year of college at Stony Brook University, in New York. She was 20 years old, overweight, and ensconced in a nine-month romance with a man from whom she is now estranged.

"I hoped Christian would bring some stability to my life," she says. The plan failed. After the birth, Andrea continued attending college for a year, but then quit to work full time. Logging 50 to 60 hours a week at the construction company, Andrea, who is five feet four, ballooned to 200 pounds. "By the time I picked Christian up at daycare," she says, "I was so tired that we just went to McDonald's or ate frozen food in front of the television. Christian wouldn't eat anything if it wasn't in a package. He was addicted to TV."

Soon, though, Andrea grew closer to her friend Dion Pagonis, who had his own unfulfilling (but lucrative) job on Long Island, working in a windowless room at Sherman Specialty, the world's largest supplier of restaurant crayons. Dion, who is also five feet four, once weighed well over 250 pounds. But he is not one to live in quiet desperation forever. He's ambitious, in idiosyncratic ways. In high school, he earned his Eagle Scout badge supervising a team that re-created a Native American village. In college, at SUNY Fredonia, he was the president of Greek life.

In 2007, Dion bought a Wii Fit and began working out three hours a day. He lost 70 pounds. Not long after, Andrea joined a gym and began working out, too. By 2011, Dion was fit enough to try the AT, solo. (He made it 200 miles before twisting his ankle.) Later, he convinced Andrea to join him for a backpacking trip in Colorado. She had never before gone on an overnight hike, and she was still smoking a pack a day. Over a weekend, they covered only seven miles. "It was very hard," she says, "but I loved it—just being outside, away from Long Island."

In spring 2012, finally, Dion engineered an escape plan. He and Andrea sold nearly all their possessions and moved west to Colorado, first to Boulder, then to Crested Butte, a ski town where Dion scored design gigs at elance.com and they operated a hostel called Butte Bunk. While Dion snowboarded, Christian (then four) and Andrea took to the bunny hill on skis. "By the end of the season," Andrea writes at buddybackpacker.com, Christian "was blowing down moguls and double blacks on one of the hardest mountains in the United States. He has the endurance of an advanced athlete with a deep love for nature. Andrea and Dion have no choice but to live epic lives with him."

The experience in Crested Butte changed the trajectory of their lives. Suddenly, the pair hoped to bring Buddy to California, so they could all learn to surf. They thought they'd like to try a long-distance mountain bike odyssey somewhere. They wanted to put themselves on a path toward adventure, and test their own endurance as well as Christian's. In Colorado, as the snow melted, Andrea envisioned another kind of adventure. "Why don't we hike the Appalachian Trail?" she asked Dion in April

2013. Crested Butte was about to button up for the off-season. So they bought the well-used Jeep for $1,500, loaded their gear, and headed east.

* * *

It's very slow hiking with Dion and Christian, and also a little bit solemn. Both of them walk with iPods and headphones. Dion listens to rock, Christian to educational music and lessons—brainy stuff chosen by Dion. (The digital lessons are the backbone of Christian's homeschooling program.) All I can hear, moving along through the woods, is the dull thud of footfalls and the rain pattering on the dead, sodden leaves. We roll along over gentle hills, passing rocky outcroppings that open onto the gray horizon, and eventually (inspired by his music, it seems) Christian begins skipping and weaving on the trail.

"Pay attention," Dion tells him. "Look where you're going."

"I love the Octopus's Garden song," Christian says when it comes on his iPod.

"Please don't sing it," says Dion. Then he adds, "Take your hands out of your pockets. Christian! Listen to instructions!"

In downtime at occasional hotels, Dion and Christian cuddle up together and watch movies on Andrea's iPad. Out on the trail, though, the dialogue is nearly all safety oriented during the 40 miles I hike with them. To me, Dion explains, "If he trips and breaks an arm, our hike is over." In New Hampshire, Dion made Christian a promise: "If you don't have any boo-boos when we get to Katahdin, I'll give you some money." Christian lost that challenge, scraping his knee in a crash.

Now, though, it's Dion who's holding us back. Still a bit chunky at 180 pounds, he isn't a particularly fast hiker, and he's plagued with what he calls "Fred Flintstone feet"—his arches are almost convex. At times, Christian and I drift ahead. Then, I ask Christian about his audio lessons. He's learning vocabulary words: *nefarious, subvert, fetid,* and *encumbered.*

"What's the teacher saying right now?"

He squints a moment, listening. Then he parrots the saccharine voice from his iPod: "We're so encumbered with red tape we can't get any real work done."

When we meet Andrea at a road crossing, Christian runs toward her, laughing, to hug her. We all get a moment of sweet reprieve, but only a moment. Andrea says, "I always feel like we're a pit crew in a car race. It's like, 'You tie his shoes. I'll put food in his mouth.' We're always rushing to get him back on the trail." She turns to Christian. "Are you ready for some Pringles, Bud?" Looking back at me, she says, "He loves Pringles— that's his favorite food."

Christian takes a small stack, and then as we step into the woods, I glance back at our mission vehicle: The Jeep is a dull red, with "buddy-backpacker.com" and a big pair of angel wings, in yellow, that Dion drew on the hood. (The wings signify trail angels, as Andrea often gives other hikers rides.) The Jeep has 150,000 miles on it, but they've been hard miles; it looks like it might die on the next hill.

* * *

The Buddy Backpacker expedition is not a well-oiled machine, and by the time I joined, there'd been a medley of calamities. On the first night of the trip, after the family rolled out of Crested Butte, Andrea left her wallet at a convenience store. As Dion dislikes carrying money, the trio was broke. They made camp after midnight near Manhattan, Kansas, in a cold wind, and struggled setting up their tent for the first time. "I was shivering," Dion remembers.

"After just two restless hours, the family pressed east, toward West Virginia and the start of their hike—and the start of their controversial trail strategies. Many hikers have attacked Andrea and Dion for being loosey-goosey—and also lazy—on the AT. Sometimes when faced with a big hill, they make things easy on themselves. They drove to the top of Mt. Washington twice, for instance, so Christian could hike down each side. (He never actually climbed Washington.) When it was snowing in the Smokies, they skipped ahead, down to Georgia, then came back weeks later. They took about 90 days off, in total, enabling Dion to earn much-needed money by doing design projects. They were simply hiking their own hike, to invoke the credo that pervades AT culture, but that counted little with backpacking's grand poohbahs, who in many cases have built their lives around the AT and come to style themselves the keepers of the trail's sacred mores.

"They were sloppy," says Warren Doyle, a retired college professor who's hiked the AT a record 16 times. "They did a lot of lollygagging, and they got into trouble because of that. They were out hiking far later into the winter than they needed to be." (Doyle, ironically, has critics himself. On his Appalachian Trail Expeditions, a support vehicle carts gear for hikers, enabling them to sashay nearly all 2,000-plus miles bearing nothing but daypacks.)

Other critics questioned if they were actually on the trail at all, suggesting that Christian's parents cheated by skipping several stretches of the AT, even as they pretend-logged the miles online.

"There are some people who are lying about thru-hiking the Appalachian Trail and, since it's almost Christmas, I'm not going to name them yet," wrote a man named Tom Bazemore on Facebook. "This will give them a chance to come clean and end their con game." Bazemore, who runs a Georgia-based shuttle company, continued by directly addressing his targets: "You are certainly not the first to lie about hiking the entire trail but the fact that you are using a little child in this con is truly beyond belief!"

Seventy-one comments followed, most of them nasty, and Andrea snarled back: "I hope you all are completely ashamed of yourselves for spewing such nonsense. I can't wait until we are finished and can laugh looking back at all you haters."

I called Bazemore to ask which sections Buddy and his folks had skipped. His complaints zeroed in on a 30.3-mile stretch of trail between Newfound Gap, North Carolina, and Davenport Gap, Tennessee. "I shuttled some hikers there exactly when [Christian and Dion] were supposed to be there," he said, "and I told these people to look for a man with a five-year-old boy. They never saw them."

Dion had anticipated such critiques, however. In his own Facebook post, he wrote, "If I wasn't hiking with Buddy, I would be skeptical of his accomplishment, too." So along the length of the AT, he took photographs with a GPS camera and then posted them to a map at panaramio.com. His pictures are mostly of Christian standing at overlooks or streams, or by trees or on mountaintops, and they do not skip the section Bazemore questions. For those 30 miles, there are more than 20 photos, each one time-stamped. I scrutinized them one morning, and a story emerged of a small boy moving over rocky terrain, through ice and snow, at a little more than 1.5 miles an hour. There is little doubt that Buddy Backpacker progressed steadily northeast, toward Davenport Gap, in two long days, on December 1 and 2, 2013.

I called Bazemore back and asked him to point me toward other skipped sections. "Look," he said, "I'm not going to go back and forth with you on this like we're all in junior high school. I know what I know and I stand by it."

* * *

The weather clears, and when we begin hiking on the second day, after camping, Christian is in high spirits. "Isn't it beautiful out today?" he says. "The trail is nice and soft, and there are no roots, and it's pretty flat right here. It's even pretty warm." He's chatty now, and he speaks of seeing orange lizards on his AT odyssey, and turkeys, and red flying squirrels, and a rattlesnake, some wild ponies, and a moose. He doesn't know the names of the plants around us. He's experiencing nature as a small animal does, sensually, as a breeze on his back and a cold bite on his brow. Listening to him, I think of Michael Cogswell, the six-year-old thru-hiker, now in his early 40s, who recently told me, "I wouldn't trade my AT experience for the world. There's a certain purity in doing something like that as a child. You can never get that back. But there are positives and negatives. By the time I was done with that hike, I wasn't really a kid anymore. I'd walked so many miles. I'd carried my own clothes and a tent and helped wash the laundry at night. I'd had all this responsibility."

Is Christian growing up too fast? He sure doesn't seem world-weary, for he keeps begging me to tell him make-believe stories. I tell him one, finally. It's about my plastic water bottle going "home," to China. The water bottle has a hard-to-pronounce fake Chinese name that Christian loves repeating, his voice a high-pitched array of scratchy, whispery sounds. When the tale is done, he spends 30 minutes detailing the plot of the film *Cloudy with a Chance of Meatballs*. Then he asks, "Should I tell you about *Cloudy with a Chance of Meatballs 2*?"

Is he lonely—starved for attention from people besides his parents? Probably a little, but when I ask if he misses going to school, he isn't entirely clear what school entails. Andrea says he enjoyed preschool on Long Island, but on the trail he only conjures up one memory. "They put me in with the babies," he says with disdain.

I ask him if hiking ever gets boring. "That's a silly question," he says. "No!"

"Do you ever hate the AT?"

"Sometimes I don't like it when it's really hard. Then I just want to be done. I want Mommy to be right there in the middle of the woods and I just want to go to sleep right there."

Later, I described my hike with Christian to Dr. W. Douglas B. Hiller, an orthopedic surgeon at North Hawaii Community Hospital and a onetime chief medical officer for the triathlon at the Olympics. He said, "I doubt they caused him any physical harm. As long as it was a happy family hike and he wasn't being pushed, or made to keep going when he was limping, he should be fine. If he got some bruises and cuts, well, that's what little kids do all day long—they run around and jump and fall and get up."

I searched at length for a child psychologist who might object to Hiller's sanguine take. I couldn't find one, and I decided that the hubbub over Andrea's parenting was rooted partly in fear: Andrea is different than most AT hikers. She's from working-class Long Island. She's combative at times. Yes, she and Dion brought Christian hiking on a very cold day. But what's the harm in dressing warmly and hitting the trail? Yes, Dion sometimes carps at the kid. As do many parents who steer their children toward more culturally accepted goals—piano, soccer, spelling bees. Why should hiking be any different? In fact, it's easy to see the experience in a very different light. Christian and his family are hiking America's most beloved and fought-over trail in pursuit of happiness, and they're happy most of the time. Together, they've found a way to engage with the world—to commune with its beauty and have an adventure. This is what matters.

On the last day I'm on the AT, Andrea picks us up at dusk, to drive us to the nearest shelter, where we'll camp. It's cold outside, so we savor the warm blast of the car's heater. When we park, Dion limps down the short path to the shelter. Christian leaps over the puddles. Andrea cooks us all dinner. Then the next morning, backing out, she runs over the gas stove. Under her breath, she says, "Shit!" Then she laughs and throws the stove into the Jeep and drives on.

* * *

I see them only one more time, eight months later, on a rainy afternoon last September in the small town of Trout Lake, Washington, as they take a break near the end of their Pacific Crest Trail thru-hike. Trout Lake is a forested Nowheresville, and after 11 straight days on the trail they're ensconced in drab tasks—laundry, e-mail, cleaning out their packs. Still, as I pull up to the Trout Lake Grocery to find Andrea standing there on the porch, with Christian entwined in her arms, she exudes a certain glow. There's an ease about her, a softness to her skin. She's happy—you can tell that without even asking questions. And she's sunbaked and lean now, 35 pounds lighter than when I'd last seen her. She's been hiking the whole way this time, with both her and Dion carrying packs. The Jeep is long gone.

"We did 23 miles yesterday before four o'clock," she says, looking down. "Didn't we, Buddy?"

"Yeah," Christian says, rocking a bit in his mother's arms. He's sleepy-eyed and determined, it seems, not to take the bait. "Actually," he says, "it was 22.8."

"What's been your favorite part of the PCT so far?" I ask.

"Whitney," he says. "It was cool. We were way up there. It felt like the end of the trail." There's still a kid's wonder in his voice, but it's more contained now. He's two or three inches taller, and there is, suddenly, a grace about his small, lanky person. It seems almost certain that in a few years girls will go crazy for him and that he'll deflect their ardor with a languid ease.

"And what else was fun?" I ask, digging a little more.

"Goat Rocks," he says, referring to a nearby boulder field that stretches on for a couple miles. "I like doing hard stuff. And this house," he says, meaning the store, where they're staying in an upstairs motel room. "At night, they light up these lights on the porch and it's beautiful. It looks like Christmas."

When Dion emerges, fresh from a shower, I see he's lost weight as well. He's more than 30 pounds lighter and also ebullient, almost jolly. The tenseness I'd seen before on the AT, as he tried to corral a restless kid and negotiate complex car logistics, has vanished. This time, the three of them have all hiked together. There is, it seems, a new calm in Dion's muscles. "This trail is easier than the AT," he says. "It's well maintained, it's graded. It's not rocky, and you can actually get a good stride going."

We walk across the street to get lunch, and Andrea and Dion update me some. Christian, they say, now likes to wield his bamboo hiking poles like Ninja swords. They've landed a host of sponsors—a tent sponsor, a pack sponsor, even a socks sponsor—and at one point, resting from the trail, they encountered a lovely 18-year-old girl who spent the afternoon teaching Christian how to twirl a hula hoop.

"You liked that didn't you, Bud?" Andrea asks.

"Yeah," he says, looking down at his fries. "That was good."

What jumps out is how steady they all seem. They're no longer the hapless outsiders of the backpacking world. No one is savaging them on Facebook anymore, and their goal of completing the Triple Crown in 2015 no longer seems outlandish. Barring catastrophe, they will get the job done. Then they'll move on to surfing or mountain biking or whatever. Everything will work out for Christian, more or less; he'll clearly be okay.

But to Christian, the unlikely peace that his family enjoys wandering the world is old news. He doesn't want to sit there and talk about it. There's a trampoline behind the store, and he keeps looking out the window toward it. Eventually, Andrea lets him go. He runs over to it, loose-limbed, his body lit with delight. He climbs inside the trampoline's protective black mesh fence, and begins jumping, giddy and laughing as he sails into the sky.

King of the Mountains

Backpacker, *August 22, 2019*

"HE MOVES," ONE HIKER HAS SAID, "LIKE SMOKE THROUGH THE TREES." "He's like a ghost," a peakbagger once told me. "You can't find a picture of him anywhere."

JR Stockwell is a real person, though. He is a 58-year-old carpenter who lives just a mile from me in tiny Gilmanton, New Hampshire, population 3,800. And for the past two decades he's explored the White Mountains so intensely that it's not hyperbole to say he knows the forested, 800,000-acre range like other people know their backyard.

JR (technically he's Leonard Stockwell Jr.) is the only living person to have bushwhacked up all 48 of New Hampshire's listed 4,000-footers in every season. He knows the names of nearly all the bird and plant species living in the Whites. He knows the whereabouts of all the crashed airplanes there, and once, when a fellow bushwhacker ran into him and reported that she'd just seen a moose carcass, JR already knew precisely where it lay rotting.

Steven Smith, the editor of the Appalachian Mountain Club's series White Mountain Guides, regards JR as a little-known treasure. "There are many places he's been that no one has visited in a long time, if ever," Smith says. He calls JR "the true heir to Guy Waterman," referencing the Whites' original all-season bushwhacker who, along with his wife, Laura, wrote books such as *Yankee Rock and Ice* that captured the Whites' wildness before he elected to end his life in the mountains he loved. On a bitter subzero winter day in 2000, Waterman hiked to the top of

Mt. Lafayette, sat down, and died from the cold. "No one has ranged as widely in the Whites as Guy and JR," Smith says.

JR has produced no books, though. He doesn't blog about his hikes. He leaves no public account of his explorations at all. He is not on Facebook or Instagram. He does not own a computer. He does not have a cell phone. There are no photos of JR online, and on the website for the White Mountains' hard-core peakbaggers (48×12.com is a gathering spot for "grid" hikers who've knocked off all the listed 4,000-footers in every month of the year), there is but a single sentence about JR, written, a tad stingily, by someone else: "Junior completed the Grid on September 29, 2013 on Mount Carrigain."

Eager to know more? Sorry, JR Stockwell is the J. D. Salinger of the New England outdoors. He stands apart from today's media-saturated hiking world and the summit photos clogging Instagram. Any one of us who's ever blogged about bagging a peak has contributed our own version of the hero shot. In the White Mountains, the phenomenon is particularly pronounced, as topping all of the region's 4,000-footers becomes an ever more popular New England rite of passage.

JR has lists to check, too, but he's guided by an antique ethic that values experience and adventure over achievement. "I want to explore the White Mountains," he says. "I want to see if there's a view from this or that peak. I want to look for the cellar holes and stone walls from old sheep farms and for the remains of old trails built in the '30s." He takes the time to find stunning sights no one has ever described in writing—for example, an unnamed, unbroken glade of white birch trees that sits just off the slope of Bondcliff, a peak that seems to draw half of nearby Boston each summer weekend. He's such an anomaly that whenever he's referred to online, the language is misty and grandiose. "JR just picks out a line on the map that interests him and goes for it," Smith has written. "Legend," another blogger wrote recently, summing up JR.

For me, the mythmaking surrounding JR is complicated. I've known the guy since 1980, when we were both teenage distance runners. Last year, I hired JR to do some carpentry at my house. I have written him checks; he's cashed them. In my experience, there is nothing ghostly about the man.

Still, I can't help but think of JR as existing beyond the tedious pale of 21st-century life, on a deeper and more meditative plane. He plans his routes by consulting his library of vintage White Mountain Guides stowed in a glass and wood case he built himself, and he has quietly absorbed the cool, restorative energy of New England's most remote places. He ventures out almost every weekend, and he returns calm and unhurried. Recently I began to wonder: Is this little-known carpenter who's worked on my house truly a hiking sage? And if so, what could I learn from him—what could we all learn—about exploring the wild places close to home? I asked JR if I could join him on the trail to find out. A full year later, he agreed. Reluctantly.

* * *

"Hey JR, you remember how you used to listen to Ted Nugent all the time? You remember that album, *Intensities in 10 Cities?*"

"What's that, bud?" It's February, and it's relatively balmy at 20°F. Carrying snowshoes, we're crunching uphill on a logging road near the Waterville Valley ski resort, over firm snow. The walking is noisy.

"Ted Nugent," I repeat.

"Well," JR says, chuckling, "as you grow older, you learn things, bud. Like maybe Ted Nugent's not the greatest guy in the world."

This is how conversations between us often go. We draw on decades of shared history and circle back on absurd moments. We pinpoint the vast differences between us (I was a Doors fan), and then in reflection, we arrive at new ways of seeing things, a path forward.

We keep crunching uphill. Our plan is to leave the trail soon, then cut upward, through the woods, across a col, and on toward the summit of an obscure peak. Sandwich Dome is the highest peak in the Whites that is not on the 4,000-footer list. As far as social media is concerned, the 3,992-foot Dome does not exist.

But it exists for JR on a list. Because once he summits it, he will be just a few peaks away from bushwhacking up all of New Hampshire's 100 highest mountains—and that much closer to completing the 20th or so list in his life. In addition to his peakbagging exploits, JR has set foot in all 259 town-like parcels in New Hampshire—every township, grant, purchase, and location. Perhaps uniquely, JR finished all 15 of New England's late 20th-century marathons.

Even if JR was inclined to discuss his achievements at cocktail parties, they're so locally focused that they might be indecipherable outside New Hampshire. They might not even register here, for his lists are arcane. They're not easily reduced to an elevator pitch, and even JR himself doesn't regard his goals as dazzling. When I ask him to explain his "obsession" with bushwhacking New England's 100 highest, he redirects me. "I'm not obsessed," he says as we hike along an open, flat section, looking out at other forested peaks. "I really don't even think about achievement." Lists are just his way of bringing order to life's clamorous array of possibilities. "A list is a framework," he explains. "It's an excuse for getting out here—for looking at brooks that I've never heard of and searching for old logging camps."

Often, JR searches for such landmarks without navigational guides, finding his way off-trail simply by eyeballing familiar features—a certain grove of maples, say. He's not boycotting technology, though. He just hasn't heeded its call. "I've never really had any reason to use a computer," he says. "There's just nothing on there that interests me." He knows how to Google things on his wife's computer, but on the two occasions he's spoken to me of Googling something, he enunciated the word with a distant curiosity, so that the "o's" sounded like the hoot of an owl.

But if a certain technology seems useful to him, he won't shy away. Today, he's using a digital altimeter and eyeing it closely. When the instrument reads exactly 2,300 feet, we step off the logging road into the conifers. Then, after strapping on snowshoes, we push through a thicket of snow-covered boughs, each ready to dump its payload at the slightest nudge—and when you follow JR into the brush, there will be nudging. Every so often I feel a cold sting on my back as snow cascades off the trees and down my shirt.

It's a minor nuisance, but also a reminder that you don't have to go far from home to find hazards outdoors. JR tells me about "spruce traps," quicksand-like holes in the snow that form atop downed branches. I'm not falling in, though. I'm cruising along. The slope we're ambling up is gentle.

But then we reach the base of a frozen waterfall and start climbing, more or less straight up the cascade. We pull ourselves uphill by grabbing onto tree trunks. Only the claws on our snowshoes bind us to the fall line. JR moves briskly, with force, and following him, I'm a little on edge. This waterfall isn't on the AMC's map. It does not have a name. I doubt any rescuers could find this place if I broke my ankle, and part of me is petrified. JR may not be an official guide, but he's carefully packaged this outing, lending me snowshoes and handling all the navigation. Over the years, he's taken several novices into the Whites, one by one, and now it's my sense that JR was born to be a teacher. Each time I absorb a morsel of White Mountains wisdom, he nods placidly as a contented smirk sprouts under his beard.

The canyon we're in is shadowed by clouds and cliffs. It's semi-dark and it carries a certain cold intrigue. When we reach the top of the waterfall, there's a frozen beaver pond off to our left, maybe an acre in size. It's not on any map, either. It's not described in any trip reports that Steve Smith, the guidebook editor, knows about. For a few minutes, JR and I just stand on its shore, savoring how, in a crowded world, there are still a few secret places.

Eventually, JR takes off his gloves so he can pull a paper map out of his pack. It's one of those tissue-thin AMC topo maps, and he squints down at it, his beard spun with tiny icicles as he figures out our route over the col. Then we shoulder our packs and press on.

* * *

Of all the things JR does in the mountains, it's his bypass of GPS that tends to spur the most conversation. Undoubtedly, GPS makes the backcountry safer and more accessible, but it can also make the wild seem a little less wild. And JR isn't the only one to find value in analog maps.

Cognitive scientists seem to concur that paper maps are good for us in ways that GPS isn't. Nora Newcombe, a Temple University psychologist who studies spatial navigation, notes that when we use GPS we don't "build up a primitive cognitive map. As we navigate, we don't refer to distal landmarks—this church steeple, that mountain. We don't build up an intersecting network of routes we've taken, so that we can start exploring."

But is it really apt to regard paper maps as sacred relics of a simpler age? Robert Moor, the author of the book *On Trails*, doesn't think so. "A modern map is a highly advanced tool," Moor told me recently. "It's the result of aerial satellite photos and the accumulated data of hundreds of years of surveying."

JR doesn't dispute the benefits of technology—hence the altimeter—but a career as a professional video game player is probably not in his future. When I first met him, he was already, at age 19, establishing himself as the quintessential ancient Yankee. He'd come to distance running via sled dog racing, where he excelled by taking his weight off the sled and hoofing it through the drifts. On account of a choppy, asymmetrical stride, he called himself "The Hobbler." Sometimes, for entertainment's sake, he bent low over a make-believe cane and spoke in a quavering voice. He seemed to embody a rugged ideal that I myself, three years younger, skinnier, and more frail and sensitive, would never attain.

I was a summer resident of Gilmanton back then, a visitor from the suburbs of Connecticut, and JR and I motored around town in my mom's yellow Volvo station wagon, which he nicknamed "the bread box." He pretended that he couldn't dare be seen in such a wimpy ride and hid under the dash each time we passed the post office.

He had local cred to protect. There have been Stockwells in Gilmanton since the late 1700s. JR's family is the namesake of Gilmanton's Stockwell Hill Road, and one of his ancestors, a mason named John Clifford, worked in the Whites in the 1920s, shoring up an iconic, face-shaped natural rock formation, "The Old Man of the Mountain," by chaining the Old Man's forehead to a cliff.

But none of JR's other ancestors ever set foot in the Whites. "They were simple, working-class people," JR says. "They lived within confined boundaries. None of them ever went anywhere."

As a solitary and inquisitive kid, JR was determined to find his way to a larger, more intricate world. After he saw a TV special on birds, he learned the cries of local species. Then, after he saw the blockbuster 1972 movie *Jeremiah Johnson*, about a burly, gun-toting Rocky Mountain trapper, he decided that it would be a good idea to venture deep into the thick woods behind his house and see what happened. "A quarter mile in, I couldn't see anything," he remembers. "I couldn't hear anybody. I was afraid I would die."

The thrill of that first terrifying adventure never left him, and when JR was 20, he pointed his pickup truck west and rambled about, visiting Alaska and Oregon as he flipped burgers for gas money.

After a little more than a year of exploring, he came home because his mother was dying. In time, after his father passed, he moved back into his childhood home and became a solid Gilmantonian. He married the gym teacher at Gilmanton School, Karen Carlson, and established himself as an expert renovator of the town's myriad old houses. His independent streak never waned, though.

Breaking from the pattern set by his older siblings, JR never had kids. Instead, he traveled the world (he's visited Namibia, Madagascar, and Tibet) and also cultivated an exacting home life. Each weeknight, to maintain fitness, JR rides an exercise bike for precisely 48 minutes (to approximate a six-mile run at eight minutes per mile). He fills the bird feeders in his yard and organizes his workshop. Then, after dinner, he pores over his White Mountain books, which include Moses Foster Sweetser's inaugural 1876 guide. He figures out the mileage of his forthcoming hikes by measuring map distances with a wooden ruler. "Three-quarters of an inch there," he muttered once when I watched him, "seven-sixteenths there, thirteen-thirty-seconds there."

JR's steadiness at home is, like his lists, a framework that yields him the solid footing he needs to bore deeper as he explores. The scheme, always, is to find, within the familiar, new intrigues and marvels.

* * *

I have to admit that even now, in middle age, I look to JR for clues as to how to live. When he came to rebuild my kitchen, for instance, I paid close attention as he contended with a construction challenge. The floors in my 220-year-old home tilt steeply, and at uneven pitches. Carpentry in such a context is less mathematical than intuitive and, as I sat upstairs, listening to JR work as I wrote, I tuned into both the high whine of his bandsaw and the crazy long silences during which, I'm sure, JR was cogitating, strategizing. I knew that it was in the silences that I was getting my money's worth, and I asked myself if I could bring the same rhythm to my writing—the same deep digging punctuated by sharp bursts of precision.

One winter I thought of JR's taste for hiking in temperatures as low as minus 20°F, and I decided to turn off the furnace and plumbing and rely on a wood stove and an old-fashioned privy. When JR came by one evening, taking a short break from the oil-heated comfort of his den, he regarded my hermitage with doubt and concern. "Dude," he asked, "what are you doing?"

Another experiment is proving more successful. It involves my exercise regime. I do a little open water swimming and a ton of cycling here in New Hampshire's Lakes Region. If I don't rack up 200 miles on Strava every week, I begin to feel guilty. I'm aware that the statistics I obsess over (elevation gained, miles per hour, average wattage) do little to afford me cosmic peace, so I decided recently to compose and tackle a list of my own—obscure and personal, just like one of JR's.

I am now endeavoring to bike to, and then swim across, each and every lake and pond that sits within Gilmanton's 80 square miles. And Gilmanton is a very watery place. Already, in consulting a New Hampshire gazetteer and my own memory banks, I have identified 18 potentially swimmable bodies of water. Reconnaissance missions will surely reveal additional lakes and ponds. I need to get off the roads. I plan to thrash my way into the woods with binoculars, for I've learned, watching JR, that lots of cool stuff is not on the map.

In a mountain range so teeming with hikers that you sometimes need to wait in line to move summitward, JR knows where to find refuge, off trail, in 20-foot-wide pools of calm black water on a terraced green slope. He's shown me that there is so much nature close to home. You just have to look. That may be the biggest lesson JR has to impart: Always keep your eyes open.

* * *

When JR and I go out for our next bushwhack, up tiny Smarts Mountain on a warm spring morning, I ask him why he never advertises his feats.

He's tongue-tied for a moment, embarrassed. "I guess I'm humble," he says finally. "I don't like making a big deal of myself. And do you really think that what I do is interesting to people?"

Well, yeah, I say, to hikers it is. JR concedes that Steve Smith, the guidebook editor, is always asking to look at the skeletal diaries in which JR records his backwoods adventures. "But I'd feel weird showing them to Steve," he says. "I'm terrible at grammar. Spelling is a mental block for me. In school, if I got a C, I was ecstatic." He adds that reading is also a trial for him: "If I get through two novels a year, I'm lucky."

As JR says this, I'm picturing his mind as a vast warehouse. The facts flow in and come to rest, each one of them, on its own neat shelf. And his mind is so orderly that the facts never leave, and they never get lost. JR may be afflicted with something like dyslexia, but when you're JR, that's a minor impediment. You find a way to bull past it, to strategize around it. You become a scholar of the White Mountains anyway, despite limitations, and you keep dreaming up lists.

Not long after our Sandwich Dome hike, JR finishes the 100 highest list, and for a couple weeks he's a little at sea, without a list for the first time in decades. The lull does not last, though, for soon enough he decides that he will climb every peak noted on the AMC's six White Mountain maps—every single one, even the dinky 800-footers with convenience stores at their bases.

No one has ever counted all the peaks on the maps, let alone climbed them, but there's probably about 1,000 of them. JR has summited more than half these peaks already (the big ones, mostly), meaning that he's got roughly 500 small ones to go. "The bumps," he's calling this grail. It'll involve 125 or so day trips, with each trip including about four peaks, such as they are.

When I hike with him again, it's late May. The lady slippers are in bloom, and the ferns are starting to flourish. We drive northwest, up into the sparsely populated hinterlands near the Vermont border, and then hike a trail up Black Mountain, elevation 2,830 feet, for a lovely view from the granite ridge at the summit. There is actually another person up here—a haggard-looking guy who's come, he says, for the "hangover cure," having killed a 12-pack the evening before. We chat with him for a moment, and then we leave society entirely, dropping off the trail into the woods to bag Howe Hill, elevation 2,681 feet, and Little Bear Mountain, elevation 1,782.

These small rises are on JR's "bumps" list, and they're unimpressive. Little Black's flattish summit is thick with trees, so that after we stumble around for five minutes, standing on various mounds, to make sure we've reached the actual peak; the only view I get is of the blackflies swarming around my head. I feel a little let down. Despite what I've learned of JR, I find it hard to believe that he's applying his formidable powers to these piddling hills. Is this how legends ease into retirement? As we descend, though, JR is attuned to the small delights all around us. "Bear scat," he says, pointing. "Moose scat. Now, there's a pitcher plant," he says, elated by the discovery. "It's carnivorous. That's only the second time I've seen one."

Gradually, I make peace with the smallness of this outing, for it's pervaded, I realize, by a certain music. I'm out here with a guy patient enough to locate minor trailside wonders—a guy who knows that the world is big and worth exploring, but that each of us lives in one place and that we can live deepest if we find things to love in that place.

We round a bend, eventually. Then we come out onto an open expanse of granite bathed by the warm afternoon sun, and JR says, "Look. That same mourning dove was sitting there when we came by the first time. Do you see it?"

I search for a moment amid the wildflowers and the waxy blueberry bushes, deep green beneath the blue sky. And then, I say, "Oh, yeah, there's that bird. I see it."

JR looks back at me. I glimpse that delighted smirk on his face again, and then we hoist ourselves up over a little crag of granite and keep moving along through the mountains.

The Long Way Home

Backpacker, *July 27, 2012*

IN SPRING 2006, KARL BUSHBY CROSSED THE BERING STRAIT FROM Alaska to Siberia, walking on shifting ice floes and swimming gaps of open water. It was an audacious endeavor, to say the least. Bushby and his partner, Dimitri Kieffer, towed 200-pound sleds through a rubble heap of fractured ice. They skittered up 30-foot-high pressure ridges, scrambled along thin shelves of ice, hoping they didn't crack, and laboriously dog paddled through 32°F pools of salt water that were often clogged with frozen slush. At one point, Bushby and Kieffer got swept 52 miles north as they tried to push west, because the ice floes moved with the wind. They ended up traveling roughly 150 miles over 14 days to cross the 53-mile-wide strait. Near the end, the pair had to jettison every ounce of excess weight in order to complete the journey. "My expedition was on the line. So we threw the supplies overboard—the shotguns, the radio . . ." Bushby recalled later.

The BBC and other media covered the successful traverse with fanfare. And not only because the pair was following, almost literally, in the footsteps of prehistoric travelers who crossed a land bridge between Asia and North America. The feat also marked the most challenging stage of Bushby's Goliath Expedition, the singular campaign that has consumed him since 1998. He aims to complete the world's longest hike, becoming the first human ever to walk and ski an unbroken path around the globe—or, more accurately, from the tip of South America back home to industrial Hull, England. Before setting off, he'd done nothing to suggest he was capable of such a trek. But when he reached Russia—with the technical crux behind him, and some half the distance done—it appeared that the one-time British army paratrooper might actually finish the 36,000-mile journey.

But what should have been the expedition's high point quickly became the low. Russian authorities arrested Bushby and Kieffer for entering the country illegally and deported them back to the United States. Kieffer, who had joined Bushby only for the Bering Strait crossing, didn't plan a return to Russia. But Bushby's efforts to resume his journey have been repeatedly hampered by visa and financial problems. Over the following six years, Bushby managed nothing but sporadic stints on the Siberian tundra, which is only passable on foot in subfreezing conditions. On his spring 2011 visit, he inadvertently strayed into one of the off-limits "security zones" Russia maintains near its borders. Authorities barred him from returning to Russia for five years. He enlisted a lawyer to lobby Moscow's visa czars, but the Goliath Expedition appeared stalled, perhaps indefinitely.

Still, Bushby had accomplished much simply getting this far. Few would have called it a defeat if he abandoned the journey. Every hike has an end, right? But Bushby didn't go home. Nor did he go forward. He simply disappeared from the adventure stage. Which is when Karl Bushby became captivating in a whole new way. Where had he gone? What happened to the record-setting hiker who couldn't keep hiking?

"I'm 42 years old and I'm broke and I'm homeless," Karl Bushby lamented as he trudged along through the coarse brown sand of a beach in Melaque, Mexico, where I caught up with him in 2018. "I'm a professional parasite. I'm a professional hobo. I'm sleeping on other people's couches. I'm 42 years old, and I have to walk other people's dogs, just so they'll feed me. My job is picking up dog shit!"

Bushby paused now, and when I looked over at him he was faintly smirking, charmed by the dolefulness he exuded as we made our way through the twilight toward the tiny village on Mexico's west coast. There was a sparkle in his blue eyes, but a fleeting one. Since late 2008, mostly living in Melaque (pronounced muh-lah-kay, population 8,000), Bushby had been undernourished, subsisting on less than 2,000 calories a day as he cadged lodgings from friends and did them occasional favors in return. His skin was pallid, as though he were back home in the north of England, where his mother still works in a confectionery factory, and his movements were restrained—sluggish, even. "I've shut down the extremities. These days I'm just preserving my core," he said. His tone was at once morose and faux dramatic. "I'm at the mercy of other people's kindness. I'm a nobody. But in a matter of months, of course, I could be conquering the world."

Well, not exactly conquering the world, but slowly plying his way across it. From 1998 to 2006, Bushby averaged about 2,000 miles a year. Not noteworthy by thru-hiker standards, but no one will question the pace if he completes the journey. The unprecedented length, along with potentially deadly obstacles like the Bering Strait's shifting ice, make it a hike no one will likely ever repeat.

The expedition began, he said, as a bad bet. "I had something to prove to my paratrooper mates." He also had something to run from—in 1998, he was still embroiled in the aftermath of a nasty divorce. He flew to Punta Arenas, Chile, with $800 and a wheeled cart full of gear.

Strangers fed and sheltered him. He scored a few meager sponsorships, and he just kept plodding along. Bushby walked up South America's Pacific coast, battling wind in Patagonia and long waterless stretches in Chile's northern deserts. He crossed Central America's Darien Gap, a guerilla-ridden jungle region where he backpacked into a no-man's-land against the advice of the Colombian military. He walked through sizzling heat in the southwestern United States and numbing cold in Canada and Alaska. Then, famously, he crossed the ice to Russia in 2006. And then, not so famously, he retreated (by plane) to this beach town in Mexico, where he could look for sponsors—film producers were nibbling—as he conserved funds. The unemployed Bushby had a grand total of $700 in his bank account when I visited him and he couldn't even access that money, having lost his bank card. The replacement was still en route. As we walked through the sand, Bushby cracked open his wallet to reveal a single 20 peso bill, worth about $1.70. "That's it," he said. "That's all I have at the moment."

His words sprouted a diagram in my mind: I envisioned life as a series of squiggly, branching lines. We make choices, and nearly all of us start out incubating some grand, youthful ambition. We want to write novels when we grow up, or scale unclimbed peaks. But then we do grow up, and we become practical. We choose lines that are easier, more conventional. We limit our adventures to what fits in the vacation schedule, and eventually, well, we do end up getting that minivan.

Karl Bushby refused to part with his grand plan, and the diagram of his life reflects that decision. He has experienced moments of triumph, to be sure, but he has also paid dearly for his stubbornness, as have others around him. When he set out on his hike almost 14 years ago, he left behind an eight-year-old son. Along the way, in Colombia, he met "the only woman who ever mattered to me." They're no longer together, though, and now Bushby passes the time in limbo here in Melaque. He is responsible to nothing but his dream. But does this make him the ultimate inspiration for adventure visionaries? Is Karl Bushby a latter-day Thoreau who's dared to live deliberately? Or is he instead a sad case of arrested development: a freeloader who has failed to see that even the best hikes must end?

* * *

We kept walking. "Even the clouds here in the tropics are dynamic," Bushby said now, looking up. "At a certain time of night, right at dusk, when the light is a certain way here, I feel like I'm in a dream state."

Every long hike has its dream-like episodes—moments when the wilderness shines out and life seems exquisite in ways that it can't amid the din of the civilized world. One winter night early in his journey, when Bushby was wending north through the Andes, he woke up in a tent covered with ice. Freezing rain dripped down on him from nearby trees. He broke camp and began climbing a mountain road, hauling his gear-laden cart—"The Beast," he called it. "Up ahead of me," he writes in his 2006 memoir, *Giant Steps*. "The clouds of fog meet the warmer air and explode into huge spirals, moving so quickly they look like giant flames, before they evaporate into nothing. On the hills to my left, huge dust devils are whipped into mini-tornadoes, sending columns of dust hundreds of meters into the sky."

A headwind whipped up against Bushby. He kept climbing, his legs burning. When he reached the peak, finally, he was "absolutely destroyed." Blowing sand stung his face. But he'd ascended more than 6,000 feet in three hours, and he was able to gaze out at the Atacama plateau and at the snowcapped peaks to the east.

And that night, as he sat outside his tent in the wind, eating pasta from a pan, he says he was "awestruck" by how clear and dark the starry sky was, looming above him, and also deeply content. "I was a very keen naturalist as a kid," he explained to me in Melaque. "I used to bring wounded birds into the house and nurse them back to health. I gathered up dead animals and then glued their skeletons back together. But then when I went into the army I had to put all that aside. On this walk—on days like that one in Chile—I've been able to connect with nature again."

Joining the military as an adolescent had changed the trajectory of Bushby's life, and it seemed this walk was his attempt to reroute it. "I was a skinny, small lad," he told me. "I was very immature, physically." Still, his father, a star paratrooper in his day, convinced him to join the British army's paratrooper unit at age 16. "I was trying to enter a division of the army where 80 to 90 percent who try out don't make it," Bushby recalled. He took the entrance test five times, and then, he said, "They cut me some slack. They let me in. It was the worst thing they could have done."

As a paratrooper, Bushby was often required to parachute out of a plane and then run 10 miles in an hour and 45 minutes with 30 pounds on his back. "I had anxiety attacks," he said. "I don't know how many times I woke up in the medical center with IVs in my arms." Bushby stayed in the army for 12 years, but always, he said, "I was considered the weak link in our unit. I was an outsider. All the other guys had pictures of motorcycles and guns by their bunks. I had a poster of the solar system over mine."

It's unlikely Bushby ever imagined anything like Melaque when he lay in his bunk, gazing at the stars. The beachside town is a winter haven for Canadian snowbirds. In the summer, when I visited, it was steamy hot, and dead. Mangy dogs could lie on the pavement of side streets, unperturbed, for hours. At La Flora Café, a rail-thin American Buddhist, who revealed only his first name, Rene, sat alone every morning, sipping his coffee and staring contemplatively into the distance. When I asked him where he was from, he said, "Well, right now I'm living in this chair."

In Melaque, Bushby was just another wandering soul, albeit more sociable than some. He was living here with just three T-shirts and two pairs of pants (his gear was stowed in Fairbanks) and mostly waiting for a call from Hollywood. A well-connected two-man production team was pitching TV networks a reality show starring Karl Bushby as a bumbling, endearing everyman explorer. "They're very close to signing the contract," he told me. "I should know by the end of the month." (At press time, Bushby was still in the dark.)

While he waited, Bushby steadfastly eschewed anything resembling a job. "I've offered him work as a housecleaner," said his friend Kyla Poirer, a Canadian who manages a swank Melaque hotel. "And other friends asked him to haul jet skis out of the water, but he always has an excuse. He says he's got to be available to talk to the film producers." Once, Bushby did a stint as a waiter at a fancy restaurant. "It was horrible," he said. "After three shifts, I was done with the clients and all their snootiness—with their sideways comments about how the tea wasn't hot enough and their food wasn't arranged on the plate the right way. If I did that for a living, I'd end up putting a plate over someone's head."

Most mornings, Bushby took his own table at La Flora. He enjoyed a bottomless cup of coffee, compliments of La Flora's owner, an admirer of his expedition, and he peered at his laptop, poaching a Wi-Fi signal from a nearby shop.

* * *

While Bushby is clearly consumed by his goal, he doesn't glorify his achievements. At La Flora, we watched a BBC video about his 2006 Bering Strait crossing, and he never got boastful. "I'm an average guy," he said. "I'm less than average. I'm an underachiever. All I'm doing is putting one foot in front of the other."

On the laptop's screen, the BBC's narrator whipped himself into a lather over how cold the Bering Sea is, and Bushby rolled his eyes, then aped the man's fretful upper-crust British delivery. "One could perish in that water in a matter of seconds," he crowed. "Seconds, I say! Mere seconds!"

The moment yielded more than a brief laugh. It also pointed toward the very quality that's endeared him to strangers across two continents. He's a world traveler, yes, and a record setter, but he remains a working-class bloke from the north of England. Encountering him, you recognize at once that his quest is not Olympian, but human and plodding. You want to shelter and feed him. You want to buy him a cup of coffee.

With the Bering Strait behind him, Bushby will likely survive if he manages to continue his journey. Though what remains isn't easy. Russia still presents formidable obstacles—skiing isn't one of Bushby's strengths, visa regulations are maddening, temperatures can reach minus 80°F, and chartered flights into Siberia can cost more than $12,000.

But once he clears those hurdles, it's just a long hike home, through Asia and Europe. Bushby's goal is to walk back into Britain via the emergency service corridor inside the Chunnel, the 31-mile train tube beneath the English Channel. Then he'll continue on to the modest brick home in Hull, England, where his mum waved him good-bye so long ago. With the ongoing visa issues, Bushby can't say with any certainty when he'll complete the journey. But he knows this: He will not touch British soil unless he gets there on foot.

The don't-go-home rule is, of course, completely arbitrary, since he's allowed himself to fly to and from Alaska, Mexico, Colombia, and other locations. But he won't allow himself even the briefest return to England. The self-imposed rule has defined Bushby's life—he exiled himself from his son Adam's growing-up. He missed birthday parties and much more. He said he's certain that, if his parents die before he walks home, he'll skip their funerals.

In Melaque, I pressed Bushby several times on the logic of the don't-go-home rule, and it was almost as though he couldn't think outside of it. "I made a commitment . . . " he'd begin. I sensed a fear of failure that's been decades in the making. In *Giant Steps*, Bushby describes reaching his late 20s and feeling "frustrated and unfulfilled." And it wasn't just his unhappy military career and ill-advised marriage.

As a youth, he often felt weak and ineffectual. In primary school, he was made to stand on a chair in front of the class because he couldn't spell (he was later diagnosed with dyslexia). His happiest childhood moments were spent outdoors, walking through the fields, exploring. So when he began contemplating a transformative experience for his post-military freedom, the answer came naturally. The world's longest hike, the biggest test he could imagine, would be his chance to prove himself in a way no one could ignore.

But Bushby had a hard time transforming himself from army misfit to world explorer. Early in his trek, he sometimes ran out of food when the distance between towns was vast. He got so hungry, he says, that he hallucinated. "Everything looked like food. I'd see food in the bushes." At times it was so windy in Patagonia that he had to walk tilting forward at a 45-degree angle—a posture that ravaged his ankle joints. In Alaska, he had to overcome snow and cold the likes of which he'd never seen. During one three-day stretch, trudging along through soft powder in a minus 40°F wind chill near Dunbar, Alaska, he covered only a mile.

Despite these trials, Bushby led a charmed life during much of his travels, receiving aid from strangers along the way, and from his parents back in England, who managed grassroots fundraising efforts. In South America, especially, Bushby found a warm welcome everywhere he went. In tiny villages, he was greeted as a windswept blond god.

"South America was like a boy's adventure story," Bushby said. "It was the happy experience I should have had in my teens—it was the best time of my life."

* * *

Every morning I was in Melaque, Bushby checked his e-mail, hopeful for a note from his producers. The correspondence was spare, though, for Jordan Tappis and Beau Willimon are busy fellows. Tappis produced the 2011 documentary *God Bless Ozzy Osbourne*. Willimon is a playwright whose 2008 drama, *Farragut North*, was the basis of a recent film, *The Ides of March*, starring George Clooney.

Early in 2011, the pair laid out about $30,000 to send Bushby from Melaque to Chukotka, Russia, with a video camera, so he could shoot two months of lonely ice road travel. Now they were hopeful that the footage would sing to Hollywood titans. "Karl has a great story," said Willimon when I called him. "He's a down-to-earth guy, and he's gone through everything in his travels. He's been imprisoned; he's fallen in love."

The tragedy of this romance was a topic that Bushby kept returning to. Bushby met Catalina Estrada when he walked through Colombia, and he returned again and again to see her, even as he traveled north. With me, he spoke of walking the streets of Medellin with Estrada wrapped in his arms. Mostly, though, the love story is a tale about craving the impossible. For three years, Bushby tried in vain to get Estrada a visa, so she could visit him as he hiked. Finally in 2008, she wrote Bushby from Medellin: "Don't come back here. We can't do this anymore."

They have not seen one another since, but when I called Estrada in Madrid, where she currently lives, she spoke of Bushby with a sweet wistfulness. "When you see a person like Karl, you can think, 'This guy is absolutely crazy,' or 'It is incredible that a person could fight for his dreams.' Karl makes me think that the human spirit is big. Karl is the big love of my life. When I was with Karl, I cried for seven years; I was so happy for seven years. It is very difficult to love a person who isn't there."

As we dined on the plaza in Melaque one night, Bushby acknowledged that he's hurt people by refusing to live a settled life. "There are moral questions involved in what I'm doing," he said, "and my son has paid the highest price. He grew up without a father at home. I don't know the guy. I don't know my own son."

Bushby is hardly the first explorer to prioritize his adventures over his parenting. Ernest Shackleton blithely left three young children behind when he sallied off on his last—and fatal—Antarctic expedition in 1921. Captain James Cook famously spent years at sea during his voyages. He had six children. Today's adventure obituaries are filled with climbers and skiers who have left children fatherless. Still, Bushby felt guilty as he told me that, throughout his adolescence, Adam was depressed. "I bear a lot of responsibility for that," he said. "And he's still lost."

Adam, now 22, works at a record store in Belfast. He has a tattoo of the grim reaper on his forearm, and he plays bass in a metal band. As his father sees it, Adam lives in a "soul-sucking, culturally deprived environment. He doesn't know what he wants in life."

Bushby believes that what Adam needs is precisely what he needed himself: a long hike. "Going to the Arctic would be a struggle for him," he told me. "But it could change his life."

In 2010, when the film producers flew Adam to Mexico, for his first paternal visit in six years, they asked him if he wanted to accompany his dad in the Arctic. With the cameras rolling, Adam Bushby entertained the idea. Later, I called Adam myself. He was genial discussing his dad, but also tentative and pained. "This long hike was something he wanted to do and I have nothing against it," he said. "But it was kind of hard not having him there as I grew up. I did suffer in a way, I suppose."

I asked Adam if he was ready for the Arctic. "Oh, the Russia thing," he said. "We did talk about that, but I don't know, that walking—that's my dad's thing. I want to stay here in Belfast and get my own life sorted out."

* * *

Of course, when Karl Bushby set out from England some 35 million footsteps ago, he too was bent on sorting out his life. Has he succeeded? If success means attaining stability and some measure of material comfort and a certainty about, say, where your next meal is coming from, well then no, he's failed miserably. But if success means being at peace with the path you have chosen, Bushby appears triumphant. Even in Melaque, at an obvious low—without money, without a certain timetable for returning to Russia—Bushby exhibited only hints of sadness. "There have been times, walking," he told me, "when I'm out in the pouring rain looking through someone's window, into their warm living room. I've felt a tinge of jealousy."

When I saw him at La Flora, just before heading to the airport, I was aware that I was leaving Bushby to fester in Spartan poverty. I just hoped that his bank card arrived soon. It seemed as though his spirits were fraying.

But when my taxi pulled up, Bushby was smirking. "OK, then, mate," he said. "It was a good time, wasn't it?"

The cab rolled off. When I looked back, Bushby was already checking his e-mail, and I knew that he was hunting for a message that would promise him a glorious future. For hope is always on his horizon. A couple of weeks later, as we talked over the phone, Bushby imagined emerging out of Russia, finally, and coming onto the home stretch of his epic hike. "Europe," he said, "is going to be nothing but one big drunken party. I won't even remember it. And I can't wait to get there."

ON THE SNOW

Taking Aim on the New Cold War

Ski, *November 14, 2017*

Just north of Coldfoot, the trees disappear.

It's too cold for them suddenly, and so as we keep driving north there are only stunted shrubs on the Alaskan tundra, and little whorls of snow dust that spin in the wind beneath the white-creased peaks of the Brooks Range. I focus on the dash, on the thermometer. When we roll down a long, gentle slope and reach the dark shadows at its base, the temperature is minus 27°F, and I fill with a cool animal dread, for we will be camping out on this trip, in tents, in the crisp Arctic air, on a mission that already has a disconcerting backdrop.

I'm traveling with the U.S. military, which has of late had reason to worry about the vast swathes of land and sea that sit north of the Arctic Circle, latitude 66°33,' occupying parts of eight different nations. A February 2017 Department of Defense report notes that, amid climate change, the Arctic is "warming more rapidly than the rest of the planet." According to the DOD report, "Human safety" is now threatened, as is the "protection of a unique ecosystem that many indigenous communities rely on for subsistence."

There are also strategic and economic dimensions to the Arctic's warming. As the ice melts in the Arctic Sea, its bounteous oil reserves will become more accessible, its now-frozen sea routes more navigable.

Russian president Vladimir Putin regards the Arctic as "a promising region" where Russia needs to "have all the levers for the protection of its security and national interests." In 2015, Putin submitted to the United Nations the long-shot claim that Russia should be granted dominion over an Alaska-sized chunk of Arctic sea ice off its shores—never mind that much of this frozen expanse now belongs to Denmark. He's also spent what would be valued as billions of dollars to build up Russia's Arctic presence, which features 16 new airfields and ports, 40 icebreaking ships, and four Arctic brigade combat teams, each thousands of warriors strong. U.S. officials are now gazing warily north.

The United States does not have a single military base in the Arctic, and one of its two ocean-going icebreakers is now broken. We are, however, making efforts to answer the Russian combat presence, and I'm here to behold an early step in that campaign.

I'm about to join 10 military men—six Army soldiers, three Marines, and a Navy officer—and our leader, a retired Army sergeant, for a three-day, 30-mile Nordic ski trip over wind-scoured Arctic terrain. We will drag 30-pound sleds through fresh, fluffy powder and test the timbre of clunky, metal-edged, camo-white "military skis" as we galumph forward wearing giant white plastic "bunny boots"—not made for skiing, but nonetheless excellent for staving off frostbite. We will boil snow to survive. My fellow travelers are all military ski instructors. They include, arguably, the nation's most deeply trained battle skiers, but no one here, save for our civilian leader, has ever undertaken a journey so cold and so long.

As we drive nine hours north from Fairbanks to our start point, there is burbling speculation as to what, exactly, is needed to pull this one off. "I've got two cans of Spam with me," says Marines staff sergeant Jonathon Campos, "and two packages of bacon. I'm gonna eat like an Eskimo."

Campos teaches cold-weather tactics at the Marines' Mountain Warfare Training Center, a base high in California's Sierra Nevada that schools about 1,200 novice skiers each year. He is a heavyset individual, 33 years old and given to patting his belly as he extols what he calls "the insulation" there. He just got deep into skiing last year, both Alpine and Nordic, and he likes bombing hills. Indeed, he's always been a thrill-seeker. When he was 10, he tells me, he rode a mattress down a rain-swollen Los Angeles River with his three brothers. "That was awesome," he says, "so much fun."

Eventually we park near remote Galbraith Lake to make camp. When I step out of the vehicle, into the minus 31°F chill, the snot in my nose instantly turns into rock.

* * *

The vibe of the whole expedition is highly militarized, so that we go "wheels down at oh-eight-thirty" and measure our progress in "klicks" as the cold air crackles with barbed remarks too f—ing colorful to be printed in a family magazine.

Our leader, Steven Decker, is a native Floridian who, decades ago, gave up his bad habits—alcoholism and bar fights—to find Nirvana telemark skiing before dawn each winter morning in the subzero chill of Alaska. Fifty years old, he runs the only other U.S. military ski facility—the Army's Northern Warfare Training Center in Fairbanks—which teaches the diagonal stride and the herringbone climb to about 350 new skiers each year. He is a stoic. Alone in our group, he will forgo a tent. He will sleep outside, on the snow, in the frigid cold, to savor the gleaming nighttime spectacle of the Aurora Borealis.

On the first day, the going is easy. We're just shuffling along—walking, basically—on gentle, rolling terrain. There's one hour-long climb that requires skins. Decker calls it "Mount Kiss My Ass," but it's not horrendous, and for me, the real challenge is the air temp, which hovers just below zero most of our trip.

It is so cold that if you accidentally spill water on your shirt, it could kill you—so cold that every time I take off my mittens I have about two minutes to tackle vital tasks demanding bare hands (changing my socks, say) before my fingertips start singing with pain.

Thickly bemittened for 23 hours and 50 minutes a day, I feel like my hands have shape-shifted into useless flippers. Worse, I feel stupid. There are many tasks I need to learn to survive this trip, like how to crush my voluminous seven-pound sleeping bag into its itsy-bitsy stuff sack, but out here the finer gears of my mind seem to have skipped town, abandoning my brain cavity to a small primal voice of survival shouting, "Stay warm! Stay warm!"

Operating deftly in the cold is a learned skill, an art form, and critical to Arctic warfare. (Imagine trying to gun down a surging enemy when you can't even get your mittens off . . .) The U.S. military spends millions of dollars honing this skill in its soldiers. At Campos's post in the Sierras, instructors lead pretend ambushes in snowfields and send low-level grunts to a plein air "hypothermia lab," where they tread water beneath the crust of an icy lake for 10 minutes, then scramble to warm up via a regimen of squats, push-ups, and piping hot drinks. I'd arrived in the Arctic with no such training, however, and so on our first night in the field, I'm the village idiot, traipsing around camp in untied boots, with driblets of Army-ration turkey tetrazzini frozen to my parka. At bedtime, when Decker mercifully gives me two sealed hot water bottles to clutch through the night, I tuck them inside my jacket, close to my heart. Then I crawl into my tent.

My tent mate, it turns out, is a Finn here on a two-week exchange.

Otso Könönen, 25, is an Army ski instructor for a nation that puts roughly half of all its conscripts on cross-country skis. He brings a sliver of Euro refinement to our expedition. His camouflage coat is a slightly sharper shade of pea green, and he's carrying with him an artisan Finnish knife that sports a curly birch handle. He tells me that in Finland every schoolchild knows about military skis; the most consequential moment in the history of ski warfare is also the crown jewel of Finnish history. In the World War II Battle of Suomussalmi, in the winter of 1939–1940, a scant contingent of 11,000 Finns, equipped with little more than skis, sleds, and rifles, staved off 50,000 heavily equipped Russians by pinioning the Russians' tanks to a single mountain road. The Finns nimbly kicked and glided through the snow-laden pines, then encircled the hapless Russians, and either shot them or waited for their food and firewood to run out. In the end, more than 13,000 Russians perished, as compared to only 1,000 or so Finns, and the Finns seized 43 tanks.

"The Russian soldiers were mostly from warm places, like Ukraine," says Könönen, whose great-uncle fought in the battle. "They didn't know winter, but we Finns, we know winter. And we start skiing almost at birth."

I'm stirred by Könönen's pride, but still I wonder: Isn't ski warfare a bit passé today, in our age of drones and super-precise sniper rifles that can hit a target at nearly a half mile? In time, I call Andrew Holland, a senior fellow and Arctic expert at the American Security Project, a Washington think tank—and I learn that in fact cross-country skis could prove quite helpful to a military that, like ours, seeks to contain an increasingly expansionist Russia. "You have to think about Russia's playbook," Holland says before musing on the Kremlin's most recent push for new turf in Ukraine. "What they did there is probe the borders. They didn't send in tanks. They sent in a few Russian soldiers with the Russian insignias taken off their weapons." The soldiers then tried to foment unrest, Holland says, by "doing sabotage and inciting local Russians to rise up against the government. I can see it happening elsewhere. We're talking about small groups of men, and to operate they'd want mobility in the mountains and forests. Skis could be just what they need."

Holland says that an on-skis Russian infiltration of the Norwegian or Finnish Arctic is possible, but he feels that it'd be more likely just south of the Arctic Circle, in the snowy Baltic—in Lithuania, Latvia, or Estonia. "Those are former Soviet states," Holland says. "Russia harbors a desire to get them back, and there are large populations of ethnic Russians there. Ski warfare? The question's not as far out there as it would have been three years ago."

On the morning of day 2, at around 11 a.m., we reach the shore of frozen Itkillik Lake and gaze left at an undulating, rocky prominence that rises 1,000 feet to a bald, windswept pass.

This pass, we learn, has no name. It is nothing on the map of Alaska, but it is our grail, the most brutal test we'll face, and for me it looms especially large. Embedded among cold-weather soldiers, I'm aware that my credentials as a red-blooded American male are dubious. I do not own a gun. I don't know even how to fire a gun. But I am, at 52, still in pretty good shape. I cross-country ski every winter afternoon when I'm home in New Hampshire. So this whole trip, I've been eyeing my co-travelers, most of them career military men in their 20s and 30s, and wondering if, on a sustained ascent, I could beat them.

I start the climb at the back of the pack. But then on the first steep pitch, I close in on Campos. He was a bull a day earlier, busting trail for miles, but now he's addled by a loose skin on one of his skis, and flagging. I slip by him, then move along a side slope, through crusty snow, and then turn into the fall line. Könönen, the Finn, is in front, high above me, toiling through powder so we can all glide in his wake. I'm in fifth now, fifth out of 11, but my elderly calves cannot endure the steep pitch, so I cut a long, laborious traverse—all alone into white space for a full 15 minutes.

When I zig back, into a now-disparate conga line, I'm in third place. But then Könönen steps trailside for a moment's rest and it's just me and Steven Decker, the leader, moving together toward the shimmering white mirage of the top. Decker cuts trail in spurts—30 or 40 strides, then a long pause as he doubles over his poles, gasping for air. Following in his tracks, I'm a leech, a parasite. I feel guilty.

So eventually I surge. For a few heady seconds, there is nothing but blue sky before me. We're now more than 90 minutes into this climb. My calves are ruined, and I reach No Name Pass in second, behind Decker, but with enough spare time to polish off a languorous lunch (freeze-dried Beef Stroganoff) before the last stragglers show.

Do I feel a little smug? Well, sure, but the patriot in me is concerned: How is it that a card-carrying member of the AARP reached the top before the Marines and the Army guys?

Soon, Decker will provide the grim answer. "The U.S. military ski program," he tells me, "is at the corner between function and dysfunction." It's strayed, certainly. At the very end of World War II, in 1945, the Army's Tenth Mountain Division, an elite cadre of skiing soldiers, became Alpine legends when they forayed into Italy's Apennine Mountains and waged a series of daring and bloody assaults to help extinguish the German resistance in Italy.

The Tenth Mountain Division still exists, but it is now focused on desert and tropical warfare, on fighting in places like Saudi Arabia, Haiti, and Somalia. The U.S. military does not have a single battalion that specializes in ski warfare. There is no Seal-type force ready and waiting to ship off to the mountains of North Korea or the snowy Golan Heights, in Israel.

For today's soldiers, No Name Pass is a killer. We descend wearily, and at about 6:30 p.m. I finish a meager supper of chicken and rice and prepare to go to bed hungry, only to detect a salty scent on the breeze. At first it is faint, but soon it amounts to a tantalizing olfactory music, a keening siren song. Staff Sergeant Campos is, I learn, cooking his Spam. He is sautéing it inside his tent.

I move toward the smell, and Campos invites me inside, and it is warm in there. It is so warm and so comfortable, so civilized, that Campos, his tent mate, and I can loll on the sleeping bags and engage in casual banter. No more of the clipped, tense dialogue that has prevailed throughout this whole frozen trip: We chat about Campos's culinary ambitions—about his scheme to cook Mexican tortillas on his next Arctic outing. He comes up with a title for a prospective cookbook, *Freeze Your Weenie Off and Eat Like a Champ*. We devour every last morsel of Spam in the frying pan and then lick our fingers. Then I slope off to my tent, sated, and sleep like a baby.

The next afternoon, after an easy final leg of our trip, Campos and I talk more about what he'll put on his next Arctic packing list. "A chocolate bar for every day," he says, "some ready-cooked bacon, some ham. More pairs of contact gloves, so I can maneuver my hands, and also lots of Spam. I'm definitely bringing Spam next time."

Vladimir Putin, say your prayers.

Cross-Country Skier as Rock Star?

Ski, *December 18, 2012*

CROSS-COUNTRY SKIING. THE VERY WORDS INSTILL A CREEPING DREAD in the average alpinist. The memories are so dreary, so dark: Do you remember that time you slogged around the golf course on toothpick-thin planks? And the searing pain in your inner thighs, and the way the warming hut loomed forever on the distant horizon? Oh, and those Spandex-clad weirdos who went wailing by you, intent and gaunt and bug-like, on skate skis?

In most quarters, cross-country ski racers are toilsome nobodies—about as glamorous as professional horseshoe players. In northern Europe, however, things are different. A skinny skier can be a rock star—a stud, even. Witness Petter Northug, who has won two Olympic gold medals and more world championships than any other active ski racer. Northug is 26 and absurdly handsome, with lamp-like blue eyes, tousled blond hair, and a GQ physique—behold his rippling six-pack. He is, famously, a bad seed. On the racecourse, he taunts his opponents, shouting, "You're nothing but a rat!" as he overpowers them with his trademark finish line kick. Off-piste, he has an eye for the ladies. Last year, when rumor held that he was dating Iranian-born porn star Aylar Lie, the Norwegian paparazzi hid in the bushes outside his apartment, waiting in vain for a photo op.

Northug is a talented poker player. In the 2010 World Series of Poker, in Las Vegas, he placed 653rd out of more than 7,000 contestants. This July he returned to Vegas for the 2012 Series. When I met him there, amid legions of shuffling tourists in the casino of the Rio Hotel, he was carrying his roller skis in a neat zippered bag and bound for a workout in Red Rocks Canyon, just west of town. We climbed into a taxi. Then, in genial tones, he mused on the perils of Norwegian celebrity.

"Sometimes I have to hide behind sunglasses," he said. "Once when I went to a club I dressed like a girl. I put on a red wig and mascara and a skirt, but then when I got all sweaty, dancing, people said, 'Hey, it's him.' It was not good."

Northug paused now, dramatically, for he had an audience. Two Norwegian journalists were traveling with him—a writer from the Norwegian men's magazine *Vi Menn*, which sponsors him, and also a cameraman from Globus Media, which is now assembling an eight-part, six-hour reality TV program on Northug's adventures. For their benefit, Northug soon told a story about a teammate of his misdeeds on a trip to Japan. He spoke with a wry smirk, and with such antic delight that I found myself laughing even as the punch line came in Norwegian.

"What did you just say?" I asked Northug.

"Oh, nothing," he responded.

It wasn't clear where we were going (the consultations were all in Norwegian), but soon we stopped off at a small stucco home occupied by Northug's friends—five young male Norwegian poker players who were in town for a month. The place was a pigsty. Cans of Pringles potato chips lay scattered about, along with numerous boxes of Lucky Charms cereal. At noon the inhabitants, pale and pasty faced, were just waking up—and were happy to have Northug entertain them as he waited for his manager to arrive.

Northug chose, at this juncture, to discuss one of the central mysteries of cross-country ski racing. Last November, as he crossed a finish line in first, he made a curious gesture, planting his thumb on his nose. He later explained that he was "honoring that fantastic animal, the rhinoceros."

The Norwegian media divined that he was simply mocking his rivals, the Swedes, but now Northug unveiled the seamy truth: His nose-thumbing was in fact a shout-out to a Las Vegas gentlemen's club, the Spearmint Rhino. "I lost a poker bet in Vegas," he said, "so I had to do that. It was embarrassing, but if you don't keep your promises, they'll send the extreme mafia after you." He added that recently he won a high-stakes poker bet against his younger brother Thomas, who is also on the Norwegian team. "Thomas had to roller ski one loop, all the way around Trondheim in a very small Speedo," he said, alluding to their hometown.

Eventually, Northug's manager, Lars Gilleberg, showed up in a red Audi S5 convertible. Gilleberg, who's 40ish, is a large man. He wore a white undershirt stretched tight over his paunch, and he looked frazzled as he handed Northug a bottle of Gatorade.

Still, Northug regarded him with affectionate awe. "My manager is never drinking sports drinks," he said to me, "only champagne."

Northug drove the convertible now, hugging the curves at 55, then 60, then 65 in a 35-mile-per-hour zone. When he hopped out to roller ski, shirtless, on the shoulder of the highway, up a long slope toward Red Rock, he kept flowing along with sleek grace and punch. He did not move fast—it was 110 degrees out and he was skiing uphill—but there was something about the power and symmetry of his motions, and the way he hurled all his weight forward, balancing on his tiptoes to stab his poles into the pavement. Even casual bystanders could tell, watching, that this wasn't some schmo on his lunch break. This was an athletic event.

One of the Norwegian poker players trailed Northug, spectating, in a rented Camaro. Gilleberg trailed, too, handing Northug his sports drinks. The *Vi Menn* writer, Thorkild Gundersen, worked his amateur racing chops, trying to hang with Northug through the warm-up. Northug simply spat him off the back, and then laughed as he burst into song. "Now it is time," he larked, "for all the old people to go home."

He kept going—up toward the looming red sandstone cliffs, the sky a cloudless blue vault above him as he shimmered with sweat. In a few years, of course, Petter Northug's reign would be all over. His cartilage would stiffen; he too would grow old. Hints of Northug's fallibility would even crop up the next day; he'd fail out of the poker tourney very quickly. But for the moment Petter Northug was at the top of his game, and he was savoring the sweet ride.

"I am not just doing this for myself," he told me as he stood by the roadside after his long workout was done. "In Norway, everybody cares about cross-country skiing. I am doing this for my family, for Norway, for all the sportsmen." He took one last slug of Gatorade. Then he shook my hand and climbed into the Audi and zipped away, out of the canyon. He had places to go.

On with the Snow

Washington Post Magazine, *February 6, 2011*

THERE ARE MANY WAYS TO CONTEND WITH THE INDIGNITIES OF BEING middle aged, but the only tack that's ever worked for me involves flight—a deliberate fleeing, I mean, from the gray reality that my cartilage is fraying as my teeth travel south. It's pathetic, maybe, but I like to chase after that sweet weightlessness I felt long ago as a kid. I try to escape.

In winter 2010, at age 45, I ran away to Minneapolis, Minnesota, to spend a season cross-country ski racing. It was a bit like going to the South of France to taste wine. The Minneapolis–St. Paul metro area boasts what is almost certainly the most extensive network of urban ski trails in North America. There are more than 180 kilometers of groomed track. The terrain is nearly all publicly owned, and a season pass, usable at several ski parks, typically runs about $45.

In the Twin Cities, high school Nordic teams typically boast 50 or 60 athletes. There are citizens' races each weekend. Some are serious; some have the loose-limbed aura of a pickup basketball game. And every season augurs toward one culminating late February gala. The American Birkebeiner, staged three or so hours from Minneapolis in tiny Cable, Wisconsin, is North America's premier Nordic ski festival, which in 2010 drew more than 10,000 skiers. There are nine races throughout the course of a weekend and finish-line family reunions. There is a pancake breakfast for the distinguished members of the Birchleggings Club, all of whom have finished at least 20 times since the Birkebeiner's inception in 1973. There is even a genre of Birkie-specific music. ("Why do they ski so far?" goes one song. "It's a long drive in my car.") But the marquee event, always, is the 50-kilometer freestyle race, which wends from Cable to nearby Hayward, along a wide, birch-lined trail, luring both Euro superstars who finish in roughly two hours and hackers who slog through in six. That race, set for February 26, 2011, is so nasty with hills that on any given subzero weeknight in January in Minneapolis, you're likely to find whole legions of earnest, Lycra-clad Birkie-ists clattering their way through hill sprints like so many nuns telling their rosary beads.

Myself, I'd never actually raced on skinny skis, but long ago, in college, I ran cross-country and track. And before I ran, I was a downhill skier in love with the magic, swooping, bird-like sensation of gliding on snow. I wanted that delight all over again, and I wanted speed, too.

So one evening last January I found myself standing on a starting line in suburban Minneapolis, amid a scattering of whip-lean 20-somethings dressed in shiny stretch suits and jiggling their calves, warming up for a throwaway little race—a weekly 5K at Elm Creek Park Reserve. "Three," said the starter, "two, one."

There was the soft sound of poles swiftly smacking the snow, then the rattling whoosh of our skis. We were going—down a short straightaway at first, then hooking left, under the lights, jockeying for position, an entire pack of skis twisting like one fast-moving snake. I had not entered a race of any sort in almost 25 years. It was revelatory how focused—how unforgiving and basic—competition can be. A bunch of kids were whaling ahead of me; my task was to shut up and throw down.

We descended a hill, all of us stooping, our bodies aerodynamically tucked. The field spread out. I lost sight of the leaders. We came, about a half mile in, to a small hill where I found a young woman faltering. I passed her (yes!) and kept pushing—and actually managed to gut past one other person, an older gentleman. When I finished, in a little over 14 minutes, I was in seventh place out of 11 and only eight seconds behind a 46-year-old racer who (I did some Googling) had done okay, age-group-wise, the previous winter. I was feeling my oats. I imagined a season of glory and upset.

But my joy was not complete until the next afternoon, when a call came in from my brother, Tim, who was studying the race results on

Skinnyski.com as we spoke. "Not bad," he said, his tone judicious and measured. "You hung right in there."

* * *

My brother is 41, and he knows how to ski. In the 2009 Birkie, he came in 45th among more than 3,300 finishers. In two other Birkies, he has likewise finished in the top 60. And let me say this: I made the boy. Proof lies in a 1974 black-and-white photo I have taped to my fridge. In the picture, taken by the side of a lake in summer, I am all scrawny and bare-chested and throwing a rock into the water. I am throwing with my left hand. My brother, 4 at the time, is watching me intently and cradling a rock of his own—in his left hand.

It was no surprise that my brother pitched lefty in Little League, then became a runner, and then (after going to college in St. Paul) a Nordic ski racer. What startled and galled me was how he surpassed me eventually, bringing to athletics a grace I could never quite muster and, in his 30s, an almost scientific precision. One day a couple of years ago, when I asked him to join me for a long bike ride, he demurred, quibbling over my "training technique."

A fraternal iciness ensued, enduring for months. But then around Thanksgiving 2009, I went cross-country skiing, and, thanks to a long summer of road biking, I felt stronger than ever. I e-mailed my brother. His response was one word: "Birkie?"

I sidestepped the question. My racing days were so ancient that I'd distilled them into myth, so when I regaled my daughter—now 16 and a runner herself—with tales of my running "career," my essential mediocrity was forgotten. I was a walking highlights reel, 24/7. I was the worst kind of has-been, and I was okay with that. Sort of. Eventually, I went down in my basement and dusted off the skinny, rubber-wheeled "roller skis" my brother had scared up for me a decade before. I began skiing the streets of my city, Portland, Oregon, each afternoon.

Most people, upon hearing of my Birkie quest, spooned me stupid bromides such as, "Oh, even finishing would be an accomplishment." My brother took me seriously. When I spent Christmas with him at his home on Long Island, he turned the visit into a skiing colloquium, rolling the meandering roads with me for two hours each day before we repaired, evenings, to his laptop to analyze technique videos starring German wunderkind Axel Teichmann.

Tim's refrain was "dynamic compression": When you ski by skating along, as I would in the Birkie, you want to engage your abs and bend your shins low toward the snow before you stab both poles, rise and repeat. The motion is musical violence: Decompressed, with his hands held high, a good skier looks like a conductor poised to render a crescendo of Wagner's. I looked more like a question mark, with my back bent and my pole plants mincing, so one morning my brother, playing coach, rode beside me in his car as I roller skied. It was 25 degrees outside and snowing so hard that I was slithering and floating along on the slippery pavement. "Nail it!" my brother shouted each time I planted my poles. "Nail it! Nail it! Nail it!"

* * *

But my brother teaches at a high school in Manhattan. He couldn't travel to Minneapolis, so when I landed there I needed a new guru. I went to Finn Sisu, arguably the Twin Cities' premier shop. Finn Sisu is the sole U.S. purveyor of a Finnish-made roller ski, Marwe, that my brother deems sine qua non. There are ancient ski posters on the wall there, and there is a little museum of vintage roller skis. The proprietor, Ahvo Taipale, is a Finnish émigré who twice coached the University of Minnesota's women's Nordic squad to a national championship. He now coaches citizen racers. He is 64 and small and owlish, with a halo of red hair and whiskery red eyebrows. When I arrived, he was in his office, reminiscing about '70s-era ski racing with a crony.

"Do you remember the Winter Carnival race in 1976?" he said. "It was 4 below that morning, and when I tried out my fiberglass skis"— Taipale waved his hand, dismissive—"very slow. I won that race on birch-bottomed skis, and I still have those skis out front—under glass by the counter."

Taipale was giving voice to a deeper aesthetic. For him, skiing isn't about snazzy gear. It is, rather, about the pursuit of perfect, Platonic technique, and he actually glimpsed such technique once, as a kid back in Finland. He listened to ski races on the radio then, and his hero was Nikolay Anikin, a Russian. Whenever Anikin's picture appeared in the newspaper, Taipale cut open a potato and, using the juice, pasted the photo into a scrapbook. Decades later, Anikin immigrated to Duluth, Minnesota. Taipale saw him ski for the first time. "His technique was exactly as I imagined it," he said. "So graceful."

Taipale's eyes welled with tears as he told the story. Usually, though, he is a crisp man—stern, even. He maintains that nearly all Birkie skiers have "terrible" form, and he says, "It takes me four to six years to teach someone to ski race. There are no shortcuts."

When I asked if it was possible, ever, to learn in a season, he saw me as a symptom of a national pathology. "Americans," he sniffed, "all they want is instant gratification. Every race, they start out too fast and then die. When I took a group over to Finland to race, they were all moaning: 'These damned grandmothers with bamboo poles passed me.'"

I had come hoping to talk Taipale into giving me a private lesson. Now, tentatively, I asked. A few days later, at 7 a.m., we met at Battle Creek Park in St. Paul.

Taipale wore a knit ski cap that did not quite cover his eyebrows. As he watched me ski, he squinted, like a jeweler inspecting a watch. His reviews were sour, and also technical, alluding to various permutations of skate skiing. After I clambered up a small hill, he said: "I don't even know what that was. That wasn't V1, that wasn't V2, that wasn't open field skate." He shook his head. "I don't know what it was."

I conceded that I struggled on uphills. "Of course," he said, "because you are not using your core. Your technique is not sustainable."

I repeated the hill five or six times, taking pains to crunch my abs and to time my pole plants so they coincided precisely with when I set my ski on the snow. I wanted so much to please him.

"That's a little better," he said finally.

It was an opening. "I understand what you're saying," I said brightly. "But I just can't make my body do it."

"That's why I say four to six years."

* * *

I kept skiing. I looped about the 25K trail network at Theodore Wirth Park in Minneapolis—over a hilly golf course and through a bog and some woods—for two hours each afternoon. I joined a team, Balance Nordic. I got a shiny gray uniform and two days a week streamed about on the snow with my gray-suited homies. I skied sometimes without poles to work on my balance. I did sustained sprints. I got better.

Still, I was trapped in a caste system. The Birkie's organizers sort all skiers into 12 separate "waves" months before the race even begins. There is my brother's wave, the "elite" men, who get to start first, when the snow is pristine and (usually) cooler and faster. There is the elite women's wave. Then, for racers with slower qualifying times, there are 10 numbered waves whose start times are separated by 10-minute intervals. By Wave 8, there is a major funk factor going on—people skiing in Halloween masks and kilts, that sort of thing.

And then there are the lowliest waves, Waves 9 and 10, reserved for skiers who have no marathon credentials at all and are hence obliged to ski in rutted tracks, amid the PowerBar wrappers shucked by their betters. I was in Wave 10, of course. I got no credit for riding my bike 150 or so miles a week back home or for keeping pace with Wave 2 skiers in practice. I was unjustly oppressed, so I wrote a plaintive, carefully crafted note to the Birkie's wave placement specialists, pleading for a promotion. No dice. I spent much of February vacillating between a smug certainty that I'd prove them wrong and a black self-doubt, a fear that they'd apprehended something that I myself lacked the courage to apprehend—that I was old and washed up: done.

* * *

The start of any long-distance race is a release—a reprieve from the waiting. And when they let us loose, finally, beneath blue skies at the Birkie, it was a glorious moment. Almost instantly, I was way, way out in front of 500-odd skiers and ensconced, along with 10 or 12 other intent Birkie rookies—college guys, mostly—in a sort of Wave 10 wrecking crew. We were the lords of the gutter. We were kings, and early on we shared sprightly banter.

"Yeah, bro!"

"Dude!"

"Wave 10 power!"

We started to climb the first incline, the infamous Power Line, a four-kilometer-long series of giant rollers that rise and undulate skyward like killer waves in a surf movie. A couple of kids passed me. I let them go. We turned left into the woods, and suddenly on the next climb there was a thick clot of skiers in Wave 9 bibs toiling along like an army of ants.

It is not easy to pass through packs of skating skiers, for they are wider than, say, runners, with their legs splayed and their poles cast wide. When I spoke to the greatest late-wave skier in recent memory—one Jason Liebsch, who stormed out of the now-extinct 11th wave in 2003 to finish 235th overall—he described a long struggle that saw him churning past more than 2,000 slower racers. "I was jumping over people's skis on the downhills," he said.

I propelled myself up some hills using only my poles, so as to be narrower. "Coming through," I kept shouting. "On your left, on your left." We worked through the eighth wave. The trail kept climbing. Fire Tower Hill, 12 kilometers in, is the highest point in the race, at 1,730 feet. My brother told me that's where he always felt the most tired. I felt oddly fresh.

But the trail was spent. On curving downhills, the snow was carved up, so that you were confronted with four or five narrow chutes shaped like luge tracks, each ice-bottomed chute walled with a couple of high berms of shaved ice. You had to pick your chute, pre-descent (no one wants to climb out of a gully at speed), and on one plunge, Bobblehead Hill, I found myself closing in on a dawdling Wave 7 skier and at risk of great ridicule.

Bobblehead is where about 300 snowmobilers gather, Birkie time, to grade skiers' crashes on a scale of 1 to 10 by holding up little numbered placards, as at a diving contest. The place brims with NASCAR-esque peril. Bryon Schroeder, the owner of Hayward Power Sports and the de facto dean of Bobblehead Hill, told me: "I've seen 40 skiers in a pile at the bottom, and if you go off the trail, there are blackberry brambles. And those are pretty hard to pull out of spandex."

I was 30 feet behind the lady from Wave 7, then 20 feet. It was going to take some crazy tricks to avoid smacking into her and wrecking my knees. I jammed my poles downward, ruddering deep in the snow. Then, slowing slightly, I leapt the berm, teetered, and skated clear amid, I believe, a small burst of hooting joy from the gallery.

* * *

By the time we reached the halfway point, crossing County Highway OO, the real race was long over. The elites were done, and yet I came across a tall, somber man standing trailside, keeping score. "You're running sixth and seventh in your wave," he shouted at me and a cohort. I was touched—someone actually cared. And I was buoyed, too, by the spectators clumped on the highway, wildly rattling cowbells. "More bell!" I said. "More bell!"

The truth is, I felt very good. My technique was a horror show still, but I had trained for this race. I felt strong. At the next water station, I dropped a couple of kids from my wave. I was still conserving, though.

The Birkie's most infamous climb, Bitch Hill, which rises 90 feet in just 200 meters, starts at the 40-kilometer mark. My brother had told me that Bitch was nothing compared with the cragged mountains we knew growing up in New England. I'm not sure I quite buy that take, but this time, at least, Bitch did not kill me. And when I crested the top, I let myself imagine the village of Hayward: the swarmed finish line, the little shops, the spectators roistering in the warm midday sun.

What was strange, indeed almost disorienting, was that my brother wasn't down there. He was still back in New York, stranded by a blizzard. He'd made absurd efforts to get out, excavating two feet of snow from around his car at 4 a.m., then driving to the airport in Newark, but all flights were canceled, and when he called on the eve of the Birkie, he was pained. "I trained 500 hours for this race," he said. Later, he recognized that this was my moment, too. He called back, leaving a message. "Bill," he said, his voice at once sardonic and sweet, "do it for us, for the victims of the Blizzard of 2010. Ski smart. Think technique. It's all you."

My brother had been kind to me. I had come shambling along, begging admittance into his world, and he'd opened the door and shared with me all of skiing's intricate wonders. He had been patient. On several occasions, he offered counsel as I hemmed and hawed over whether I should be using poles that were 160, as opposed to 165, centimeters long. Such conversations were always urgent and clipped. We spoke a common language stripped of superfluous gesture. We were brothers.

On the ice on Lake Hayward, fighting a headwind, I tried to ski like a machine punching nails. I wove through a traffic jam of Wave 5 skiers. Then I climbed a tiny slope onto the snow-packed city streets and kicked in. My finish time was 2 hours, 46 minutes, and 3 seconds—a string of digits that at first made my blood sing with ecstasy. (In 2009, the winning time was 2:11:48.) Soon, though, I learned that on the morning's firm, fast snow, Fabio Santus had set a course record of 1:56:58 as he became the seventh Italian to win the 50K freestyle race. Everyone blazed, and I was, well, the 723rd-place finisher of 3,645. I'd missed qualifying for Wave 1 by less than two minutes, and I felt a shade of chagrin. Why had I left so much in the tank? And all that hollering I did on the highway ("More bell, more bell")—why had I stooped to such junior varsity horseplay?

But my self-recrimination was slight, and contained. When I sidled into the Moccasin Bar on Hayward's main drag, what I felt mostly was a physical potency. For years, I had hungered for one more hit of that clean agony that only racing can yield: that taste of blood in your wheezing throat, that knowing that you have to push, and that you will, and that you will survive. I had not skied a perfect, all-out Birkie, definitely not, but I had come close enough to feel quite alive.

And so when a friend jostled toward me through the crowd with a pitcher of beer, I commenced drinking. And somewhere in the back of my skull there lurked a bright, splendid thought: In five years, I'll have the technique licked. I'll be 50, sure, but there'll still be plenty of fight left in the dog.

That's right. Read my lips. The Italians are going down.

From the Margins of Endurance Sports

Stairway to Hell

New York Times Magazine, *January 27, 2013*

WHEN YOU WATCH THE VIDEO FROM THE START OF LAST FEBRUARY'S
Empire State Building Run-Up, an 86-story stair race, one man stands
out. Thomas Dold, a 28-year-old German wearing Bib No. 1, is already
a few inches ahead when the starting horn blasts. His shins are canting
into a run, and with his left arm he's pushing at the chest of a runner to
that side of him. A split second later, his right arm juts up to block more
runners.

All around Dold, the racers are wincing, for what's coming is harsh.
There are 1,576 steps ahead of them, 10 to 12 minutes of suffering. And
before that, less than 10 yards from the start, there's a door to get through.
It's standard size, 36 inches wide, and everyone, Dold especially, wants to
be the first one there. The jockeying is desperate. In 2009, Suzy Walsham,
an Australian, was shoved into the wall next to the door. "The impact was
so great," she says, "that I initially thought I had broken my nose and lost
teeth." She fell and was trampled before she rose and ran on to victory.
"I get super nervous and anxious whenever I start" at the Empire State
Building, says Walsham, who has won the women's division three times
and will be one of about 650 competitors at this year's race, which takes
place February 6, 2013. "I really dread the start."

What the racers may dread even more, however, is the sight of
Thomas Dold dashing up the stairs two at a time, yanking along on
the railings. Dold has won Empire State (known as Esbru among the
stair-racing community) a record seven consecutive times. He is the only
person in the world who makes a living at stair-racing (his sponsors

include a German health care company), which makes him the lord of an obscure but nonetheless codified sport. According to the World Cup rankings on towerrunning.com, Dold finished 2012 in first place, with 1,158 points, 157 more than the runner-up, Piotr Lobodzinski of Poland. Four hundred of those points came from his victory at Esbru, tower racing's unofficial world championships, and its oldest contest, dating to 1978. Another 156 stair races, held in 25 nations, generate World Cup points as well.

Dold also sits atop the Vertical World Circuit, a championship tour of eight celebrated races—among them, Esbru—and he is a minor celebrity on YouTube. In one clip, you can see a smiling Dold sprinting stadium steps at a photo shoot for a print ad. In another video, from the Corrida Vertical, a 28-story dash in São Paulo, the announcer cracks, "A shortcut to win the race is break Dold's legs . . . or giving him some sleeping pills." Dold wins and, as he crosses the finish line, still running, peels off his plain white race jersey to reveal a sleek undershirt emblazoned with his web address, run2sky.com.

In New York in 2012, Dold may have gotten away with a false start; the video is fairly incriminating. "I was moving before the start," he told me recently. But then, he said, he caught himself and stopped. So he was actually at a disadvantage, he said, "moving backward when the others are moving forward."

In interviews, Dold is chipper and exudes supreme confidence. "I can run backward faster than most people can run forward," he boasts. (He is in fact one of the world's premier backward runners, having completed a heels-first mile in 5:46, a world record.) At times, he lapses into the third person, like a major-sports star, or Donald Trump. "It's all about beating Dold," he told a German reporter not long ago, summing up the stair-racing world. "That's the goal for hundreds of participants."

* * *

Most of the important stair races happen in Europe and Asia. A tiny cadre of die-hards—roughly a dozen men and three or four women—travel the globe chasing minuscule cash prizes. The largest single prize, in Taipei, is less than $7,000. Esbru offers no prize money. The race sites are often architecturally significant: the Messeturm tower in Basel; the Palazzo Lombardia in Milan; the Swissôtel in Singapore, designed by I. M. Pei. "There's something very elemental about climbing an iconic building," says Sproule Love, a New Yorker who has finished third at the Empire State Building three times. "You can survey the area and see how far you have come."

Still, the stair racers don't experience architecture so much as stairwells. I assumed their races are characterized by a mind-numbing sameness, but Walsham assured me I was wrong. "Some stairwells turn to the left," she said. "Some turn to the right. Sometimes the stairs are shallow, sometimes they're steep. And the number of floors always varies."

Walsham, who works in Singapore as a manager for a computer-security firm, spent about $12,000 traveling to races last year. In the United States, a small contingent of stair climbers are shelling out similar sums to get to the 100 or so American races offered each year. When I went to Los Angeles recently, for the 51-story Climb for Life race, I met Daniel Dill, who flew in from Texas, happy to pay the $50 entry fee and the requisite $100 donation to the Cystic Fibrosis Foundation for a race that would take him less than 13 minutes. Dill, a large man dressed in articulated-toe sneakers, brought with him a special warm-up tool, an Elevation Training Mask. It was designed for Mixed Martial Arts fighters, he said. "It's supposed to stimulate red blood cells and open up the lungs."

* * *

Nearby was Zivadin Zivkovic, who came up from San Diego, more than two hours away. The drive was old hat for Zivkovic: twice a week he commutes to Los Angeles to train with the nation's premier stair-climbing squad, West Coast Labels, which doubles as a quasi family. Its 50 members call one another "step siblings" and shower one another with high-stepping affection on a Facebook group, Stair Race Training Buds. At races, members will sometimes brace and push injured teammates up the stairs as they falter. After races, the step sibs like to go out for cigars.

That sense of hard-won camaraderie must be the draw, because running in an unventilated stairwell may be the least pleasant form of recreation ever conceived. The lungs are so taxed that "climbers' cough" is a well-known affliction. Every climb is a redline endeavor, with the heart rate often topping 180 beats a minute.

But stair-racing also has the appeal of newness. Most endurance sports are by now highly evolved, their training regimens a matter of science: if your goal is to become a world-class marathoner, for example, you will almost certainly run between 110 and 130 miles per week. Stair-racing is guesswork, comparatively, and there is room for all sorts of experimentation—Dill's face mask, say, or choreography. One stair-climbing devotee, Stan Schwarz, a computer-systems administrator, publishes detailed charts enumerating the stair counts and riser heights for each racecourse. Flights that have an odd number of steps present special challenges, for good stair racers go two steps at a time, and in one recent Facebook thread a correspondent calling himself Stair Climblunatic bravely contemplated a building with 23-step staircases. "I'll be doing a triple step on every flight," Lunatic said.

At bottom, though, stair climbing's appeal may lie mostly in its simplicity. It is suffering distilled, and its practitioners embrace the agony with an almost religious ardor. On Stair Race Training Buds, there is a lyrical video of the elite stair climber Justin Stewart wending his way up the glass-encased stairwell of an eight-story parking garage at night. The stairway is bathed in amber light, and as we watch Stewart's lonely labors from a distance—from across a desolate stretch of asphalt—we see a monk in devotion.

On Facebook, there is also a photo of Schwarz lying facedown in a stairwell, almost dead from exhaustion, and an earnest post from one Nelson Quong: "Up at 4 a.m. to go climb the college stairs, then to the gym for an hour of intense physical therapy, then some weight training. Since meeting my wonderful step sibs, this never feels like a lonely workout."

* * *

In March 2012, I entered my first stair race. My father had just died of pulmonary fibrosis. The American Lung Association was staging a fund-raiser, a 34-story Tackle the Tower race, in my dad's hometown, Hartford, so my brother, Tim, and I put together a memorial team. We are both cross-country ski racers, and Tim, in fact, is one of the two top racers competing for the Manhattan Nordic Ski Club: the other is his training partner and best friend Sproule Love.

Love, 41, is a professional stair racer; last year, West Coast Labels paid him $500 for travel expenses. In other words, we had ringers, which meant we had a chance to defeat the Northeast's preeminent stair squad, a multistate team called the Tower Masters.

One star of Tower Masters is Alex Workman, a 36-year-old engineer based in Schenectady, New York, who arrived at the Hartford racecourse early to measure the riser height of the stairs (6.8 inches). Workman sometimes climbs with a metronome clipped to his shirt to regulate the pacing of his strides. When we met him in the elevator, he was exceedingly perky. But the vibe was tense—he was familiar with Love and my brother. Last year on his blog, *Climbing to the Top*, he titled one entry "Schooled by Sproule" after a race at One Penn Plaza. A later entry, about another New York stair race, one at which my brother set a course record, was headed "Schooled by Sproule's Friend at 30 Rock."

After chatting briefly with Workman, we moved to a stairwell, and Love told me about his training, which takes place in his 40-story Manhattan apartment building. He used to climb with his young son, Mazin, strapped to his chest. "We started when Maz was 14 months old," Love said, "and at first he was cooperative. He'd sing; he'd sleep; he'd point to things on the stairs, to ask questions." For a few golden months, Mazin burbled, "Go, Baba, go," from his pouch. But then, Love said, "he got impatient, and one day, he just told me, 'I'm done, Baba.'" Love replaced him with sandbags. Carrying the weight upstairs, he said, is "miserable, masochistic."

But it paid off for Love, who works as a mortgage loan analyst. He won the Hartford race. Workman finished second and my brother third, and I managed to take seventh, out of more than 550 runners. Our team won, beating the Tower Masters—who were at less than full strength—as well as dozens of ad hoc squads, among them the Freeshipping.com All Stars. (Team finishes were determined by cumulative times.) Later, after the awards ceremony, as Love and I rode our bikes away in the rain, we were all but singing with joy. "It feels good!" Love exulted. "It feels good!"

In our giddiness, we began to dream of another upset. We wondered: Could Thomas Dold be beaten at Esbru 2013?

* * *

There are reasons to think so. In summer 2012, at a steep 91-story race in Taipei, a onetime Australian mountain-running champion named Mark Bourne nipped Dold by four seconds. Dold would later say about that race: "I'd been training for a marathon. I'd been running long distances, rather than stairs." Nonetheless, Taipei offers evidence of Dold's vulnerability—as even last year's Esbru victory does. His winning time at the Empire State Building was his slowest ever: 10:28, almost a minute off the course record of 9:33.

That record was set in 2003 by an Australian cyclist named Paul Crake, who won Esbru five times. Crake, however, can no longer run—a 2006 mountain-bike crash rendered him a paraplegic—so who could beat Dold next week?

"A lot of guys could," says Rickey Gates, a professional mountain runner and onetime Esbru runner-up who writes for *Trail Runner* magazine. "I'm 100 percent sure that if you offered a million-dollar purse at Esbru, the winning time would be in the low nines."

Who would win? Track runners? Three-thousand-meter specialists?

"No," Gates says. "They're probably too skinny. It's a sport that favors cyclists—they've got the sheer quad strength and the high lactic threshold it takes. Cross-country ski racers would do well, too, but you'd have a hard time convincing a world-class skier to run up the Empire State Building in the middle of February. And really, there's no incentive for anyone to do Esbru. There's no prize money, and you have to train specifically for the race—you have to run stairs. And the whole time you're thinking: Why am I doing this? To get my picture in the paper?"

* * *

Of the probable contestants at the 2013 Esbru, Gates himself looks like a favorite, as does Bourne. An Australian has won Esbru 11 times, making the country a kind of Kenya of stair-racing.

I'm rooting for Love, though, and not just because he's a friend. No New Yorker has won the race since 1979, when Jim Rafferty prevailed, and this strikes me as sad, given that Esbru began as a stunt involving almost no one but New Yorkers. That first race was won by Gary Muhrcke, a retired New York City fireman. At the time, Muhrcke was receiving an annual tax-free disability pension of more than $11,000, because of a back injury. He was pilloried in the press—the *Times* editorialized that he should give firehouse Dalmatians a course in jogging—and he never entered Esbru again. But the race still bears the rough-and-tumble spirit of his era.

Consider the mass start. It is dangerous, and some voices within stair-racing have pressed the New York Road Runners, which hosts Esbru, to start racers at intervals. The Road Runners club has made some concessions. It now pads the doorway, for instance, and in 2012 began limiting the mass start to two heats. This year 21 top men will start en masse, as will 10 women. Everyone else will begin at intervals—and will most likely feel lucky even making it into the race. The Road Runners received 1,955 applications for 650 spots.

For these runners, sharp elbows will probably be a part of the experience. The director of the race, Peter Ciaccia, seems to regard physical contact as part of the Esbru brand. When I asked him about Dold's starting-line skirmishing, he chuckled and said: "We call that the Thomas Dold wingspan. Yeah, there's gamesmanship to this race." Ciaccia went on, "A lot of that goes on in the stairwell—that's why stair-racing is an extreme sport."

Even the Empire State stairs have some perverse charm. "It's grim in that stairwell," Love says fondly. "It's like the inside of a battleship. Everything is gunmetal gray. And the layout is crazy—on the early floors you'll have only 8 or 10 steps before a turn. Later, there's 20." Almost every racer I spoke to described the course in hallowed tones. "It's Fenway Park," Love says. "It's Wrigley Field."

* * *

Love is a long shot. His best Esbru finish time, 10:51, came back in 2006, when he was 34. Since then, he has all but given up running outside the stairwell, a concession to plantar fasciitis (pushing off stair steps on a flat foot, however, causes him no pain). He stopped competing for five years. In late 2011, however, he left his job as an energy consultant. Sparsely employed over the next six months, he spent nearly all his waking hours circling Central Park on wheeled roller skis with my brother. He did stair workouts—Mazin, then almost 2, watched from the family's apartment-door frame, slightly terrified by his dad's grimaces—and he went on a winning streak. In one five-month stretch, he won five successive North American stair races. He broke the course record at the world's longest stair race, at Willis Tower in Chicago, climbing 103 stories in just over 13 minutes.

"He came back out of nowhere, at the age of 40," Alex Workman says, marveling. "Ten years from now, even if he fell off the face of the earth again, I'm sure people would still be talking about Sproule Love."

Then in February 2012, fit and race-ready, he tore a calf muscle en route to Esbru while jogging through Midtown. "The Empire State Building was in plain view," he says. "That was one of my lowest moments as an athlete." But in June, having planned his family's spring break strategically, he showed up in Frankfurt and finished a solid fourth at a European Championship qualifier. Now he gets another chance at Esbru.

On February 6, Sproule Love will be among the chosen 21 elite men to start the 35th running of Esbru, along with Thomas Dold. "In '02," he says, "I got to the door first. I led the race for the first 50 stories. Then I blew up—on the stairs, you can't recover. But you get smarter as you get older; you get a little bit wiser. This time, I'm going to start slow. I'll be the last one into the stairwell, probably. It's always a good idea to keep your powder dry."

Bounding Ambition

Northwest Magazine, *September 10, 1989*

MY BEST FRIEND ERIC—WELL AT LEAST HE WAS THE KID I HUNG OUT with most—became the Slurpee-slurping champion of the neighborhood early that summer. His eyes bulging, he snatched the ice cold paper cup from my hand then sloshed the green slush down his gullet—in 14.3 seconds.

David Maloney, who'd just moved onto the street, was also a sort of champion. On a drizzly evening that June, he balanced on one foot for nearly two hours—and his picture appeared in the *Farmington News* for doing it.

And Eddy Fitzsimmons had notched the achievement that lingered most in our memory. On the eighth day of July that summer, Eddy sunk his hands and knees and crawled three miles without stopping. And in doing this, he nearly made it into that book that Eric and I read through every day, the fascinating book whose pages we had dog-eared and annotated in orange felt tip pen and almost memorized: The world's record for crawling, as chronicled in *Guinness Book of World Records*, was 5.33 miles.

Eddy, in short, had nearly become famous. And we all wanted to become famous because being a neighborhood champion was not really enough. You were still just a kid and you still had to take out the trash.

People who were famous seemed immune to problems and uncertainty. "We came here to play baseball," my Red Sox heroes would intone as they were interviewed in the locker room, "and that's what we did out there today. We played good baseball."

My own forte, as a skittish, skinny 10-year-old growing up in the suburbs outside Hartford, Connecticut, was obscure. I could pogo stick. No one else on the street (except maybe Eric) really cared about pogo sticking; certainly no one else owned a pogo stick. But I did—and I could make the thing work.

I could lunge over a puddle or a hole in the pavement. I could clench the shaft between my thighs, tense my abdomen and bounce 17 times with no hands and only one foot touching the stick, and execute perfectly those tiny, one-inch-off-the-ground sewing-machine hops you need to do if you wanted to conserve your energy and pogo for a long time. Even Eric—a sly, manipulative kid who usually wrote the rules to fit the game and then beat you and then made you remember that he had beaten you—could not do these things. I was the best pogo sticker in the neighborhood, in the whole town, perhaps. But I was silent about my prowess. I never pogoed in public, and I never told anyone of my skills. I was a closet champion.

Until, that is, the muggy August afternoon I stepped into our garage, pulled my pogo stick down from the wall, and started in on those sewing-machine hops. And kept going—past Eric's consecutive jump best, 478 pogos, then past my own record, 862, then past 1,000, past 2,000, past 3,000, and on up toward the exhausting, exhilarating heights of five-digit pogo-stick jumping. When I hit 1,000, my legs felt springy and strong, and the staccato beat of the pogos—the jolt! jolt! jolt! that thuds through your thighs each time you land—was smoothing out. The jumps were flowing together into a slinky rhythm that echoed against the walls, and the coal-black spring was compressing and expanding, compressing and expanding, over and over, dancing on the shaft of the stick.

I hopped over to the corner and pulled open the overhead door. I stripped off my shirt and lofted it onto the driveway. A few minutes later, my mother squinted into the garage and peered at me with one of those, "Well, at least it's keeping you busy" looks.

Eric sauntered into the garage just after I reached 8,000. "Eight thousand, three hundred and fifty-one," I said. I looked at the floor then out through the spider webs that encrusted the windows. I did not look at him. "Fifty-three, 54, 55, 56," he said, his voice a bit fresher and sharper than mine. "Fifty-seven, 58 . . ."

He stood there counting for maybe two minutes. then he ran inside to get a clipboard and a pencil. I was, you see, halfway there. The world's record for consecutive pogo stick jumps was 17,323. Danny Kloster, of Clinton, Michigan, had set this record, in two hours and 50 minutes.

* * *

"If anything happens," Eric said a while after I passed 12,000, "if you have to go on TV or anything, I'm your manager, all right?"

A thousand or so pogos after that, he was peeling his bike across the Fitzsimonses' lawn and heading toward his house. He wanted to get some decent clothes on. He wanted to look nice just in case the press did cover this.

My mother was in the garage with her camera when I hit 16,000. She was fiddling with the light meter and, every so often, pressing her hand down on Eric's head—as though he were in danger of floating away. "No," she was saying to him, "you can't call the TV stations yet. Wait until he gets the record."

Once she'd fixed her camera, she crouched to the floor, snapped two quick pictures and then shuffled to the trash barrels at the back of the garage.

I could tell that she was terrified of rattling me, that she knew I would hate her forever (or at least a week) if she caused me to fall off. But I was only vaguely concerned with her and Eric and what they were doing and thinking. They didn't seem to matter.

The only thing in the world that mattered, really, was that I stayed on that pogo stick until 17,323. I was on the verge of making history—and I was also on the verge of crashing to the garage floor. The shaft of my stick was squeaking for lack of oil. The muscles in my thighs were shaking, and my knees, which had been wrapped around the stick for two hours now, were red and swollen. And I knew this: Anyone who made it all the way to 16,000, and then fell off, was a loser.

* * *

"Seventeen thousand, three hundred and nineteen, 20, 21." Eric was squatting on the driveway now, his hands pressed before in a prayerlike pose as he counted the jumps. "Twenty-two, 23, 17,324!" He burst from the asphalt, his arms thrust high over his head, and then bounded up and down, keeping pace with me as I eked out a few insurance pogos. For a moment, the sight of Eric hopping all over the place, in the bright white shirt and pants he'd donned for the press, was hilarious. But even as I got down off the stick at 17,353 and limped to our porch, Eric kept going. He kept tearing around our driveway, prancing first toward the basketball rim, then toward the brown and yellow grass at the edge of our lawn— and I became frightened somehow that I would get no credit for what I had done, that Eric would hog all the glory.

We sat on our porch, Eric in his resplendent white suit and I in an undershirt that he had emblazoned with "17,354," and waited for the TV trucks to pull into the driveway.

The first reporter to arrive—and it took her two hours to get there— was a woman who wore sandals and was a friend of my mom. We went into the backyard. She sipped root beer and chatted about her son (I knew this kid; he was a jerk). Occasionally, she tossed me a question. It was even worse when the TV trucks came. Two young men, hulking fellows with mustaches, emerged and loped across our lawn. One of them was still sucking the remnants of some drink he'd bought at McDonald's.

They told me to pogo on the driveway—it didn't matter to them that I'd actually set the record in the garage—and then the taller of the two men panned his camera over me as I thudded through 100 or so painful, wobbly hops.

After that, they talked with Eric. They spent two or three minutes filming him, asking him questions. And then they started up the driveway toward their truck.

My mother seemed confused. She stepped toward them, then asked if this was going to be on the evening news.

"Sorry," said the man with the camera. "But we can't promise anything. We don't make those decisions."

That night, as we watched the evening news for nearly an hour, all they'd talked about, really, was President Nixon. My father, who sat beside me in the gray suit he'd worn to the office, was dozing off. My mother, giving up, had gone to the kitchen to carve up the pot roast. But then the anchorman said, "A 10-year-old boy . . ."

"Mom! C'mere! Quick! Check it out! I'm on TV!"

* * *

I am 25 years old now, and of course, I have never been famous—and invulnerable and larger than life—in the way that I hoped I would be. Actually, I wasn't famous that night I got on television; my mother still made me dry the dishes after dinner. I didn't make it into the *Guinness Book of World Records*—Guinness, we learned, only acknowledges feats witnessed by two impartial adults. And the only person who's curious about every detail of my life is the bill collector who keeps calling to say he'll cut off my electricity.

But I'm not entirely jaded.

* * *

The other day, as I sat in my apartment trying to write, there was this kid pelting a tennis ball at the brick wall across the street—throwing, catching it on the bounce, throwing it, and so on. This kid had been out there for several hours, or at least it seemed that way. And the noise that he was making was incredibly distracting.

I decided to go out into the street. I figured that, if the kid saw me and I looked adequately annoyed, he would go away. But when I got out there, he was shuffling all over the street and pulling quickly at the bill of his cap after each throw—and he didn't notice me. I changed my tactic; I would reason with him.

As I paced back and forth in the street, I was not quite sure what was running through his mind. Maybe he was angry at someone, and just venting steam. Maybe he was trying to break a neighborhood record. And maybe (who knows?) this kid was driven by some vague and blind hope that, by tossing a ball against a wall, he could launch himself out of kid world, out of the world of chores and broken tops and become a world champion, famous.

So I decided, finally, not to say anything. And I just stood there beside him, watching the ball now spinning smoothly off the bricks, now ricocheting off the mortar in the wall, now dancing madly, dangerously, off some crack in the sidewalk—watching, glad each time the kid caught the ball.

Cleetus Fit

Outside, *November 5, 2018*

FOR ME, THE BIGGEST MYSTERY SWIRLING AROUND FITNESS GURU KALE Poland is why the retail giant Walmart has thus far failed to offer him corporate sponsorship. A few years ago, when Kale was competing in the excruciating Peak 500 footrace in Vermont, running a muddy mountain loop over and over amid torrid rainstorms, his mildewed, blistered feet swelled up like balloons. His running shoes became skin-shearing straitjackets, so Kale made a strategic move that would now be legend, if only Walmart had been paying attention: he sent his wife to the nearest Supercenter to buy him a pair of $13, size-13 Walmart-brand boats.

After the missus came back with the shoes, Kale proceeded to wear them through the race's remaining 320 miles. He wore them as he ran through the midnight chill. He wore them as he stumbled through the race's final loop, hallucinating, somehow seeing mannequins in the woods and letters printed on boulders. He wore them as he crossed the finish line, victorious.

And in the aftermath of his Peak 500 triumph, Kale Poland, who's 36, has only proven himself more qualified to be a Walmart spokesmodel. An amiable, can-do country boy who grew up in a tiny Maine farm town, he is the mastermind behind Cleetus Fit, a one-man school of exercise science meant to evoke a mythical, slack-jawed hillbilly.

Cleetus Fit flourishes on Facebook, where some 3,000 friends lap up Kale's wry three-a-day posts about, say, his dog Sage's stick-fetching habits, his swim workouts, and his he-man runs through raging blizzards. It also lives and breathes in the green hills of New Hampshire's

Lakes Region, where 25 or so of his personal-training clients join Kale in eschewing the gymnasium to build muscle by towing dumpsters across parking lots and doing push-ups atop the underside of a wheelbarrow. The Cleetus juggernaut at times strays into relatively more esoteric corners of the fitness universe—with a partner, Kale recently opened Yoga Jaya, a studio in Meredith, New Hampshire—but a chummy, hat-backwards dudeness permeates all things Cleetus. See, for example, Kale's eloquent Facebook diss of highfalutin cross-country skiers ("I don't drive a Subaru or a Volvo and I don't lie awake at night dreaming about how I am going to win the waxing debate tomorrow"). Or consider a recent selfie that captured Kale out on a 185-mile training ride dressed in a cotton hoodie and stuffing pizza into his maw.

"BEAST!!" wrote one friend, adding a comment to the robust dialogue that accompanies all Kale posts.

"I thought that was raw bacon," wrote another.

"You," rejoiced a third, "are a marvelous hack."

On November 6, the world's largest retailer will once again miss a chance to embrace this populist hero. That morning, Kale will leap into a University of New Orleans swimming pool to commence Decaman USA, the first-ever Deca Ironman—that's 10 Ironmans in a row—to be held in the continental United States. The race will see 16 brave athletes attempting to swim 24 miles (in other words, 792 laps) before they shuttle to nearby Fontainbleau State Park to bike 1,120 miles (160 mind-numbing repeats of a flat seven-mile loop). The sufferfest concludes on foot, with no less than 262 out-and-back repeats of the same half-mile-long patch of dirt. The clock will be running constantly, meaning that front-runners will likely retreat to their course-side sleeping tents for maybe three hours a night before finishing in roughly nine days.

The deca, born in Mexico in 1992, is still only held two or three times a year worldwide. It's gaining popularity, and there are now even occasional double and triple decas for the most depraved sadists. None of these races draw the fun-run multitudes, however. When Kale came in second in his first deca—the World Cup Ultratriathlon Challenge in Monterrey, Mexico, in 2012, crossing the line in 12 days, 10 hours, and 20 minutes—he was also the last-place finisher.

In Louisiana, race director Wayne Kurtz says Kale is most likely to distinguish himself by spending very little money on the race. "If you give Kale a T-shirt," Kurtz says, "he'll wear it for 10 years." As Kurtz sees it, Kale is a possible dark horse at Decaman. (It's almost impossible to handicap a race that so brazenly courts human decay, but a wise bettor would do well to back Ferenc Szonyi, a 54-year-old Hungarian who was the lone finisher in June's Hell Ultra, a 300-mile running race that traversed the Indian Himalayas, summiting five peaks.) "Kale's weak in the swim," says Kurtz, "but the guy can ride, and he's great on sleep deprivation. We know he can grind through the night, but his biggest asset, really, is his calmness—and his dad's calmness."

Kale's father, Wes Poland, who runs the parts department at a tractor dealership in Auburn, Maine, is his son's pit-crew chief. It's a challenging job with its own adventures in sleep deprivation and stormy emotion. "The deca is a soap opera," explains Kurtz. "At one race last year in Mexico, three or four people on this one crew started screaming at each other in Portuguese. Soon enough they were leaving, midrace, and flying back home to Brazil. Kale and Wes, they're steady. I can see Kale going top five."

* * *

As it happens, I live near Kale's current home in the Lakes Region. We're in the same cycling group, and in early September, I decided that America needed to hear his story. A few days later, at dusk, he and I were road-tripping to his parents' cabin in western Maine, so that he could do an all-night-long trail run followed by a punishing, sleep-deprived morning bike ride over a mountain pass.

"The thing about the deca," Kale says, driving along, "is you're miserable most of the time. It's not like there's joy in the misery. It's just misery, so the training is all about building mental toughness."

In the lead-up to that first deca in Mexico, back before Kale was a sought-after, $50-an-hour personal trainer, his daily life had such hardships built in. He was living in Laconia, New Hampshire, pulling a graveyard shift as a supermarket shelf stocker then and also working full-time at Eastern Mountain Sports down in Concord, and even though EMS was 26 miles from home, he commuted on a bike—on a single speed, in the winter. "Sometimes," he tells me, waxing nostalgic, "I'd look at my schedule and realize, 'Oh, God, I can't sleep for the next two days.'"

In the years since the Monterrey deca, Kale has sought out new ways to sabotage his sinew. In 2015, he established an ultramarathon cycling record, traversing a 255-mile-wide swath of Maine in 15:01. More recently, he's taken to running the trails of New Hampshire's White Mountains in pursuit of fastest known times.

We keep driving. The lawns around us are still bearing Trump signs two years after he was elected. We get passed by a pickup truck fluttering two American flags from the tailgate. We're on Kale's home turf. He grew up in Turner, Maine, which the *Portland Press Herald* has called "one of Maine's most conservative towns," a "farming community that prizes self-sufficiency and low taxes."

Turner, it so happens, is home to one of New England's largest chicken farms, a sprawling environmental nightmare whose scent permeated the town. "In the spring, when it got warm," remembers Kale's old friend Nick Harrington, "the manure started to thaw out at the chicken coops, and you'd need to put up fly strips. You'd need a few dozen fly swatters in your house."

"You could never get anyone to come to Turner for barbecues," remembers Linda Poland, Kale's aunt.

In Kale's childhood, motor sports were holy. "We might have had a shutoff notice from the light company," says his uncle and neighbor, Dan Poland, a mechanic, "but we still had boats, four-wheelers, snowmobiles, campers, go-karts, and minibikes."

Kale was 5 when he was given his first snowmobile, a 295cc 1972 Polaris Colt. By the time he was 10, he and his buddies were ranging miles from home and changing out their own spark plugs and belts. Their favorite pastime involved climbing into plastic sleds, so they could be snowmobile-towed at blistering speed to the crest of a hill.

When Kale began dabbling, at age 12, in cross-country ski racing, his cronies regarded him as a defector. They called him a "forest fairy," Kale says, and at first he steered clear of his new sport's most effete practices. He refused to wear Lycra and instead raced in wind pants and a hoodie.

He brought the same raw ethic of his adolescent forays into triathlon. In his first tri, he swam more than a mile with his head up, out of the water (he'd never learned the crawl). His borrowed department-store road bike had a ruined bottom bracket, and even though he was a formidable runner, he finished deep within the bottom third of the field in a lowly all-comers race.

The seed was planted, though, and in his undergraduate days at University of Maine–Machias, Kale bought his first real bike. Glory was only a few thousand workouts away.

When Kale and I reach the cabin, Wes Poland is already there, seated at the kitchen table, drinking a Coors wrapped in a beer cozy. A merry and slightly jowly raconteur with a bushy salt-and-pepper mustache, he launches right away into comic stories. He tells me how at one quintuple Ironman, when the balls of Kale's feet became two giant blisters, he duct-taped sandals to his son's ravaged dogs, giving them a chance to air out as he hobbled along. "We fixed the problem," he says, before gesturing across the table at his wife, Belinda, who is a nurse. "Your mother wouldn't be too impressed by how we fixed it, but we fixed it."

"I just can't watch Kale's races," says Belinda, who has aided Wes in crewing, along with numerous relatives. "My job is to make people better."

Wes shrugs, snickering. Then he lays out his philosophy, which he honed partly by crewing at rural Maine stock-car races back in the '70s and '80s. "You just gotta suck it up if you want to finish what you started," he says. "You can't have any sympathy for the athlete. You can't let him wallow in self-pity. You've just got to keep him moving and fed. And you've gotta stay focused. I don't pay attention to what anyone else is doing—that's their business. And I try to keep things consistent. Kale is excellent at consistency. On the bike, you could set your watch by his laps."

By now Kale is stuffing three headlamps into his backpack. It's 10 p.m., time for his run up the two peaks of nearby Baldpate Mountain, elevation 3,812 feet. I've already elected to forgo the outing in favor of a little shut-eye, but when Kale gets back to the cabin at 3 a.m., dripping with sweat, we touch base, whispering in deference to his dad who needs to wake at 4 a.m. for a busy day at the dealership. "Right now," he says, "I do not feel like getting on my bike, and I think that's exactly how I need to feel. I need to be exhausted."

"Noted," I think, and then drift back into sleep.

At dawn, with Kale still gone, I head out for a walk on a winding back road. After maybe an hour, I hear something behind me, a bike, and then Kale and I are ensconced in a pivotal moment. He has full license to just zip past me, head down. It'd be kind of a dickish move, sure, but he's training, and it's cold outside. Does he really want his muscles to stiffen up in the damp?

Kale slows down until he's right beside me, moving at a piddling three miles an hour as he and I shoot the breeze. "Did you go up to that quarry?" he asks. There's a sweetness in his tone, a caring. The original plan had been for us to ride together, but I tweaked my back. The injury's put me in a slightly maudlin mood, and Kale, it seems, has picked up on this. He rides all the way in beside me, chatting. It's no big deal—just an easy gesture of kindness—but it makes me realize that there's so much more than sweat and snideness to the Cleetus program. There's a humility and an unrehearsed warmth.

Everything Kale does in fitness has a welcoming vibe. His mission in life is to make outdoor sports fun for all, even if they're not ectomorphic gear geeks. A decade ago, while living in Maine's northernmost county, he dreamed up a footrace, the Aroostook Dirty 30, to rebut the Tough Mudder, which he regards as a "fake tough race for fake tough people." He obliged competitors to linger at "torture stations" as they slogged 30 miles through boggy river bottoms and over old railroad beds. The fitter the runner, the more often they were asked to chain themselves to a truck tire or lug cinder blocks up a hill or push helmeted volunteers through the woods on a refrigerator dolly. There was no entry fee and no trophies, but Kale rewarded all finishers with a rusty railroad spike. One competitor so loved the Dirty 30 that he got a spike tattooed on his calf.

The Dirty 30 is no more (for liability reasons), but in recent years, Kale has continued to accrue fans—from personal training and also from the Gunstock Mountain Resort, where he's taught cross-country skiing to grade-schoolers and also led mountaintop yoga, often luring

30 or 40 pilgrims who climb to the summit to partake of Kale's guidance through downward dog.

The man is not unaware of his cult status, and at times his Facebook posts seek out a sonorous, sermon-like depth. "Everything I have seen," he wrote one morning last July, after the early death of a beloved Gunstock employee, "validates a theory I have had all along: Life is short. DO IT NOW. SPEND THE MONEY. TAKE THE TRIP. LIVE WILD."

One hundred and thirty likes ensued, along with 55 loves and 27 comments:

"Word."

"Truth!"

"Amen to that!"

* * *

The next time I see Kale, on a warm September afternoon, he's heading to a small, crunchy New Hampshire preschool—Saplings, it's called—to do a 90-minute session in his new role as the school's mindfulness/yoga instructor. We ride there together in his pickup, and in a way it seems odd that a self-described redneck—a man who voted for Donald Trump in 2016—would take such an assignment.

But Kale's interest in yoga is sincere, even if he first took to the mat for branding reasons. ("People were afraid of doing personal training with me because they figured that I was too hard core," he explains. "I wanted to soften my image.") Over the last couple of years, he's gone all-in. He's partaken of a heart-chakra-opening yoga workshop on a blood moon, and recently on Facebook he drifted into the namaste mists when he proclaimed, "I am still in my infancy as a yogi."

Kale's woo-woo credentials are seriously undercut by his taste for beer yoga, which involves swilling large quantities of Pabst Blue Ribbon, but whatever. This fall on Facebook, he wrote with thrilled lyricism about

Saplings: "You guys. I went to a special place today. Kids were muddy and jumping off rocks and playing with frogs."

When we reach the 22-acre wooded campus, the children are inside a yurt, their teacher hushing them upon the sound of our footfalls. "Owl eyes and mouse mouths, everyone," she says. "Kale is here."

He stoops low and enters the yurt wearing a long-sleeved plaid shirt, tattered shorts, and a ski hat, and soon the day's mindfulness regime begins. It consists, basically, of running around in the woods, with Kale leading the pack. "Let's go to the stump circle!" he shouts. We all scramble out there, snaking through the trees and the brush. When we sit down to pass the sharing stick, one little boy says that his favorite thing about Saplings is "going on adventures and running."

"Yeah," Kale says, nodding solemnly as he clutches the stick. "I second that. Definitely."

We quack like ducks as we weave along toward the Big Rock, then climb atop it before clambering on toward the muddy shores of the brook. Then a moment later, it happens: some kid steps on a yellow-jacket nest, and suddenly we're all sprinting down a hill, the children screaming in terror, the adults scooping them into their arms. The yellow jackets move with us, a black menacing cloud, and each time a child gets stung, an anguished cry pierces the forest.

We keep running. The wasps go into hiding now, lodging under everyone's shirts. Kale and the teacher begin stripping clothing off kids. One little boy looks up at me, the interloper, and in tears he asks, "Are the bees going to keep chasing us forever?"

We reach safety on the leafy playground, finally, and a week later, after I've spent many hours icing my welts, I learn that every single sapling has fully recovered. "They didn't even say the word *bee*," Kale tells me after his next visit. I start imagining these kids as future deca stars. I mean, they've got the whole pain-tolerance thing down . . .

Kale is in focused-training mode now. As autumn comes on—as the leaves flame orange and then drift down onto the roads, becoming cold slime under our tires—his Facebook feed attains a quiet and sober timbre. Anyone who has ever entered a race knows the goose-pimply chills that precede the call to the starting line. Now that feeling seeps into Kale's words, so that one morning in late October, he dials in on the specific agonies his trial will entail. "Contact and extended exposure," he writes. "The sun on the skin. The chlorine from the pool where the goggles press your eyes. The weight of your body on the bike seat pressing up against your ass. The wind in your eyes."

Sage the dog is momentarily left unmentioned. In these last, critical days, the PBRs retreat into the dark recesses at the back of the fridge. Homeboy's got a race to run—a long one. He needs to be ready.

Naked Joe

Boston Magazine, *March 26, 2013*

AT FIRST, AS THE TRAIN ROLLED INTO NORTH STATION ON THAT CRISP autumn morning a century ago, it looked like the police might lose their rein on the mob. There were an estimated 200,000 people on hand to greet the world's most unkempt celebrity, Joe Knowles, who was arriving from Portland on October 9, 1913. Men stood atop railroad cars, waiting. Female admirers lingered by the tracks, hoping for a private audience with Knowles, who, according to the *Boston Post*, had just completed "a most extraordinary experiment never before attempted by civilized man." The stairs to the subway were so crowded that they resembled a "grandstand at a football game," the *Post* would report, and the crowds spilled out onto Causeway Street and around the corner onto Canal.

The throngs first spied Knowles sitting beside the window of the train's drawing room. A middle-aged man with an unruly gray beard and a long tangle of gray hair, Knowles was no Adonis. Indeed, he was a bit portly, at five feet nine and 180 pounds. His muscle tone was about what you'd expect of a 44-year-old professional illustrator with a predilection for hanging about the taverns of Boston, where he regaled the boys with exuberant tales of his glory days—the 1890s, when he worked as a trapper and hunting guide in the woods of his native Maine. His gut hung. His arms bore some flab. Still, a few days hence, 400 coeds from Dr. Sargent's Physical Training School for Women, in Cambridge, would stand in line waiting for the chance to touch his worn skin. Now, the crowds simply surged. Scores of policemen endeavored to hold them back as they rushed the train, and for a moment it seemed that chaos would erupt.

This was a happy and civilized moment, however, and soon Knowles's fans stopped shoving and began bellowing cries of affection. "Great work, Joe! . . . You're all right! . . . You're my bet!"

Then Joe Knowles emerged from the train, wearing a crude bearskin robe and grimy bearskin trousers. It wasn't a costume, exactly—Knowles had established himself as the Nature Man. Two months earlier, he had stepped into the woods of Maine wearing nothing but a white cotton jockstrap, to live sans tools and without any human contact. His aim? To answer questions gnawing at a society that was modernizing at a dizzying rate, endowed suddenly with the motor car, the elevator, and the telephone. Could modern man, in all his softness, ever regain the hardihood of his primitive forebears? Could he still rub two sticks together to make fire? Could he spear fish in secluded lakes and kill game with his bare hands? Knowles had just returned from the woods, and his answer to each of these questions was a triumphant yes. In time, he would parlay his Nature Man fame into a five-month run on the vaudeville circuit, where he would earn a reported $1,200 a week billed as a "Master of Woodcraft." He would publish a memoir, *Alone in the Wilderness*, that would sell some 30,000 copies. He would even have his moment in Hollywood, playing the lead in a spine-tingling 1914 nature drama also called *Alone in the Wilderness*.

Knowles was the reality star of his day. On the Sunday after he set off, the Boston *Sunday Post* ran a whole special section on him, complete with a banner headline reading, "Naked as Cave Man He Enters Woods." There was a ponderous studio portrait of him (he appeared in profile, with his head bowed as smoke plumed skyward from his cigarette), and there was also an affidavit, signed in cursive by 17 witnesses, affirming that Knowles had entered the woods at 10:40 a.m. on August 4 "alone, empty-handed and without clothing." In an adjacent think piece, the *Post* quoted Dr. Dudley Sargent, the founder of the Physical Training School for Women, and also the "physical director" at Harvard. "His attempt to live like primeval man will have a scientific value," Sargent declared. "We will be interested to know how the lack of salt will affect Knowles."

Knowles would soon become an asterisk of history. For now, though, after he emerged from that train, he followed the police out into the streets, then stepped into a waiting automobile for a parade. As the car began to move, he stood up, and pandemonium ensued. "Those nearest to the machine," the *Post* reported, "threatened to smash the running boards as they mounted the rims and mud guards."

Eventually, Knowles reached Boston Common, where as many as 20,000 people were waiting for what, presumably, would be the most critical speech of Knowles's life—the one public address that would distinguish him in the annals of American history.

Knowles climbed out of the car, made his way to the bandstand, and began to speak. "I will tell you one thing," he told the crowd. "It is a whole lot easier being in the woods than it is making a speech."

He made a couple of vapid remarks. Then he got back in the car.

* * *

Joe Knowles lived in the golden age of publicity stunts. In 1901 a woman named Annie Taylor became the first person to descend Niagara Falls in a barrel. In 1911 Ralph "Pappy" Hankinson, a Ford dealer in Topeka, Kansas, invented the sport of auto polo to sell Model T cars. In 1924, to promote a movie, Alvin "Shipwreck" Kelly sat atop a high pole outside an L.A. theater for 13 hours and 13 minutes, launching a short-lived American craze for flagpole sitting. According to a condescending and scathing 1938 *New Yorker* story on Knowles, the Nature Man stunt was dreamed up by Knowles's drinking buddy, Michael McKeogh, a freelance writer. McKeogh read *Robinson Crusoe* and marveled over how the book, published almost two centuries earlier, was still selling briskly. Then, one night in 1913, in a smoky Boston saloon, as McKeogh listened to Knowles ramble on about his long-ago Maine adventures . . . light bulb! In his mind's eye, he saw old Joe naked in the woods. "We'll make a million," he told Knowles. Then he drafted an outline of the drama (and of a prospective book) onto a notepad. "Tuesday: kills bear," he wrote, then asked, "But are you sure you can do it, Joe?"

Hunched at the bar, Knowles described five or six ways that he could.

Knowles had recently worked at the *Boston Post*, a sleepy workingman's newspaper that was trying to stay alive in the nation's most competitive media market. The city had 10 daily papers in 1913, and the *Post* was bleeding readers to the flashy upstart *Boston American*, which was financed by William Randolph Hearst, the father of yellow journalism. Knowles met with the *Post*'s Sunday editor, Charles E. L. Wingate, and proposed that the paper could boost readership by sending him to the Maine woods. He promised to produce drawings and status reports on birch bark, using charcoal, and to leave the documents in the crook of a designated tree. Hunting guides could then fetch them for McKeogh and other reporters, who would linger near Knowles, in a small cabin, and cast the whole tale as a fine, purple-tinged melodrama.

Wingate said yes to the scheme and agreed to pay Knowles a now-forgotten sum. His decision would prove brilliant. Between August and October 1913, the *Post* would later report, its circulation rose from 200,000 to more than 436,000.

* * *

The expedition began on a drizzly August morning, in a sort of no-man's-land outside tiny Eustis, Maine. The spot was some 30 miles removed from the nearest rail line, just north of Rangeley Lake, and east of the Quebec border. Knowles showed up at his starting point, the head of the Spencer Trail, wearing a brown suit and a necktie. A gaggle of reporters and hunting guides circled him.

Knowles stripped to his jockstrap. Someone handed him a smoke, cracking, "Here's your last cigarette." Knowles savored a few meditative drags. Then he tossed the butt on the ground, cried, "See you later, boys!" and set off over a small hill named Bear Mountain, moving toward Spencer Lake, three or four miles away. As soon as he lost sight of his public, he lofted the jockstrap into the brush—so that he could enjoy, as he would later put it in one of his birch-bark dispatches, "the full freedom of the life I was to lead."

* * *

On his own, Knowles kept hiking. It was raining. In bare feet, he slipped in the mud, but still he trudged on over the flank of Bear Mountain. Eventually, he spied a deer. "She looked good to me," he wrote, "and for the first time in my life I envied a deer her hide. I could not help thinking what a fine pair of chaps her hide would make and how good a strip of smoked venison would taste a little later. There before me was food and protection, food that millionaires would envy and clothing that would outwear the most costly suit the tailor could supply." Knowles resisted the temptation to kill the deer, deciding to live within the game laws of Maine. He was hungry, wet, and cold, and also still a bit thrilled and agitated about being out there sans jockstrap. He could not sleep. What to do? He tossed off a few pull-ups. "On a strong spruce limb I drew myself up and down, trying to see how many times I could touch my chin to the limb. When I got tired of this, I would run around under the trees for a while."

If Knowles made himself sound like Tarzan, it was perhaps intentional. One of the most popular stories in Knowles's day was *Tarzan of the Apes*, an Edgar Rice Burroughs novella. Published in 1912 in the pulp magazine *All-Story*, it starred a wild boy who goes "swinging naked through primeval forests." The story was such a hit that in 1914 it was bound into book form.

Pulp magazines (so named because they were published on cheap wood-pulp paper) represented a new literary form, born in 1896. They offered working-class Americans an escape into rousing tales of life in the wilderness. Bearing titles like *Argosy*, *Cavalier*, and the *Thrill Book*, they took cues from Jack London, whose best-selling novels, among them *The Call of the Wild* (1903) and *White Fang* (1906), saw burly men testing their mettle in the wild. They were also influenced by Teddy Roosevelt, who insisted that modern man needed to avoid "over-sentimentality" and "over-softness" while living in cities. "Unless we keep the barbarian virtue," Roosevelt argued, "gaining the civilized ones will be of little avail."

Both Knowles's dispatches and the pulps represented a sharp departure from the pious nature writing that had prevailed in this country until about 1900, especially in New England. Thoreau had died in 1862, but at the turn of the century his heirs were still fixed on seeking wisdom, as opposed to adventure, in the outdoors. Boston's principal hiking group at the time was the Appalachian Mountain Club, and its members, says Christine Woodside, the current editor of the AMC's journal, *Appalachia*, "were often high-level academics, people from MIT or Harvard, who told themselves: 'We are deep thinkers about the wilderness and what it does for our character.' They'd come home and deliver academic papers or write journal articles."

The editor of *Appalachia* from 1879 to 1919 was Charles Ernest Fay, a professor of modern languages at Tufts, and also an unabashed snob. In a 1905 *Appalachia* essay, "The Mountain as an Influence in Modern Life," Fay dismissed country people as incapable of enjoying the splendors of nature. "The mountain dweller," he wrote, "may even look upon the towering masses that surround him as so much waste land, as occupying space that might otherwise come under tillage." Fay advocated for a superior species: the mountaineer, who, though he sees the mountain only rarely, loves it "for the grand anthem its forests sing to him, for the rich and varied gallery of Nature paintings that in sunshine and in storm, in the day-time and in the night season, it reveals to his eyes."

Fay's bald elitism had, of course, a long legacy in Boston. For most of the preceding century, the city had been lorded over by the Brahmins—the Quincys, the Cabots, the Lowells, the Lodges—who sequestered themselves on Beacon Hill and shored up their wealth as they championed high-minded cultural institutions such as the Museum of Fine Arts and the Boston Symphony Orchestra. By 1913, though, the city had changed. With a population of 670,000, it was home to more than 200,000 recent immigrants, most of them Irish and Italian. In 1914 it would elect as its mayor James Michael Curley, a Catholic born in Roxbury's Irish ghetto. Curley was so beloved that he was reelected as mayor three times, even though he was twice imprisoned for fraud. He was not a restrained individual. Once, in attacking an allegedly communist WASP political foe, he said, "There is more Americanism in one half of Jim Curley's ass than in that pink body of Tom Eliot."

As a newspaperman with artistic ambitions, Knowles was, socially speaking, a notch above the factory workers, bakers, and dockhands who made up Curley's core constituency, but he was still solidly ensconced in Boston's rising underclass. A grade-school dropout, Knowles grew up in Wilton, Maine, a tiny town about 40 miles northwest of Augusta. His father was a disabled Civil War veteran. His mother supported the family's four children by selling moccasins, as well as firewood and berries gathered in the forest. They were poor, and the subject of local ridicule. "The schollars [*sic*] poked fun at my homespuns," he wrote in an unpublished memoir, "tore the patches off my clothes, and stole my lunch. . . . And to make a good job of it, they broke up the bread and threw the crumbs to the birds."

As Knowles tells it, his father bullied him, too, and when he was 13, after a paternal beating, he ran away, lying about his age so that he could work aboard cargo ships and travel the world. Knowles would eventually visit Cuba, South America, the Mediterranean, China, and Japan. By the time he was 17, he'd enlisted in the U.S. Navy and had returned to Wilton with a tattoo of a young woman twirling a snake. On another teenage return home—a surprise visit made after two years at sea—he arrived with a bottle of whiskey, a gift for his dad. His father did not say a word and did not touch the bottle. "He just gave me a look," Knowles wrote, "that was all. That hurt more than all the lickings he'd ever given me."

* * *

As dawn broke on his second day in the woods, Knowles fashioned a basket out of birch bark and began gathering berries. He speared two trout, but a mink stole them. He tried to light a fire, but the woods were still damp from the rain, so he simply built a shack out of dead sticks, fir boughs, and moss, and lay down, naked and hungry, in the forest duff.

The next day, Knowles sewed himself some witch-grass leggings and constructed a dam across Little Spencer Stream, to channel fish into a trap. On his fourth morning, he built a fire and ate baked trout for breakfast.

Then the reports stopped. For 11 days, no birch-bark dispatches appeared. The *Post* milked this silence for drama, reporting that Maine woodsmen believed him injured. Meanwhile, the paper squeezed all sorts of entertaining side dramas out of the Knowles saga. One story, titled "Joe Knowles Blew His Way to Fame," recounted the Nature Man's naval career. Another piece was titled "Boston Hunters Admire Knowles' 'Cave Man' Feat."

Readers did not hear from Knowles again until August 24, when, on page 1, the *Post* ran a Knowles sketch of a wildcat, along with an alarming headline: "Knowles Catches Bear in Pit and Kills It with Club." The bear was a yearling. It wasn't bear-hunting season in Maine yet, so the *Post* now had license to tantalize readers with the prospect of their hero's arrest. One story read, "The wardens are mustering the courage to tackle the Forest Man in his lair and drag him out."

Did Knowles apprehend his legal danger? Did he flee to Quebec? For an October 5 story, an anonymous reporter made a "long, hard tramp" of two days into Knowles's camp to answer these questions. He came away stumped and shivering, so he dwelled theatrically on the primitive trappings of Knowles's solitary existence: bits of bark chopped with blunt instruments, broken branches marking a crude trail, and a small lean-to. "Here was the scene of a great struggle," the story read in a crescendo worthy of Jack London himself, "not the marks of a physical battle, but the deeper, more impressive signs of a mental battle. For it was here a human being lived the strange life of self-imposed loneliness after he had fought and won his battle with nature. It was here he gathered crude comforts that would enable him to conform the civilized mind to primitive conditions."

The *Post*'s dispatch noted that black bristles from the vanquished bear were "found on many projecting points and on the upturned roots near the camp. On a rock was more hair, where evidently the forest man had been doing his tailoring." But Knowles's bedclothes were absent, according to the story, and the bearskin was nowhere to be found.

* * *

Why? Because Knowles had taken it west. On the morning of October 5, the *Post*'s front page blared, "KNOWLES, CLAD IN SKINS, COMES OUT OF THE FOREST." A subhead continued, "Boston Artist, Two Months a 'Primitive Man,' Steps into the Twentieth Century near Megantic, Province of Québec." Subsequent copy read, "Tanned like an Indian, almost black from exposure to the sun. . . . Scratched and bruised from head to foot by briars and underbrush. . . . Upper garment sleeveless. Had no underwear."

Picked up nationwide, the *Post*'s piece explained that Knowles had just traversed the most inhospitable portion of the Maine woods, after which, when he had emerged on the outskirts of Megantic, he had made his first human contact—a young girl he had found standing by the railroad track. "And the child of 14, wild-eyed, stared at him," the story said, "and into her mind came the memory of a picture of a man of the Stone Age in a history book."

"Something within him rose," the story continued, "and forced a cry from his throat, and kindly tears into his eyes. He smiled, and the girl saw the gold in his teeth flash. 'He is a real man,' she said to herself."

* * *

Not everyone believed the story. In late October, after he had returned to civilization, an editorial in the *Hartford Courant* wondered whether "the biggest fake of the century has been palmed off on a credulous public." Meanwhile, a reporter from the rival *Boston American* had begun working on a long story about Knowles. The paper specialized in blockbuster exposés, and its investigative bloodhound, Bert Ford, had spent seven weeks combing the woods around Spencer Lake, aided in his research by a man he would call "one of the ablest trappers in Maine or Canada," Henry E. Redmond.

On December 2, in a front-page article, Ford went public with the explosive allegation that Knowles was a liar. He zeroed in on Knowles's alleged bear killing, noting that the Nature Man's bear pit was but four feet wide and three feet deep. In boldface, the story asserted, "It would have been physically impossible to trap a bear of any age or size in it." Knowles's club was likewise damning evidence. Found leaning against a tree, it was a rotting stub of moosewood that Ford easily chipped with his fingernails.

According to the *Boston American*, Knowles had a manager in the Maine woods, and also a guide who bought the bearskin from a trapper for $12. The bear had not been mauled, but rather shot. "I found four holes in the bear skin," Ford averred after meeting Knowles and studying the very coat he was wearing. "Experts say these were bullet holes."

Ford argued that Knowles's Maine adventure was in fact an "aboriginal layoff." He wasn't gutting fish and weaving bark shoes, as the *Post*'s dispatches suggested. Rather, he was lounging about in a log cabin at the foot of Spencer Lake and also occasionally entertaining a lady friend at a nearby cabin.

Knowles responded to Ford's story by filing a $50,000 libel lawsuit. In December he returned to his bear pit in Maine, this time with a small captive black bear. Then, watched by both reporters and Maine locals, he clubbed the poor animal to death and began picking at its skin with a sharp piece of shale. "In less than ten minutes, he had the hide off one of the bear's legs," Helon Taylor, a 15-year-old witness, would marvel late in life. "We were all impressed."

But it was a sham. The bear was ready to hibernate, and so sluggish that Knowles had to prod it with a stick to make it put up a fight. Later, as Knowles and the spectators hiked out of the woods, Taylor spied a "nice, tight little log cabin," so new that "the peeled logs hadn't even started to change color." Out behind the cabin, there was a pile of beer bottles and tin cans four feet high. Taylor suspected that Knowles had stayed there for the whole of his adventure, never once camping out.

A quarter-century later, in 1938, the *New Yorker* would corroborate Taylor's hunch—and would also allow Knowles's ghostwriting "manager" to reveal himself. He was none other than Michael McKeogh, the tavern habitué who'd dreamed up Knowles's wilderness stunt in the first place. McKeogh described Knowles as a melancholic louse. The Nature Man, he said, showed up at the cabin just hours after leaving his sendoff party at the foot of Spencer Trail.

According to the *New Yorker* story, Knowles entered wearing his jockstrap, sat down, and said nothing. He stayed for weeks. He was so morose and lethargic that when Maine's game wardens came looking for him in late September, following the *Post*'s report about the vanquished bear, he shrugged off McKeogh's entreaties that he run. McKeogh cried, "You'll be put in prison, Joe, you'll be put in prison!" But Knowles moved only when he heard footsteps. And he only began his march toward Quebec after McKeogh hired an Indian guide to lead him through the forests that he had supposedly conquered.

* * *

Knowles was a nightmarish roommate for McKeogh during their time in the cabin—a hog who deprived McKeogh of life's simplest pleasures. The worst of it came one day when McKeogh walked to the village of Eustis, 12 miles away, bought himself an apple pie, and carried it all the way back to the cabin. McKeogh placed it on the windowsill, to keep it cool overnight. The next morning, he heard the scuffling of feet behind him. He turned to see someone swiping the pie and trundling it off into the wilderness.

It was Joe Knowles. He ate the whole thing.

* * *

Nobody in Boston knew about this, of course. When Knowles finally returned to town, the city fathers embraced him as an emblem of virtue and hope. On October 11, an august assemblage—"a host of New England physicians, sportsmen, and professional men," as the *Post* described it—honored Knowles with a black-tie banquet at the Copley Plaza Hotel. The gala was calibrated, it seems, to preempt naysayers and to sound hurrahs for a proud and growing city that had just opened the Franklin Park Zoo and was building its first real skyscraper, the 16-story Custom House Tower. The Honorable William A. Morse presided as emcee, and Dr. Samuel W. McComb, a psychologist, spoke, noting that Christopher Columbus had, much like Knowles, faced doubt after discovering the New World. "The world is full of skeptics," McComb said. "However, I think we may disregard them all." Soon, Dudley Sargent, Harvard's physical-education guru, rose and argued, improbably, that the 45-year-old Knowles was stronger than Harvard's hardest football men. "With his legs alone," Sargent marveled, "he lifted more than 1,000 pounds."

A few days later, Knowles went on the vaudeville circuit. He worked on his book. And then, late in 1914, he made it to Hollywood, where in his one film he rode horseback through the ostensibly Canadian woods, over snowdrifts and across raging rivers, as he was chased (and falsely accused of murder) by Canada's North West Mounted Police. His mission was to save a beautiful starlet.

Knowles tried to get more movie gigs after that. A circa-1915 publicity shot shows him pitching himself as a heartthrob. Sitting on some porch steps in a fringed buckskin suit, he stares pouty-faced at the camera, his dreamy eyes filled with pained longing. Perhaps he was shilling for his own screenplay, *The Poacher*, an undated drama that was, as he himself described it, "a story of outdoor life in the game country of the Canadian Northwest." The screenplay lists Joe Knowles in the starring role.

Knowles's movie career went nowhere. But in time, after settling on Washington state's Long Beach Peninsula in 1917, he would reinvent himself and find celebrity once again, as the illustrator of schlocky, canned images celebrating the American West. Knowles's drawings and paintings of Indians, shipwrecks, and animals were so popular that when his pet chipmunk, Mr. Peabody, died in 1939, the *Oregonian* ran an obituary. Knowles, the newspaper noted, habitually fed Mr. Peabody fresh green beans.

With humans, though, Knowles seems to have been less endearing. In his memoirs, he dismisses his working-class neighbors in Long Beach, saying, "The natives do not interest me. They do not understand me, but I understand them, and they do not know it."

* * *

Joe Knowles died in 1942. All of the 200,000 people who gathered at North Station to greet him are now probably dead, too, and his book is available in only a few libraries. A biography of Knowles, *Naked in the Woods*, by Jim Motavalli, appeared in 2008, but on the whole, this common man's hero has in death met a common man's fate: He has been forgotten. Or almost.

Today the world's most important repository of Joe Knowles material, arguably, is the Long Beach Peninsula Trading Post, a rambly antiques shop where, amid old postcards and license plates, there's a little shrine to Knowles—a glass case displaying several of his etchings, as well as a few yellowing manila folders containing his memoirs.

Last fall, I traveled up to the Trading Post from my home in Oregon, a couple of hours away. I went as a pilgrim. In poring over the dusty troves of old news clippings, I'd developed a warm appreciation for Knowles. He was a dyspeptic coot and a hard drinker, I can't deny that. He had no stage presence, and he was a liar. But by my lights he was still an American hero. He was like the Great Gatsby. He had chutzpah and grandiose ambitions, and in his own bumbling way he chased after his dreams.

I visited the Trading Post on a sunny Saturday morning, where, lounging on a couch, I leafed through the last musty remains of Joe Knowles. I read of a skirmish Knowles had late in life with an aging neighbor. In a long letter to his lawyer, he alleged that 65-year-old Hatty Harmon tried to poison him so as to take possession of his home, and called her an "old witch" and an "old harlot." In his unpublished memoirs, under the heading "Passing Thoughts," he set down what could be construed as his closing argument. "Life is a queer game," he wrote. "Cheat a little here, bluff a little there, smile when it hurts, hide the truth, grab what you can while the grabbing is good, hold what you have. If you play the game according to these rules, you will win materially."

Later, across the street, 94-year-old Adelle Beechey told me she remembered Knowles as a "free thinker." During the Depression, she said, he bought a car, even though he owed money at the local grocery store, and then took some friends out for a drive. "His friends were nervous because, of course, he imbibed a bit," she told me. "And when they came to a railroad crossing and found a train coming, Joe just kept driving. 'Don't worry,' he said. 'She's fully covered by insurance.'"

In the end, I wanted to have my own moment with Joe Knowles, so I drove into the village of Ilwaco, parked my car, and walked down toward the beach. For the last two decades of his life, Knowles resided there, in what Motavalli calls a "crooked cabin made of driftwood." But that cabin vanished long ago, and even the topography of the place has shifted. The bluffs and fishing rocks that Joe Knowles walked by every day are now mostly erased. So I just strolled alongside the ocean as beachgoers flew kites and built sandcastles nearby. The sun was still high in the sky. It felt warm and good on my back, and I watched as its slanting light played tricks on the water.

Notable Updates

"Wonder Boy." After running 37 miles at age 4, Budhia Singh proved a mediocre schoolboy athlete. When he was eight, he failed to qualify for the second round in a one-leg hopping competition. Still, in 2016, he was the subject of a Hindi-language documentary, *Born to Run*. In 2021, 19-year-old Budhia was living with his mother and sister in the Bhubaneswar, India, slum of his childhood and raising money on Twitter in hopes that he could compete in the 2024 Olympics. Neighbors had not seen him run in years, however, and he raised only $42. At the time of this writing, February 2024, his Twitter account (@Budhiasingh_Ind) was suspended.

"The Challenger." Immediately after my profile of Evans Chebet ran online, he defied the oddsmakers and defended his title at the 2023 Boston Marathon. Favorite Eliud Kipchoge finished sixth.

"Pre-destined." After I profiled 19-year-old Galen Rupp in 2005, he went on to win the silver medal in the 10,000 meters at the 2012 Olympics and the bronze medal in the marathon at the 2016 Olympics. In 2019, his longtime coach, Alberto Salazar, was banned from coaching for four years by the U.S. Anti-Doping Agency. Rupp got a new coach and he is now, at age 37, in the twilight of his storied career.

"Henry II." In 2019, Henry Rono moved back to his village in Kenya, Kiptaragon, settling into his brother's home near the thatched hut in which he grew up. A 2022 news story said that he was sober but also estranged from his wife and two children. In February 2024, he died in a Kenyan hospital of an undisclosed illness. He was 72.

"The Last Naturalist." In 2021, at age 81, Bernd Heinrich published a new book, *Racing the Clock: Running Across a Lifetime*, and also ran a 50K race. In July 2023, at the 5.7-mile Raven Run, held in Weld, Maine, in honor of his bird research, Heinrich finished 31st out of 74 runners, covering 5.7 miles, most of it on gravel roads, in 59:38—a 10:27 pace.

"Nairo Quintana, Colombia's Cycling Hero." Quintana finished sixth in the 2022 Tour de France, but postrace testing found that he'd illegally taken tramadol, a drug that reduces the body's perception of pain. He was retroactively disqualified and also cut from his team, Arkéa Samsic. Still beloved in the Latin world, he is now a promoter for amateur races such as the Grand Fondo de Nairo Mexico.

"Million Mile Man." Cyclist Danny Chew continues to ride, despite his paralyzing 2015 accident. These days he mostly logs miles in his hand-powered wheelchair. He recently moved out of his old Squirrel Hill neighborhood in Pittsburgh to take up residence on the city's North Side, where, he says, "The flatter streets are better for me to push my wheelchair on." Lifetime, he is now at about 788,000 miles. "My new realistic lifetime mileage goal," he writes at dannychew.com, "is 800,000 miles."

"The Long Way Home." Explorer Karl Bushby was finally able to get a Russian visa three years after I met him, in 2014. He then walked across Russia, Mongolia, and Uzbekistan. When he reached Iran, he found himself stalled again, by war, COVID-19, and visa problems. His decades-long global crossing continues, though, and he is now poised to swim 150 miles across the Caspian Sea, with hopes of reaching his home in England in late 2026.

"Cross-Country Skier as Rock Star?" In 2014, while driving drunk at more than 100 miles per hour in Norway, Petter Northug crashed his Audi A7. His passenger incurred a broken collarbone, but Northug fled the scene and was found only when police sicced search dogs on him. After the skier tearfully retired from the World Cup in 2018, he was caught speeding again and was permanently stripped of his driver's license. He remains wildly popular in Norway, where he is a TV commentator, the impresario behind Northug brand ski wear, and also an elite amateur ski racer. In 2024, he finished 29th out of nearly 5,000 competitors in the Marcialonga, an Italian marathon.

"Bounding Ambition." In 1976, I bettered my pogo personal best, hopping 18,512 times. Already, though, the world record was more than 40,000 and out of my reach. (I was only 12 at the time.) The current world record is 115,170 jumps (James Roumeliotis, Boston, 2023), and there are now also records for most cars jumped on a pogo stick (six, Tyler Phillips, 2022) and most underwater jumps (3,647, Ashrita Furman, 1987, in the Amazon River, in eight feet of water, while wearing a mask and a snorkel).

ACKNOWLEDGMENTS

I'm indebted to the many great magazine editors who worked with me on the stories in this collection. A special thanks to Charlie Butler, Greg Ditrinco, Peter Flax, Leah Flickinger, Mark Jannot, Barry Johnson, Toby Lester, Dennis Lewon, Gloria Liu, Nora O'Donnell, Dean Robinson, and David Rowell.

Christen Karniski edited this book with grace and aplomb.

My late mother, Barbara Donahue, was a fine writer who shaped my love of words. I am forever grateful for her guidance.

My daughter, Allie, issued her first critique of my writing when she was about eight. ("Too many commas," she said.) She is now a high school English teacher, and I am grateful for her ongoing refusal to let a bad sentence stand.

My brother, Tim, is a fellow cyclist, cross-country ski racer, and writer. Many of these stories benefited from my conversations with him.

There have been many key supporters of my work, among them Sheila Baraga, Frank Bures, Mala Cline, Dave Clingan, Jane Donahue, Georges Nicolas, Chris Polich, Robin Starbuck, Tricia Snell, and Dwight Trainer.

Scott Chapin, Lynn Jennings, Shadrack Kochong, and Delmar and Misty Stevens offered substantial help as I was reporting these stories.

All these stories are informed by the zillions of hours I've spent running, cycling, and skiing with true friends. In particular, I'd like to thank Scott Clark, JR Stockwell, Jamie Sullivan, my fellow White Mules, Gunstock Nordic, Nina Gavrylyuk, the Rippers, and the maestros of the Tuesday Night Ride.

My partner, Verna, is a scholar, writer, and runner, and she was gentle and wise and patient with me as I brought this book, decades in the making, to the finish line. For now, she still lives a little over 100 miles away from me. Every time I ride my bike to her house, I'm so happy I did.

Sources

"The Bike Wanderer." First published in *Bicycling*, April 14, 2022. Copyright © 2022 by *Bicycling*. Reprinted with permission of Hearst.

"Bounding Ambition." First published in *Northwest Magazine*, September 10, 1989. Copyright © Bill Donahue. Reprinted with permission of Bill Donahue.

"Breaking up the Boys Club." First published in *Outside*, October 2, 2019. Copyright © 2019 by *Outside*. Reprinted with permission of *Outside*.

"The Challenger." First published in *Runner's World*, April 14, 2023. Copyright © 2023 by *Runner's World*. Reprinted with permission of Hearst.

"Cleetus Fit." First published in *Outside*, November 5, 2018. Copyright © 2018 by *Outside*. Reprinted with permission of *Outside*.

"Cross-Country Skier as Rock Star?" Adapted from a story with this title published in *Ski*, December 18, 2012. Copyright © 2012. Republished with permission of *Outside*.

"Fixing Diane's Brain." First published in *Runner's World*, February 2011. Copyright © 2011 by *Runner's World*. Reprinted with permission of Hearst.

"Henry II." First published in *Runner's World*, September 2007. Copyright © 2023 by *Runner's World*. Reprinted with permission of Hearst.

"Kindergarten Can Wait." First published in *Backpacker*, June 10, 2015. Copyright @ 2015 by *Backpacker*. Reprinted with permission of *Outside*.

"King of the Mountains." First published in *Backpacker*, August 22, 2019. Copyright © 2019 by *Outside*. Reprinted with permission of *Outside*.

"The Last Naturalist." First published in *Outside*, December 15, 2017. Copyright © 2017 by *Outside*. Reprinted with permission of *Outside*.

"The Long Way Home." First published in *Backpacker*, July 27, 2012. Copyright © 2012 by *Outside*. Reprinted with permission of *Outside*.

"Million Mile Man." First published in *Outside*, November 22, 2016. Copyright © 2016 by *Outside*. Reprinted with permission of *Outside*.

"Nairo Quintana, Colombia's Cycling Hero." First published in *Vice*. July 3, 2015. Copyright © 2015 by *Vice*. Reprinted with permission of *Vice*.

"Naked Joe." First published in *Boston Magazine*, March 26, 2013. Copyright © 2013 by Bill Donahue. Reprinted with permission of Bill Donahue.

INDEX

About the Author

Bill Donahue has reported stories from more than 20 countries. His writing has appeared in *Outside*, *Harper's*, the *Atlantic*, and *New York Times Magazine*, and also in *Best American Sports Writing*. A three-time winner of the Lowell Thomas Gold Medal for Adventure Travel Writing, Donahue lives in rural New Hampshire, where he is a devoted cyclist and cross-country ski racer. This is his first book.

GRACE SCOTT